AMERICAN CHRISTIANITY

Discovering
AMERICA

Mark Crispin Miller, Series Editor

This series begins with a startling premise—that even now, more than two hundred years since its founding, America remains a largely undiscovered country with much of its amazing story yet to be told. In these books, some of America's foremost historians and cultural critics bring to light episodes in our nation's history that have never been explored. They offer fresh takes on events and people we thought we knew well and draw unexpected connections that deepen our understanding of our national character.

AMERICAN CHRISTIANITY

THE CONTINUING REVOLUTION

STEPHEN COX

University of Texas Press

AUSTIN

Requests for permission to reproduce material from this work
should be sent to:
Permissions
University of Texas Press
P.O. Box 7819
Austin, TX 78713-7819
http://utpress.utexas.edu/index.php/rp-form

♾ The paper used in this book meets the minimum requirements
of ANSI/NISO Z39.48-1992 (R1997) (Permanence of Paper).

LIBRARY OF CONGRESS CATALOGING-IN-PUBLICATION DATA

Cox, Stephen D.
    American Christianity : the continuing revolution / Stephen Cox. —
First edition.
        pages   cm. — (Discovering America)
    Includes bibliographical references and index.
    ISBN 978-0-292-72910-0 (cloth : alk. paper)
1. Christianity—United States.   2. United States—Church history.
I. Title.
    BR515.C69   2014
    277.3—dc23   2013034801

doi:10.7560/729100

To Paul Beroza

CONTENTS

= CONTENTS =

ACKNOWLEDGMENTS

My first debt of gratitude is to Mark Crispin Miller, the editor of the Discovering America series, who accepted my proposal for this book with no apparent concern except that it be a good book. At the University of Texas Press, Theresa May, editor-in-chief, and Robert Devens, assistant editor-in-chief, adhered to Mark's curious standard. The intelligence, friendliness, and scholarly informality of these three people have been worth the Seven Cities of Cíbola to me.

Chief among the other friends who helped me was my superb colleague in the history of American culture Joseph Ho. Several of the photographs in this book are his, and his help was essential in presenting the others. Joe also gave me the benefit of his large knowledge of contemporary church music and of Asian American experiences of Christianity.

Colleagues in libraries, archives, and church offices gave me crucial help. I especially want to thank Bonnie Balloch of the Crystal Cathedral; Mark Edwards and Michael McKeon of the Cathedral of St. Mary of the Assumption, San Francisco; Wayne Kempton of the Archives of the Episcopal Diocese of New York; Jeannette McDonald of the Jackson, Michigan, District Library; and Lois Rosebrooks of Plymouth Church, Brooklyn, New York.

I received unique and uniquely instructive help from Mark Bennett, James Lawrence, and Ted Vaughn of the pastoral and production staffs of the Rock Church, San Diego; Jessica Haughton of the Vineyard; Carol Phillips of the Bridgeport, Illinois, Presbyterian churches; Edward Ross of First Methodist Church, Jackson, Michigan; and Rosemary Taylor of the Taylor Prayer Chapel, Farmersburg, Indiana—all of them interesting and generous friends.

Mehmet Karayel assisted my research in Michigan and New York and followed the book throughout its development, asking questions, reminding me of things that readers would want to know, and in general acting as Greek chorus—supposing that Greek choruses had Mehmet's common sense.

In concluding these acknowledgments, I remember the help I received from many Christian and non-Christian friends whom I have not mentioned by name. Most of them didn't realize how much they were helping me; they just did. The scripture verse applies: "Ye are the salt of the earth."

AMERICAN CHRISTIANITY

†

SEP-12-07

FIGURE 1.1. *The Cathedral Church of St. John the Divine: a "ruin" at its birth. Courtesy of the Archives of the Episcopal Diocese of New York at the Cathedral of St. John the Divine.*

RUINS OR
FOUNDATIONS?

On Amsterdam Avenue in New York City stands the Episcopal Church of St. John the Divine, the largest cathedral in the world. Designs for the church were drawn in 1887. Work began in 1892. But the structure remains unfinished.

The first fourteen years were slow—"not entirely," it was said, "because of a lack of money." There were also problems with soils and materials: the church, built in a medieval style, was supposed to be constructed entirely of stone, like the medieval cathedrals, and that wasn't easy. In 1906 the building consisted of a crypt, one chapel—about the size of a country church—and a granite arch 150 feet high. Tourists asked, "To what ruin does that arch belong?"

In the next year, unpredictably, new life came to the ruin. More chapels appeared, radiating from a beautiful chancel. Enormous granite piers arose, prepared to support the great tower that was planned for the crossing of the nave and transept—a tower 425 feet high, with a bulk that would dwarf every other feature of the church, as the church would dwarf every other religious structure on the continent.

Then, suddenly, the building committee fired the architect

and for no known reason commissioned a Gothic church of a radically different design. The new architect, Ralph Adams Cram, was daring and original. He spent the rest of his life trying to convert one type of church into another type of church while creating an organic unity between the present and the past.

Cram never solved that problem. "We ourselves," he said, "shall never be called upon to complete the work unless some miracle happens."[1] It didn't. At Cram's death, in 1942, St. John the Divine was nowhere close to being finished.

In the 1970s construction resumed in a modest way, but the cathedral is still an agglomeration of strange, fantastic, and discordant parts—a gargantuan façade and nave, chapels of many shapes and architectural periods, wall and window ornaments representing every historical and cultural movement under heaven. Near the high altar, surrounded by masterpieces of modern medieval sculpture, stand two giant Japanese vases, the gifts of Emperor Hirohito in his youth. But the traditional altar is no longer the one ordinarily used. Its replacement is a nondescript platform that presents no obstacle to the many nonreligious events held in the church, such as a birthday bash staged in 2007 for the pop singer Elton John, a vocal opponent of Christian churches. Near the entrance to the nave rests an equally trendy, though permanent, attraction: a huge section of tree trunk called, for some reason, a "peace table." Midway on the south wall of the nave is another work of art, a metal sculpture by the contemporary artist Peter Gourfain showing scenes of freeways and automobiles and of hunters massacring animals—an apparent protest against the despoliation of the natural environment.

Perhaps the most thought-provoking feature of the cathedral is the decorative dome above the crossing. It was installed in 1909 as a temporary substitute for the vast lantern tower intended to cover this space, but advocates for historic preservation now insist on keeping it, even if the church

FIGURE 1.2. *St. John the Divine, early 1920s: the largest dome in America (Byzantine-Romanesque), with a white space awaiting the addition of a gothic nave. Courtesy of the Archives of the Episcopal Diocese of New York at the Cathedral of St. John the Divine.*

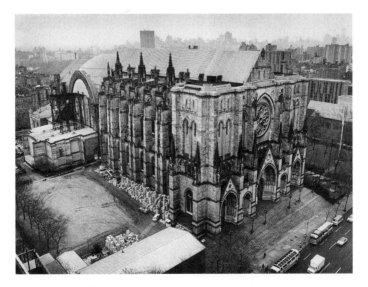

FIGURE 1.3. *St. John the Divine, early 1970s: the only solution is to keep on building. Courtesy of the Archives of the Episcopal Diocese of New York at the Cathedral of St. John the Divine.*

FIGURE 1.4. *The Crystal Cathedral, Garden Grove, California: the abode of flying angels. Courtesy of the Crystal Cathedral.*

raises enough money to complete the plan. When the traditional becomes temporary, the temporary naturally becomes traditional.

In the meantime, hundreds of other cathedrals have been constructed in America. They come in every imaginable shape and flavor. There is the Cathedral of Hope in Dallas, Texas, which began as a local congregation of the predominantly homosexual Metropolitan Community Church. Until recently there was the Crystal Cathedral in Garden Grove, California, an enormous glass auditorium designed by the modern and then postmodern architect Philip Johnson. The congregation that occupied the Crystal Cathedral, an offshoot of a traditional Protestant denomination, first met at a drive-in movie theater, then worked its way up to a building that could accommodate the church's signature events—holiday pageants with Bible animals and ladies suspended from wires,

impersonating angels. In 2012, following the church's bank-
ruptcy, the building was purchased by a Roman Catholic diocese that plans to make it a cathedral in the traditional sense,
thus completing the spiral from old to new to old again.

The term "cathedral" comes from the Latin *"cathedra,"*
a word for a bishop's chair. But even if your church doesn't
have bishops (and few American churches do), you can still
have a cathedral. Detroit alone has sixteen of them: the Abundant Faith Cathedral, the Christ Cathedral of TRUTH, the
New Beginnings Cathedral . . .

That last name, New Beginnings, is the most appropriate. It's true, American Christianity always wants to keep
its contact with the past. A pointed arch, a pungent passage
of scripture, the very word "cathedral"—these are things too
valuable to be left behind. But a church that doesn't promise
new beginnings can never prosper in America. American theology has always presented a demand for motion. Even when
church people attempt a wholesale return to the past, to "traditional values," something strange always happens.

So it was with the Cathedral Church of St. John the Divine.
The planners wanted a building that would replicate the past.
But which past? And how should they replicate it? They had
to decide, and they did. First they decided one thing; then
they decided another and another and yet another. What they
got was a monument to volatility, to uncontrolled revision, to
a vitality that never achieves stability or even apparent harmony. It's an image of American Christianity throughout its
existence, the picture of a religion in continuous revolution.

This book argues that American Christianity is now and
always has been a triumph of unpredictability. It also argues
that American Christianity's history of change cannot be
adequately explained by political or social conditions; by
the rise, progress, tragic conflicts, and comic aspirations of
that darling of the social historians, the "middle class"; or by
the grand ideological narratives of intellectual historians.

The only way to explain it is by reference to Americans' strange and incalculable ways of reaching out to God, and to their churches' strange, incalculable, but generally successful ways of reaching out to them. To say this is to admit that there is no theory that can really account for the evidence: no coherent story of American Christianity's origins and variations, deaths and resurrections; no all-embracing epic, myth, or intellectual romance of American belief.

That idea will seem strange and unwelcome to many people who have a stake in the subject. It contests the normal assumptions of the social scientist, for whom religion is secondary to the forces at work on it, *social* forces that can be quantified and conclusively analyzed. It may appear to contest the assumptions of devout believers, for whom Christ's Church is primary and the only "forces" truly at work are the ones that God exerts miraculously on its behalf. It will certainly be unwelcome to those people, on both the religious right and the religious left, for whom the story of Christianity miraculously coincides with the stories deduced from contemporary political assumptions. The idea is unsettling even for the author, a student of literature who enjoys finding coherent explanatory patterns in the texts he studies.

But American Christianity is not a text. It is something even more interesting—more colorful, more troubling, more amusing, more challenging, more emotionally demanding—than the greatest, strangest poem. It demands appreciation for itself as a structure that is always visible but always mysteriously shifting its form, a structure that cannot be finished because, in a way, it was never really started: no one agreed on its plans, and no one agreed on the revisions of the plans. Everyone just built.

To put this in other words: if we want to appreciate what we see around us, in the religious (or antireligious) attitudes of our friends or of ourselves, we should stop trying to explain what nobody ever saw: the undeviating "faith of our fathers" that is said to be "living still" in our national life.[2] Many people think this faith has always existed in America and always will exist. Others think it once existed, but it has gone to eternal death, the victim of relentless "forces." Many others fear, or rejoice, that it will soon return. But fortunately or unfortunately, that cathedral of unchanging stone was never there to begin with.

FINDING OIL

The most famous film about American Christianity begins with a woman singing, or rather droning, a traditional gospel song: "Give Me that Old-Time Religion." As her voice continues—eerie, slow, hypnotic—an ominous group assembles on the streets of an unnaturally dim and empty town. Led by a minister of the gospel, they head for the school, where they arrest a wide-eyed young teacher for expounding the theories of "Mr. Charles Darwin."

This film is *Inherit the Wind* (1960), a dramatization of the Scopes "monkey" trial of 1925, famous for its encounter between a fundamentalist account of Christianity and a Darwinian account of biology. The film suggests that there really was, and continues to be, an old-time religion, and Christian fundamentalism is it: an unchanging, oppressive, tremendously dull set of dogmas, militantly resistant not just to science but to any breath of air blowing in from the modern world.

One might get a different impression if one were told that the trial in Dayton, Tennessee, was an advertising event arranged by city bigwigs in collusion with prominent agnostics and representatives of the American Civil Liberties

Union to publicize the town and contemporary religious con-
troversies.[1] One might also get a different impression if one
were told that William Jennings Bryan, Dayton's champion
of the old-time religion, was one of America's foremost political progressives, nominated for the presidency by the Democratic Party after his spectacular reinterpretation of Christ's
Passion as a picture of labor's martyrdom by the capitalist gold standard. "You shall not press down upon the brow
of labor this crown of thorns!" Bryan shouted in what many
regarded as the greatest speech of the age. "You shall not cru-
cify mankind upon a cross of gold!"

Bryan was not a man of the past; he was a man of his time.
And fundamentalism—an attempted return to the "funda-
mentals" of Christianity—was far from the old-time religion.
Its context was new, its leading personalities were unconventional, and its ways of cultivating its forms of devotion were
hardly those of pious farmers conning Holy Writ by firelight.
Its means were the mass meeting, the PR campaign, and at
Dayton the show trial spectacularly staged for the benefit of
newspapers and radio. Fundamentalism may have been dis-
graced by that trial, but it didn't go away. Eventually it found
newer and more vital ways of re-creating itself in a world of
television, the Internet, and political agitation on the conservative side. In the meantime, the fundamentalists' liberal and
modernist foes in the "mainline" or "mainstream" churches
had also re-created themselves—and also in ways that could
not have been predicted.

In *The Secular City* (1965–1966), the most influential work
of American theology published in the past fifty years, Harvey
Cox pictured Christianity as a pilgrimage, a constant encounter with new worlds. The kind of encounter he anticipated
for the near future would be prompted by modern liberal
social action, although he left the details tantalizingly vague.
About one thing he was clear and clearly right: Christianity
is always on the move. Yet there are endless ways in which it

can engage itself with the world, and Cox proved no better at predicting its engagements than anyone else. During the five decades since his book appeared, the high places of the mainstream denominations have become increasingly liberal or even radical, but the bigger movement has been an intended return to traditional values, a movement appearing almost everywhere else in American Christianity. Yet somehow, without anyone's predicting it, tradition itself has changed. It now expresses itself in "megachurches," "Christian rap," best-selling novels about the end of the world, "outreach" and "inreach" programs about everything from hiking and biking to the problems of single dads, and political campaigns for causes never dreamed of in the past.

Who can keep order in the household of God? What can prevent revolution? The obvious candidate is the Bible, the authority to which every faction of Christianity appeals, each in its own way. This is true and important: the Bible sets limits to Christian belief. It never leads its readers to embrace polytheism or to contemplate an uncaring or capricious deity. It always inspires belief in one God, active in human history and revealed through human story, a God who wants to be reconciled with humanity and with individual human beings. But scripture that is freely available for individual interpretation, as the Bible has been throughout American history, is not just a magnificent stabilizer of belief and practice; it is also a magnificent destabilizer. To its text every question that arises among a Bible-believing people eventually returns, and from it new and usually surprising answers regularly emerge.

Of course, new scriptural concepts can always be asserted, in the absence of actual scriptures. More commonly, however, scripture itself is a provocation of change. The New Testament continually emphasizes the importance of conversion and transformation, and the importance of individual people as agents of transformation. As I have argued elsewhere,[2] this emphasis is an essential part of what can be called the DNA of the New Testament, the array of ideas and literary methods by which Christianity reproduces itself. That scriptural DNA has been continuously reproductive in America. This has nothing to do with whether individuals' specific interpretations of scripture are right or wrong. It is simply a fact about the Bible's influence.

Another source of both stability and instability has been the major Christian denominations. From the beginning, they have been caricatured as monuments of repression, enemies of the new. Yet even the most hierarchical churches have been swept by revolution in virtually every period of their existence. Some revolutions were open and violent. They involved agitations, schisms, hysterical denunciations, mass firings and defections of clergy, and America's favorite weapon of war, litigation. Other revolutions happened behind the scenes. These were revolutions from above, produced by the very people charged with maintaining stability and continuity—the seminary teachers, the well-placed preachers, the staffs of denominational headquarters, the theologians, such as Harvey Cox.

Much has been written about the "democratization" of American Christianity but comparatively little about its official revolutionaries. Yet they are one of the main reasons it is impossible to find an American religious group that turns the same face to the world today that it did one hundred or even fifty years ago. Instead of staying in one place, American churches have wandered across the landscape, abandoning old sources of support and discovering new ones, in a continuous process of self-conversion. Often their changes of character have been urged or imposed from above, not demanded from below or dictated by any of those social-economic "forces" sometimes represented as the final explanations of religious belief. Often new versions of religious experience have been implemented over the impassioned protests of the people in the pews. "Old people" left their seats, and "new people" took them. The church moved on, in whatever direction church leaders identified as traditional, progressive, or (most often) both—or in whatever direction disaffected Christians took when they rebelled against the leadership.

American Christianity would be easier to understand if a predictable pattern could be found in all these motions. Many patterns have been suggested. Two of them are constantly evoked in debates about what America is or should become.

The first pattern is discerned by cultural conservatives who believe that America is inherently a "religious nation" or a "Christian nation." There is some truth in this belief. As two prominent social scientists have noted, "historically, whatever their degree of religiosity, almost all Americans have identified with one religion or another"—ordinarily the Christian religion.[3] Seen from this distance, no religious changes have ever amounted to fundamental change.

The second pattern is a favorite with opponents of religious belief. The American Christianity that they see is constantly being eroded by science and the necessities of life in a secular society. Their view is itself an American tradition: for two centuries, people have been arguing in this way. But their opinion is also supported by evidence. The great majority of American Christians long ago abandoned a literal reading of the Bible's historical books. The churches' most restrictive moral customs are no longer dominant in most communities. And according to the writers quoted in the preceding paragraph, about one-quarter of the population coming of age after 2000 reports no specific religious affiliation.[4] By this analysis, the real story of American religion is a continuing revolution against religion itself.

Here we have two vivid and plausible images. We can choose to imagine America as a thousand acres of rich midwestern soil, endlessly generating crops of religiosity, or we can imagine it as an island populated by primitive fauna that are slowly but inexorably being replaced by more highly adaptive species.

Unfortunately, neither image could really satisfy a social scientist. Neither has enough facts to support it when considered from anything like a scientific point of view. The emphasis of social science, and the historical theories derived from it, is naturally on social and economic circumstances. Most social-scientific theories describe American Christianity as a class phenomenon ("the middle class and its religion") that developed in response to the social and economic insecurities that afflict the middle class or to its growing prosperity and confidence—either explanation will do, or both at once.[5]

This approach has been fruitful, to a point. It is obvious that religious movements are involved with their social and economic surroundings and that no one should make statements about American religion while neglecting the mountain of facts that social scientists have discovered about its social settings. It is also obvious that American churches are, by and large, managed by middle-class people: the rich are too few, and the poor have too little money. What affects the middle class will probably affect the churches and, indeed, America's general religious outlook. Therefore, to most social scientists who address the issue, the history of American Christianity isn't the story of a perennially productive field or an island gradually losing its ecological health; it's the story of the great social storms that blow across the American heartland.

But how exactly does this work? What is the seed of the heartland's faith? Who plants and harvests it? Why does economic depression "produce" religious revival at one time and religious lethargy at another? What economic circumstances inspired multitudes of Americans to believe that the world would end in 1843—or 1844, 1914, 1975, 2011, or twenty other times? What threats to social stability produced churches—and large churches, too—devoted to the idea that Saturday, not Sunday, is the Sabbath? Or to the idea that ancient inhabitants of the Americas migrated here from Israel and were visited by the resurrected Christ? Or to the idea that minimal consumption of alcohol, then abstinence from alcohol, then state prohibition of alcohol is a necessity of the Christian life? Yet these purely religious notions have all had startling effects on American social history.

Consider figure 2.1, an outline of Presbyterian movements in the United States. To follow the mainline Presbyterian Church from its American beginnings in the First Presbytery (1706) to the denomination now called the Presbyterian Church (U.S.A.) is like watching a locomotive slowly switching its way through a yard in which new tracks are constantly being laid. To discover what economic conditions laid the tracks, what social circumstances drew the blueprints—that would be a challenge, to put it mildly.

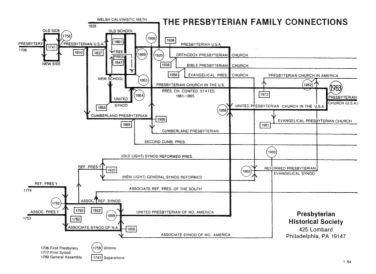

FIGURE 2.1. *The Presbyterian Church(es). What can explain all this? Courtesy of the Presbyterian Historical Society, Presbyterian Church (U.S.A.), Philadelphia, Pennsylvania.*

There is clearly something incomplete about the social-economic explanation of religious history. The absent factor is the connection between social backgrounds and individual foregrounds, between the conditions that influence people and the decisions—often the strange and unexpected decisions—that these people make.

Such connections are extraordinarily difficult to evaluate with the quantitative methods of the social sciences. People decide to become, or remain, or never become Christians because they think that is the best course for them. Choices are by nature individual and qualitative, not collective and quantitative, and the intensity of experience they represent cannot be explained by statistical analysis. What one person experiences as "crisis," "the tipping point," or the final "commitment" may register as only a minor variation in another person's life.

Personal decisions always take place in some social context, which can almost always be represented by some kind of numbers. Most people who make over $100,000 a year would never think of joining an inner-city church 30 miles away or going on a 10,000-mile missionary journey. But some of them do, and their decisions have had significant effects; they have saved old churches and started new ones. Why these things happen, and what their results can be, cannot be settled by statistics or reference to social contexts.

If people's religious attachments, choices, and beliefs were actually determined by social and economic forces, then someone who knew the history of the latter ought to be able to predict the history of the former. But while social scientists and other intellectuals have frequently predicted the demise of religion, or particular kinds of religion, their predictions have never come true.[6] Nor have anyone else's prophecies, optimistic or pessimistic, about the shape, size, and intensity of American religious belief. The big events that you, I, or anyone else would have expected to exert an enormous influence on religion—the Civil War, the two world wars, the Great Depression—produced no corresponding changes on that side of the ledger. But odd new ideas, eccentric religious personalities, a few ordinary people determined to communicate Christian ideas in a new way—these have often had the shaping force that great national events have lacked. This is worth remembering when one reads speculations about the religious effects, so far not discernible, of the great economic downturn of 2008.

One social development was indeed crucial to American Christianity: the eighteenth-century breakdown of the state church system. At the time, many people predicted that Christianity would die if it (that is, one version of it) was no longer established by law. What happened was that Americans' religious choices increased dramatically, and so did Americans' involvements with particular religious bodies. People were free to choose the religious approach that inspired them most, for whatever reason: because it was traditional, or untraditional; the faith of their fathers, or *not* the faith of their fathers; rational, or beyond all reason; what everybody else believed, or what nobody else believed. The charter of choice put an end to predictability, once and for all. One might make generalizations about what had happened in the past, and some of those generalizations might be true. Predictions and deep insights into fundamental patterns were another thing.

A sophisticated attempt to map the history of American Christianity by using a theory of choice is contained in a deservedly well-known book, *The Churching of America* (1992; 2nd ed., 2005). The authors, Roger Finke and Rodney Stark, try to measure not just reported affiliation but real church membership, attachment, or "adherence." Religious adherence, they find, has greatly increased during the past two centuries of scientific enlightenment. In 1776 only 17 percent of Americans adhered to a church. Adherence increased to 51 percent in 1906 and 62 percent in 1980. It was still 62 percent in 2000. On this scale, a reported "seismic shift" from 7 percent (1972) to almost 20 percent (2012) in the proportion of Americans who "do not identify with any religion" looks somewhat less serious.[7] Nevertheless, the mainline Protestant denominations, the old churches in the center of town, now enjoy a much smaller "market share" of Christianity than they did in 1940. Other groups—Pentecostals, Southern Baptists, and the many "fellowships" and "ministries" of born-again believers—have greatly increased their market share.[8]

This, the authors suggest, is because churches that are not mainline, that advertise their distance from prevailing social trends, can offer more compelling choices for people shopping in the religious "marketplace."[9] They set a high price for their goods; they make special demands on their adherents; and for a significant segment of the population, their distinctiveness increases their value. Their crop can weather the storm and even benefit from the droughts and floods.

Finke and Stark provide a persuasive view of religious change. Perhaps necessarily, however, their explanation flirts with tautology. It shows that churches requiring more commitment from their members retain more committed members. Compelling messages compel; uncompelling messages do not. People—some people—respond to a challenging message; others find it too challenging, or challenging in the wrong way, and do not respond.

This is no critique of Finke and Stark's research. Causes of change in American Christianity are simply too complex and volatile to be explained by any general theory. There is always an uncertain relationship between the story of the churches, which is Finke and Stark's major concern, and the stories of their individual constituents, who cannot be expected to choose the same church (or express the same intensity of devotion to that church) for the same reasons.

Most varieties of Christianity offer people many more than one religious attraction and challenge. In this country, there are reported to be 68 million communicants of the Roman Catholic Church.[10] Some of them are attracted and held by the church's concern with sexual purity and its respect for the unborn, but some adhere to the church despite what it teaches about those subjects and because of its teachings on others. They are all members of the same church, whose growth or shrinkage can be "explained" by reference to any or all of the tendencies they represent. This is true of any religious movement of significant size.[11]

Finke and Stark identify some prominent features of growing churches—the distinctive messages, the challenging demands. But they aren't able to say as much about the challenges that become too challenging. Jehovah's Witnesses are one of America's most demanding denominations. In 1940 it required an average of about 1,000 hours of religious work for them to convert someone into an active adherent; by century's end about 6,000 hours were necessary to bring someone to baptism, and half a lifetime of work (about 40,000 hours) to make an active Witness.[12] At the other extreme there is the standing problem of the mainstream denominations. These vast, ungainly bodies have been losing market share for generations, but despite their perceived lack of challenge, they retain tens of millions of adherents, with local churches embracing an almost incredible range of options. The Congregational Church, the church of the New England Puritans, now includes the megachurch of Reverend Jeremiah Wright, President Obama's flamboyant former pastor. San Francisco's Ebenezer Lutheran Church, founded in 1882 by religiously conservative Swedish immigrants, now calls itself Her Church, worships the "God/dess," and prays "the Goddess Rosary."[13]

Clearly, even mainstream denominations can offer challenges that social science cannot easily quantify or explain.

And it isn't just "ordinary" churches (if there are such things) that offer them; it is "ordinary" people too. This is not, unfortunately, the impression one derives from standard denominational histories, which are often written as if institutions sprang naturally out of the soil, without the creative work of individual people, especially people without an official title. We read that the Baptist Church "grew" in one state or another, or that Reverend So-and-So "went" to such and such a place and "started a church."

The idea of an automatic institution has also been projected by people who speak in solemn tones about the decline of American Christianity. They have been doing this for a long time. "The day has passed," opined an evangelist of the 1920s, "when you can ring a church bell and expect a crowd." But when was that day? Even when churches were established by law, no one could simply open a church and expect it to succeed. Established churches in the colonial South met with the indifference of people from all social classes, who found it remarkably easy to withhold their support. In the Puritan colonies, the church regime was much stricter, but even such pious people as Anne Bradstreet hesitated before joining a church, and after joining still suffered temptations from the variety of Christian ideas in circulation.[14]

During the nineteenth century, churches that had formerly been established faced heroic struggles to survive and expand. The experience of an Episcopal bishop can stand for that of many would-be planters of churches: "For the first fifteen years," he recalled, "I was at home only about one-fifth of the time."[15] The rest of it he spent visiting settlements, where he went from house to house passing out advertisements, hoping that people would turn up for services in a sod school or a borrowed church. He generally got a welcome, but when it came to starting a church, he could never predict who, if anyone, might be inspired to give some money or do some work, although women were the likeliest to be interested. The life of the church was its women volunteers.

American churches were the lengthened shadows of individual men and women, people who were willing, for reasons best known to themselves, to start a church and keep it going. Some denominations provided small subsidies to new churches; many did not, and if there was a subsidy, it was never enough. It was up to the local people to support the project year by year. Standard histories seldom report a fact that is starkly visible in virtually any church records you care to consult: American churches and their pastors have generally lived cheaply, if not from hand to mouth. In 1906 the average ministerial salary for the top payer among Protestant denominations, the Unitarians, was a princely $1,653 (about $33,000 in today's money), with $663 as an average for all Christian ministers. In 1968 the Unitarians were still on top, with a median salary of $8,117 (about $55,000 in today's money). Methodists stood at $6,232; Southern Baptists, at $4,504. Total income would include not just salary but also allowances for housing, transportation, and so forth. When these are added, however, the median income of 5,000 ministers surveyed about their pay for 1968 goes up to only $8,037. Experience affects salary, but in 1968 only 8 percent of ministers with more than fifteen years' experience received $10,000 or more in salary.[16]

Ministers are still underpaid, compared with people in other skilled occupations, even though salaries often constitute most of a church's annual budget. In most churches today, contributions that come in on Sunday are spent by Saturday. If the core members, the people who, for whatever reason, value the church enough to make themselves responsible for its existence, fail to show up and contribute, the church dies.

This account of individual choice and responsibility applies not just to the oldest, whitest denominations but even more to African American churches. We know that during the forty years following the Civil War, black churches experienced phenomenal growth, achieving a member-ship of about 3.6 million by 1906—and this out of an African American population of about 9.5 million.[17] What this means is that millions of people who had not belonged to a church and whose parents had not belonged to a church or perhaps had not been allowed into a church had now chosen a church for themselves, usually one that was run by African Ameri-cans. That in turn means that young people (and some not so young) were seeking appointments to the ministry, either from struggling denominations with even more struggling seminaries or from local congregations that had identified their talents. They were investing their lives in what old-fashioned Christians called a "new work."

But formal organization, membership, and ordination are only part of the story. Congregations could not survive with-out the voluntary commitment of their members, the men and women who contributed their garden money and their egg money and a tithe of their small wages to buy a bit of land to build a church, then contributed their sweat to raise the building, then discovered ways to get and keep a minister, and after that discovered ways of passing their connection with Christianity on to the next generation.

While doing so, these people created or remolded larger institutions, some of which now span the nation. For minis-ters and laypeople alike, this generally meant travel by train, in the cheapest seats, to conferences where threadbare pas-tors debated the things of the spirit, arguing about which among the hundred possible connections to God their tiny denomination should endorse; failing agreement, it meant founding a new denomination. By the late twentieth century, African Americans had formed almost two hundred separate church organizations of the Holiness variety alone.[18] Each of these groups—and each of the big African American denomi-nations, such as the African Methodist Episcopal Church,

FIGURE 2.2. *A church in an African American neighborhood of Cairo, Illinois, 2005. The scripture on the sign quotes Romans 8:28: "And we know that all things work together for good." Author's collection.*

the African Methodist Episcopal Zion Church, the Christian Methodist Episcopal Church, the National Baptist Convention, and the Church of God in Christ—crafted its own ways of ministering to the needs of people vigorously exercising their powers of choice.

Most scholars have stopped talking about "the black church," as if there were only one kind. In their ungovernable diversity, African American churches offer a remarkable instance of a larger pattern, or lack of pattern—the mutual enterprise of religious "leaders" and religious "followers" that constitutes American Christianity.

William James, the most distinguished American writer on the psychology of religion, made a serious mistake when he proposed to examine religious experience as it appeared in the consciousness of a few people of "genius," not in the experience of the "ordinary religious believer." "It would profit us little," he says, "to study this second-hand religious life."[19] But James abandoned his own distinction. His book *The Varieties of Religious Experience* (1902) presents abundant information about the intense religious lives of people who did not claim to be geniuses. James couldn't resist these ordinary people, and he was right not to. In America, revolutions in religion are often produced by eccentricity, but they seldom wait for genius to appear, among either leaders or followers. The vast reservoir of potential religious experience—what James called religious "propensities" or "appetites"[20]—is waiting to be tapped by anyone who has the tools to do so.

James never produced an exact definition of religious experience; the varieties were too many. He suggested, however, that it was a psychological phenomenon of a highly distinctive type. He called it one of humanity's "genuine keys for unlocking the world's treasure-house" of ideas and feelings. It was the kind of experience capable of discovering something beyond itself—life seen from a new point of view, a vantage point provided by the self's perceived connection with God. It was a revolution in perspective. By means of this "communion," he said, "new force comes into the world."[21]

Yet if religious experience is a "key" to something, what are the keys to religious experience? What are the means by which a capacity for this experience can be discovered and brought to light?

About 1816 a farmer from the New York–Vermont frontier with the extremely common name of William Miller began a systematic study of scripture. He found in the Bible's mathematical symbolism a prediction that Christ would return, and the world would end, sometime around 1843. What no one except God could have predicted was that Miller's dry studies of biblical numerology would open a new intensity of experience to people throughout America. Some abandoned their unbelief; others abandoned their churches. When 1843 and then 1844 came and went, Miller's followers suffered what was called the "Great Disappointment." Many fell away. But there were enough men and women still ardently expecting the second coming, or "advent," of Christ to continue the movement. They created adventist fellowships, adventist churches, and eventually adventist denominations. Some of their institutions extended themselves around the world—the denominations now known as the Seventh-day Adventists, Grace Communion International, and Jehovah's Witnesses.

Like someone prospecting for a precious substance without knowing exactly where it might be found, Miller had discovered a hidden propensity for religious experience, a readiness for religious involvement that ran far and deep in the American people. This vein of readiness was nothing as visible as a field of corn. It was nothing as predictable as the return of spring. The best image might be the irregularly spreading veins of a great oil field. If you strike such a vein, your success may be explained, after the fact, by the circumstances in which it happened: an expanding economy in need of oil or a contracting economy in which other enterprises offer less reward. These purported explanations will of course have nothing to do with your ability to find the oil.

The same after-the-fact problem occurs with explanations of American religion. The two major social-scientific explanations for adventism describe it as (1) an optimistic and progressive response to a developing capitalist economy and (2) a pessimistic and reactionary response to the economic downturn of the 1830s.[22] Yet the fact is simply that William Miller found a vein that other people had missed. Maybe they misjudged the terrain. Maybe their tools weren't right for the job, in some way that couldn't be discovered except by experiment. In any event, he found the vein.

At roughly the same time, in roughly the same region of the country, and often among the same people, another vein was found, the vein that today flows mightily through the Church of Jesus Christ of Latter-day Saints—the Mormons. That process of discovery began in the 1820s, in the farm country surrounding Palmyra, New York, with revelations delivered to another man with an ordinary American name, Joseph Smith. These revelations were not about the end of the world; they were about its hidden history. Smith was twenty-four years old when he published the Book of Mormon, which his followers call "another testament of Jesus Christ." Whether or not Smith actually heard the voice of God and found the early history of the western hemisphere written on golden plates in a "reformed Egyptian" script, he had indeed found something: the hitherto unknown readiness of Americans for a new recovery of an ancient past, for a new community based on revivals of ancient customs.

Smith and his successors also found a willingness for continuing revelation that constituted a mandate for revolution. In 1847 the Mormons began to leave the existing states and embarked on the creation of a new society in the deserts of Utah. In 1890 they renounced their attempt to restore Old Testament polygamy. In 1978 they began admitting men of black African descent to their priesthood. Today, followers of America's most exceptional large religion—the one most often regarded by other churches as not only heretical but positively non-Christian—are almost indistinguishable from their neighbors. Their salient characteristic, achieved through successive revolutions, has become their ambition to represent both the normal and the norm of American life. Even Joseph Smith, the Prophet, could not have foreseen that a consecrated normality would be the Saints' most powerful means of attracting and holding followers.

This book will consider, among other things, certain religious movements that, unlike the Mormons, seemed likely to capture large fractions of the populace but didn't. It will also consider religious ideas and approaches that succeeded in such unlikely ways that one can only echo an observation made by the estranged mother of a great evangelist, contemplating her daughter's oddly successful ministry: "If God continues to bless His word and save souls under those conditions, it is very wonderful."[23]

One reason the course of Christian movements can seem so *wonderful* is that no one can graph the individual scales of values and interests of hundreds of millions of believers, past and present. Another reason is that religious messages often identify values and interests where they weren't known to exist before. Finke and Stark are correct in viewing religious change as an alteration in people's scale of values or "preferences" in response to the successful communicating or "marketing" of religious options. But they are only half-correct in believing that "when people change churches, or even religions, it is usually not because their preferences have changed, but because the new church or faith more effectively appeals to preferences they have always had." Preferences can be "had" only when they are recognized and acted on. Confronted with new religious options, people often discover *at that point* that this was what they were "always looking for."[24] Until then, their preference was merely potential; something had to happen in order for them to identify it and connect it with a new religious practice. Crude oil, oil in the ground, becomes valuable and interesting only when someone has the tools to find it, bring it to the surface, and make something out of it. The same can be said about people's religious inclinations, real and potential.

Charles Grandison Finney, one of the most important evangelists in American history, declared that *"religion is the work of man"*; it is a tool, a set of "measures" to accomplish a specific task, a way of making potential experience into something actual.[25] Today, "measures" might be called "techniques" or even "technologies." Americans have used many techniques in making their versions of the Christian religion: apocalyptic forecasts; idealizations of heart and home; ethnic identifications; architectural innovations; new ways of preaching, praying, and singing; new ideas of "community"; odd forms of biblical interpretation; and political crusades for every conceivable cause. These are a few of the measures by which American Christianity has prospered. No cynicism is implied; those who created and used these measures almost always believed in them, and sometimes the measures worked.

An African American pastor has said that people attend church in response to one of the "four *I*'s": information, influence, inspiration, and ignorance. Some people are seeking knowledge of God (information). Others are seeking a power that can affect the lives around them (influence), or the power of the Spirit on their own lives (inspiration). Still others just show up unreflectingly (ignorance). This pastor's church, and every church that keeps its doors open, has its own ways of addressing the "four *I*'s." Some methods work better than others, at least for now; the methods don't stay the same. As the pastor says, an active church doesn't stand still just waiting for the Lord.[26] It hopes that its measures will attract more people than they repel—something that isn't easy to calculate. The measures are therefore subject to revision. And whatever the churches do, there will still be Christians, ardent Christians, who aren't affiliated with any church at all.

To say this is to recognize that there is a place where institutional histories and social theories stop, and the histories of individual men and women start. Consider the story of Frances Jane (Fanny) Crosby, one of the greatest celebrities of nineteenth-century Christianity. A prolific hymn writer ("Blessed Assurance," "Pass Me Not," "To God Be the Glory," and hundreds of other songs), Crosby had—and continues to have—more influence on religious feeling than an army of clergy. Yet after her conversion to Christ, she waited more than three decades to join a church.[27] Until that time, she wouldn't have counted in any statistical study of Christians in America. But of course, she wouldn't have cared.

Members of churches or not, people like Crosby are the heart and core of American Christianity. These are the people who have found a vital connection to the faith, a means of transforming potential interest into actual engagement. No one, including them, can predict where such connections will be found, in what church or denomination, movement or creed, if any. The task of religious movements is to locate *them*, and no one can say which methods will work or when.

For Crosby, as for many others, what worked was a combination of the very old and the very new. In 1850, at the age of thirty, she visited one of the new metropolitan churches where revival meetings were held. In each service, the high point was an invitation for sinners to come forward and be reconciled with God. It was called "getting happy." Crosby came forward twice; twice she was prayed for, and twice she departed without finding the experience. On the third night, she was the only sinner at the "altar." Then, she said, "They began to sing the grand old consecration hymn, 'Alas, and did my Savior bleed, / And did my Sovereign die?' And when they reached the third line of the fourth stanza, 'Here Lord, I give myself away,' my very soul was flooded with a celestial light. I sprang to my feet, shouting 'hallelujah.'"[28]

Apparently, many measures had to be used—a specialized

FIGURE 2.3. *The Queen of Gospel Song: Frances Jane (Fanny) Crosby. The book in her hand is not the Bible; she simply liked to hold a book. Courtesy of the Bridgeport History Center, Bridgeport, Connecticut, Public Library.*

service, an altar call, and a 143-year-old song of Christ's sacrifice, inviting a new song of self-surrender. Eventually these measures had their effect. But the flood of celestial light—that was surprising, ironic: Fanny Crosby had been blind since early infancy.

Years after her conversion, Crosby began to explore new ways of converting others. She offered her songs to publishing firms that were using the newest, cheapest means of printing and distribution, and she traveled the country, a little blind woman, alone, preaching Christ to the huge crowds that turned out to hear her.[29] By the end of the century she had become "the Queen of Gospel Song."

Crosby was far from a theological innovator. She adhered to a basic form of evangelical Christianity—the old-time religion, if you will. Yet she was one of the most important participants in a revolution in nineteenth-century Protestantism, the change from a contentious, proudly dogmatic religion of divine justice to a religion of the heart, ever listening (in Crosby's words) for "echoes of mercy, whispers of love."[30] A century and a half later, multitudes of Christians—old and young, rich and poor, male and female, of every ethnicity and political persuasion—have her words on their lips every Sunday. They sing them in various arrangements, "traditional," "contemporary," whatever, and they find their own meanings in the words, just as she found her own meaning in "Alas! and did my Saviour bleed." But more people recite Fanny Crosby than Walt Whitman or Emily Dickinson, and more people are influenced by her than by any author who today proclaims the end of faith.

This is how a simple story—"Blessed assurance! Jesus is mine!"—can become so complicated that no theory can contain it. Yet one thing to notice is that wherever Crosby's songs are sung, they have the potential to revive the experience of conversion, of revolution on a personal scale. Another thing is that this revolution can take place in any social context, including contexts that are themselves revolutionary. Crosby's songs may be part of a service in which a Korean American pastor solicits donations for a campaign against AIDS in Africa, or a gay marriage is blessed by a woman pastor. All this would have puzzled Fanny Crosby. It wasn't something she could have predicted.

It would probably puzzle most twenty-first-century Christians, too, if they happened to reflect on it. Supposing that they did, however, I think they would be more bemused than shocked. They understand that practical Christianity requires tools that identify religious "appetites" and can satisfy them, right now, in any social context. These people seldom use the word "revolution," because the normal idea of revolution is something that occurs once, and annihilates everything before it. Of course that's naïve; it never happens that way. The vital tension of American Christianity is that of a revolution which is always happening, and always needs to happen. The old-time religion must always be made new. No one can predict what new measures American Christianity will invent, or how—if at all—they will be reconciled with the old measures. We are living at a time when the Southern Baptist Church, originally severed from the northern Baptists by its defense of slavery, has elected a black pastor as its head. And we are living at a time when believers in a literal interpretation of Mark 16:18 ("they shall take up serpents") still die from snakebites received in religious services—which these days are advertised on Facebook.[31]

No theory can encompass these tensions and ironies. Yet American Christianity survives not by theories or systematic theologies. It survives by what transcends them all: life, individual experience, the way things actually happen, and the means by which they are made to happen, means that are strange, diverse, generally unpredictable, seldom sensible, often inspiring, and just as often annoying or unsettling, but remarkably informative about the American people.

THE MAINSTREAM
AND THE CATARACTS

Today, Jackson, Michigan, is a decayed industrial town. But if you had visited it in the 1880s, half a century after its settlement, you would have found a progressive metropolis—a center of manufacturing, a junction of seven railways, the commercial hub of a dozen smaller towns. Inspecting its big, comfortable homes and the conveniences and gadgets on display in its wide store windows, you would have seen a picture of the nation's "heartland" as people often imagine it: a hopeful yet traditional, old yet recognizably modern America, the stereotype of themselves that modern Americans either attack or defend. You would also have seen a map of American Christianity in its supposedly classic form.[1]

Within three blocks of Jackson's main intersection were five large brick churches, built in either a Gothic or a Romanesque style, each possessed of at least one Hardy Boys tower, and each, when properly equipped with snow, well qualified to appear on any twenty-first-century Christmas card. These churches were Baptist, Congregational, Episcopal, Methodist, and Presbyterian—the mainstream Protestant denominations of heartland America, then and now.

Each congregation had existed in some form since Jackson's early years; they were considered old, even historic. The buildings themselves were new, but they were made to look old and to seem eternal. Their air of antiquity, their harmonious architecture, their shared prominence in the center of town were evidence of a massive, unchanging religious core. Ten blocks away, on the outskirts of the city, rose the spires of St. John's Roman Catholic Church, another bulky presence on the religious landscape, harmonious in its way and indicative of yet another congregation dating to the 1830s, though located at a significant distance from the Protestant center.

Here is the collection of denominations that continue to represent "the Church" in the broad generalizations often made about American Christianity. The prominence of these six religious bodies can be easily, though perhaps superficially, explained by their connections to main currents of America's development.

The Episcopal, or Anglican, Church is the American descendant of the state church of England. It was the established church in several southern and middle colonies. The Congregational Church, planted by English dissidents in the northern colonies, was the established church in most of New England. The Presbyterian Church was the special denomination of Scotch-Irish immigrants who had settled on the Appalachian frontier and then on more westerly frontiers. These three churches were visible proof of America's connection with the Old World.

Methodists and Baptists also had European roots, but in the early nineteenth century they were largely convert, not heritage, denominations. Their American growth had been fast, strong, and recent.

Methodism was developed by people within the Church of England who met to consider ways in which life could be more "methodically" ordered by God's word. Their mission was to revive Christianity and return it to its roots; their specialty was evangelism to unconverted, merely nominal Christians. The movement's greatest evangelist, George Whitefield, came to North America during the "Great Awakening" of religious fervor in the 1730s and 1740s. More than anyone else, Whitefield inspired the Awakening, addressing the largest crowds yet seen on the continent (25,000 or more) and stirring many of his listeners to frenzy. Benjamin Franklin, who had no theological sympathy with Whitefield, wanted to hear him preach but resolved not to contribute any money. He wound up putting everything, "Gold and all," in the collection plate.[2]

After the American Revolution, the Methodists organized themselves as a separate denomination, the Methodist Episcopal Church. Their traveling evangelists were usually the first preachers to show up in a frontier community. By 1850 they were the biggest religious body in America, with a third of all church members.[3] Early Methodists were frequently regarded as a wild frontier sect, but they were never confined to the West and South. Unexpectedly for a "frontier church," they prided themselves on organization—bishops, a national convention with real authority, and an elaborate rule, or "discipline."

The Baptists, though socially and economically similar to the Methodists, had few organizational ambitions. One of the first Baptists in America, Roger Williams, the eccentric founder of Rhode Island, was too religious to participate in any religious organization, considering none of them authorized by apostolic authority.[4] When Baptist congregations started appearing in large numbers in the early nineteenth century, they were small, independent attempts to replicate New Testament congregations. They were "Baptist" because they insisted that baptism be undertaken only by people of adult understanding and administered only in the New Testament way, by immersion. The Baptists' idea of the independent church was well adapted to frontier life, but like

FIGURE 3.1. *George Whitefield, religious revolutionary. Courtesy of the University of Pennsylvania Archives.*

the Methodists, they enjoyed strong growth in every social climate. By the end of the 1880s, Baptist adherents were approaching 10 percent of America's population.[5]

In most communities, Roman Catholics ("Romanists" or "papists" to their competitors) had become visible even more recently than Methodists and Baptists. There had been Catholics in English America almost from the beginning; a Catholic had started one of the English colonies, Maryland. But their strongest association was with recent immigrants, especially the Irish. Relations between Protestants and Catholics were poisoned on many levels. Many Protestants asserted that Catholics could not be saved; many Catholics returned the compliment. At great cost to themselves, Catholics formed their own schools, chiefly because the public schools routinely provided small amounts of generically Protestant religious instruction, chiefly readings from the King James Version of the Bible—a translation similar to the Catholics' own Douay Version but dismissed as "Protestant" by church hierarchs. Meanwhile, "nativist" movements organized to deny political power to Catholic immigrants. The construction of the Washington Monument was delayed for twenty-five years after the pope dared to donate a stone for it.

Catholics in Jackson were mainly Irish immigrants and their children. Many had come to work for the railroad as common laborers, but in 1889 they were numerous enough to support two large churches—the second one only four blocks from the city center—and two schools to go with them. So Catholics ran their own schools, but they were not civically isolated. At the funeral of Father Moutard, Jackson's first resident priest, thousands of citizens, representative "of all opinions, religious and political," marched in his honor.[6] National tensions were not necessarily local ones.

On a purely social or institutional view of religion, the Catholic Church completed the array of organizations necessary to maintain Christianity in Jackson. Irish immigrants had their own church; various kinds of Protestants had their churches, also. According to a plausible theory, one reason church adherence increased during the mid-nineteenth century is that growing towns like Jackson could offer a menu of churches, not just the single church in reach of the old farmhouse. If you didn't like one church, you could easily find another.[7]

Under these circumstances, one might expect to find a state of happy complementarity among Christian congregations. Even Methodist evangelists sometimes expressed their "scorn" for "the contemptible business of proselyting members from other Churches."[8] And sometimes Christians did cooperate handsomely. Whitefield was warmly welcomed (at first) by many Congregationalists and Presbyterians, despite the fact that he was a minister of the Church of England, with which they had a long record of enmity. Cooperation was especially frequent when members of competing denominations found themselves isolated together in some makeshift frontier settlement. In the 1830s Jackson's Congregationalists and Presbyterians, grown from similar intellectual roots, formed one "Presbyterian" church. Forty years later, when the Presbyterians sought an independent existence, they met in a Baptist church, then in the Jewish synagogue, then in the halls of fraternal organizations, and finally in their own newly erected building. Religious tolerance continued to be symbolized by the synagogue, which stood on the city square, across from the city hall.

But even the Christian mainstream was far from an untroubled current. In nineteenth-century America, there was almost as much skepticism among Baptists about other Protestants' chances of salvation as there was among Catholics about the Baptists' own chances. And contrary to stereotypes, people didn't respond to a diversity of religious choices by quietly segregating themselves in congregations that might be considered socially appropriate for them: wealthy people in the proud, intellectually cultivated Episcopal Church; ambitious tradesmen with the enthusiastic Methodists; poor people with the bare-bones Baptists. Churches avidly competed for members from the same social-economic groups. In Jackson, as in other cities of moderate size, each church had its share of prosperous merchants and professional people, and of economically struggling people too.[9]

Even the Episcopal church, the supposed resort of substantial wealth, had trouble paying its bills. Like the great majority of nineteenth-century churches, it took in enough during a normal year to provide a meager salary for its minister, and not much else. To raise money for their first building, completed in 1840, Jackson's Episcopalians followed the example of most other congregations and sold pews in the prospective structure. You could buy a pew for as little as $55 or as much as $155, but the average was $84. Pews could also be rented for as little as $13 a year. Despite all that, the church had to take out a mortgage.[10] Unless it attracted and kept a broadly representative population, it would go under. Complicating the situation was the fact that members and even officials of Jackson's churches kept wandering from one denomination to another. No church had a secure position in the marketplace.

When one looks at the architectural history of these churches, one sees how interested they were in competing with one another, no matter how adventurously they had to invest in doing so. In 1870 the Methodists, the city's largest group of Protestants, spent $75,000, an enormous amount for the place and time, on a new church on Main Street. They spread the rumor that their church was "free from debt" on the day it opened. That wasn't true—the building had been financed merely by pledges from the membership. A financial downturn a few years later meant that the pledges couldn't be paid. Creditors were ready to evict the congregation when a wave of fear swept up enough donations to save the church.

FIGURE 3.2. *First Baptist Church, Jackson, Michigan: taller is better.*
Photo by Joseph Ho; used by permission.

The Methodists, however, long constituted a competitive menace to other congregations. When the Baptists opened their downtown church in 1872, it looked just like the Methodists', except that its spire was somewhat taller. The Baptists' attempt to compete left them, too, heavily indebted. The Methodists installed an organ that was said to be audible six miles away; the Episcopalians, with a smaller congregation, dug deeper into their pockets and spent $4,000 on an even better instrument.[11]

All of America's big denominations except one (the Congregationalists) competed throughout the nation, a sign that their theological differences were broadly significant. Whether to christen infants or immerse adults was an issue that aroused strong passions almost everywhere. Virtually any aspect of governance, procedure, or symbolism could provoke violent controversy among Protestants or between Protestants and Catholics. Before the mid-nineteenth century, few Protestant churches were "papist" enough to raise crosses on their steeples. In Jackson, only the Lutherans and the Episcopalians were willing to do so at any time during the century.[12] But beneath the national, denominational differences lay something more intricate and vital: the competitive or constructive enterprises—active, detailed, and personal—of local communities. To paraphrase a late twentieth-century political slogan, churches may think globally, but they have to act locally. A group of people has to come up with something that will not only identify who they are but also attract and hold other people.

Consider the way in which Christianity came to Jackson. In 1830, the year when the place was founded, a man named Isaiah Bennett, who had been a licensed Methodist preacher but had "backslid," called a religious meeting at his log house. Having scruples about his own qualifications to lead the meeting, he summoned a "praying-man" (a layperson) from a nearby settlement. Around the same time, almost all the women of the community started holding their own Christian services. Several of the men eventually joined them, and after a year or so, seven men and women organized a Methodist church, with services led by circuit-riding preachers who visited on the Sabbath.

It's a common story. The people involved in it wouldn't amount to much in historical statistics or generalizations. Yet these men and women were organizing churches for themselves and finding others who would help them. Even the Episcopal church of Jackson was started by laypeople, on their own. And until 1857, Jackson's old Catholic families worshiped in a log church that they built themselves, served from time to time by a visiting priest.

This doesn't mean that Jacksonians couldn't also participate in religious movements that went beyond the local churches. Today the most spectacular of those movements is represented by the superb Civil War memorial that stands at the top of Jackson's main street, the creation of the great Midwestern sculptor Lorado Taft. From the 1840s on, Jackson was a center of religiously motivated opposition to slavery. It was an important stop on the Underground Railroad that helped slaves escape to Canada. In 1854 a convention at Jackson gave a name—Republican—to the new antislavery party. Soon what was called a "revolution" occurred in the town's political affairs as control shifted from Democrats to Republicans. During the war that followed, an astonishing one-eighth of Jackson County's total population enlisted in the Union army or navy.

It took strong religious inspiration for this to happen. But there was religious dissension as well. In 1841 Jackson's Presbyterian church went over to the Congregationalists when its pastor and most of its members objected to the national Presbyterians' failure to act against slavery. Yet abolition wasn't universally popular in Jackson; a decade later, Jacksonians refused to finance a college because they knew it would favor abolition. What got the Congregationalist pastor into serious trouble with the community, however, was his participation in another crusade that mobilized people across denominations: the fight against alcohol. His property was vandalized, and he had to hide in the fields from a mob of outraged "friends of whiskey." His successor continued preaching temperance, whereupon that man's beloved fellow citizens tried to burn his church.[13]

But denominations were shaped more by internal than by external conflicts. The churches' most devout adherents, the people who cared most about religion, quarreled among themselves, locally and nationally, with even greater enthusiasm than they quarreled with anybody else. Internal warfare was as recurrent and destructive as the plagues of Egypt. Out of the wars came new churches—and old churches, revolutionized.

Presbyterians, Congregationalists, and Baptists originally shared the Calvinist belief that God gives his grace as he wishes, regardless of what people do. That belief was contested by the events of the Great Awakening, during the eighteenth century, and of the Second Great Awakening, early in the nineteenth. The success of these movements implied that it wasn't only grace but also human measures—evangelism, revival meetings, and preaching and praying designed to induce conversion—that led people to decide for Christ. Conflicts about these measures and the assumptions behind them prompted bitter divisions between Calvinist and Free Will Baptists; Old Light and New Light Congregationalists; Old Side and New Side, then Old School and New School Presbyterians. The result was shattered congregations, expulsions of clergy from their pulpits, charges and countercharges in the public press, and the warfare of rival ministerial associations and colleges (Yale advocating the traditionalists, and Princeton, the renegades). These were some of the tamer means of combat. In the days of established churches, traditionalists could also use the law to restrain their competition.[14]

By the early nineteenth century, Congregationalists found themselves embroiled in an even deeper theological conflict. Many of their churches were denying the ancient doctrine of the Trinity—one God in three persons—and asserting that Jesus was not God but only an especially beneficent man. They were becoming "unitarian." It was a revolution from above: the unitarians seized the commanding heights of Harvard and the pulpits of the stylish New England churches. When challenged, they were capable of insisting that nothing, after all, had happened. William Ellery Channing, their most distinguished personality, calmly noted that both the unitarians and the trinitarians believed in a Father, a Son, and a Spirit; in this sense, he suggested, they all believed in the Trinity: "As the word Trinity is sometimes used, we all believe in it. . . . Christians ought not to be separated by a sound."[15]

Such words concealed nothing, mollified no one. The old faith of the Pilgrims had been shattered by its leading intellectuals. Without losing its lofty intellectual tone, Congregationalism changed from a denomination that specialized in traditional dogma to a denomination devoted to modern humanitarian causes, convinced that "practical righteousness is all in all."[16] Some ministers and congregations abandoned their old institutional ties and formed a unitarian denomination. Meanwhile, dissidents from every denomination were forming Universalist churches, dedicated to the idea that Jesus died for *all*, not just *some*. By 1852 there was a Universalist church near the center of Jackson, and in due time a Unitarian church joined it.

For a while, Universalism was a dynamic movement, with a strong appeal both to Bible believers and to rationalists and progressives. But like many other religious movements whose continued success might seem to have been predictable, Universalism stalled. One explanation is that some of its advocates discovered intellectual reasons to migrate to still other religious movements formed around the damaged framework of the Calvinist churches. Another is that Universalism was limited by its own intensity, its own strong focus on a single concept, the theological "measure" by which it had first gained adherents; it absorbed the core audience for this message and then found no other interesting idea. A third explanation is that other Christian denominations stopped focusing on damnation and started letting their members assume that everyone (or nearly everyone) might be saved. This revolutionary change in emphasis may have helped their own membership statistics, but it must have hurt the Universalists'.[17] Such after-the-fact explanations may or may not be true. What is certainly true is that in 1961, the Universalist denomination ceased to exist, being institutionally absorbed by the Unitarians.

It is interesting, however, that none of the proposed explanations has to do with social classes or economic trends. True or false, they are all appropriately religious explanations of a religious phenomenon. Purely theological disputes were prominently displayed on the map of Jackson. By 1849 the town had a church of Free Will Baptists as well as a church of the standard, Calvinist variety.[18] Soon it possessed a Free Methodist church as well as several standard Methodist churches, and (to illustrate the fact that theology often trumps ethnicity) an African American Baptist church in addition to the African Methodist Episcopal church. These distinctive congregations were all pursuing the common quest of American Protestants: the search for the original, "primitive," and therefore authentic church. By 1900 a visitor could find a dozen examples of this church not "made with hands" within a dozen blocks of the railway station.[19]

Some churches were built and rebuilt, repeatedly, on both the national and the local level. The movement associated with the name "Disciples of Christ" is one example. Its adventures began in 1801, at Cane Ridge, Kentucky, at the start of the Second Great Awakening. In the midst of a sacramental meeting—a solemn communion service called by the Presbyterians—the frenzy of the Holy Spirit erupted with an intensity that surprised everyone. Many people were convinced that this was a second Pentecost. Some took it as a mandate to restore the Church as it had been at the Spirit's first descent. In 1832 veterans of Cane Ridge joined with members of a primitive-church movement started in western Pennsylvania by Thomas and Alexander Campbell and formed a new religious body. Its sympathizers called it simply the Christian Church. Outsiders identified it with its visible human architects; they called it the Campbellite Church.

Campbellites rejected appeals to any authority except individual study of scripture, thus preempting, they supposed, all quarrels about official creeds. This left them free to quarrel about scripture itself. In the early twentieth century, following much debate, the denomination fractured. The issue was the logical one: whether any religious practice was forbidden if it was not specifically permitted by the New Testament or whether any religious practice was permitted if it was not specifically forbidden by the New Testament. The latter position was adopted by the largest group, whose official name is now "the Christian Church (Disciples of Christ)." It is one of the most important churches in America, and its members are some of the wealthiest and best educated. Its doctrine allows local churches to become "liberal" or "conservative" about virtually any matter one could name. Yet these congregations have retained a strong propensity to split. In small towns, people say, there are always at least two Disciples churches.

In Jackson the difficulty of holding together a generically Christian congregation was obvious from the start. A "Christian" missionary appeared punctually in 1836, and a church was built; then the congregation dissolved. In 1852 another missionary arrived and gathered believers by offering the Bible "as the only creed and discipline for the new organization," but "an unfortunate division occurred," and the congregation dissolved again. It revived a few years later, and another church was built. Within a few years, a talented "liberal" pastor brought people into the congregation, and then "alienated" them. The congregation couldn't make its mortgage payments, and its church was sold. The next Christian pastor was openly a Unitarian.[20] Latent interest in the Campbellite way had always been present, but the means of ministering to it hadn't worked. The Christians didn't return to Jackson until the 1920s.

Some of Jackson's religious history was a bit more predictable than that of the Campbellites. German families naturally established a Lutheran church (1864). And it was natural that African Americans, shunned by most of their white Christian brethren, should have established their own institution as soon as they could (1865). This branch of the venerable African Methodist Episcopal Church began when there were only about 250 black people in Jackson, most of them working in service occupations or as laborers. Yet their church, which in 1871 had only thirty-three members, still exists. Religious commitment can't be measured by the census; it can be estimated only by its own vitality.

Religious vitality was unmistakable in Jackson during the last two decades of the nineteenth century. Churches sprang up in all parts of the city, contesting the hegemony of the costly steeple houses downtown. By 1900 there were three more Baptist churches (besides the Free Will Baptists); a second Congregational church; two more German-oriented churches; the African American Baptist church; the second Catholic church; a Seventh-day Adventist church; a Salvation Army barracks; and five more Methodist churches.

There were also institutions that provided an approach to Christianity for people who had freed themselves completely from Christian tradition. One was the spiritualist society (1868), part of a movement that had begun in upstate New York in 1848 when spirit beings initiated communications with three young women, the Fox sisters. Spiritualism appealed to people who wanted practical evidence of religious claims, to people who expected "scientific" progress in religion as in every other area of life, and to people who, like King Saul, had personal questions to ask of infinity.[21] Women as well as men could ask such questions, and answer them too, by becoming spirit mediums and lecturers. One of spiritualism's special "measures" was its appeal to women, to whom it offered a freedom and authority denied by traditional denominations.

Spiritualism was a response to obvious social as well as religious needs, but it was hardly a response to specific social events. It is often said that the country's interest in spiritualism increased after World War I because of the war deaths, but whether this is true or not, the first and biggest craze for spirit communication had nothing to do with war. It was a reaction to people's immemorial desire to discover a life beyond this life. It addressed this desire with a new technology—spirit rapping, table tipping, automatic writing, mediumship of many kinds. These techniques and the worldview behind them were widely reproducible. Spiritualism could crop up anywhere. Even the tiny town of Leslie, fifteen miles north of Jackson, built a spiritualist church. In the early twentieth century, Jackson itself had several spiritualist congregations. One of them—the occupant of a standard Romanesque building with a standard churchly tower—appealed to the widest possible audience, offering an array of banquets, games, "socials," and Sunday morning services broadcast on radio. Its genial slogan was "We Need You. We Want You."[22]

The reason spiritualism declined during the later twenti-eth century and never fully recovered is the subject of many speculations, none verifiable.

In 1900, however, America's largest neo-Christian move-ment, and the one with the deepest penetration into Ameri-can society, was Christian Science. "Science" was the dis-covery of Mary Baker Eddy, a woman of unique force and determination. A stranger and a sojourner in many small New England towns while writing her foundational work, *Science and Health With Key to the Scriptures* (1875), the independent Mrs. Eddy offered her book in service to the deity she called, in her paraphrase of the Lord's Prayer, "Our Father-Mother God."[23] Her idea was that sickness, death, evil, the physical body itself, are nothing but illusions, ready to be dispelled by the intellectual light—the *science*, or *know-ing*—of the Christ who healed the sick and vanquished the grave. Since matter doesn't really exist, neither do disease and death. To know this is to accept Christ's healing.

That realization—so simple, so complete—gave birth to no elaborate ritual or hierarchy. The outward forms of Christian Science are little more than readings from the Bible and the works of Mary Baker Eddy. "Science" was her way of exploit-ing a particular vein of religious feeling, the impulse to cut straight through to ultimate reality and see results in the real terms of physical and mental health. By the time she died, in 1910, she had made the Church of Christ, Scientist, a major American institution, a triumph, as Mark Twain remarked, of its creator's ability to "organize" potential experience and make it real.[24] In 1925 Christian Scientists erected the stately temple that stands today on Jackson's main street, two blocks from the city center, across from the Civil War memo-rial. Anyone who tries to explain that neoclassic monument by reference to industrial output, class conflict, economic fluctuations, or the ruling patterns of American social or intellectual history will have a difficult task.

One other temple should be mentioned here. In 1889 the industrialist Andrew Carnegie published an essay entitled "The Gospel of Wealth," in which he argued that rich people have a duty, before they die, to give their money away to charitable institutions—not an idea that broadly characterized his social class, or Christians of any class. Carnegie repudiated all the ordinary teachings of Christianity. Nevertheless, on the strength of his ideas about the moral significance of rich people, he concluded that because he donated to charity, he was a disciple of Christ, one of the "true laborers in the vineyard," fulfilling the maxim that "man does not live by bread alone" and anticipating the millennial day when all men shall "indeed be brothers." Of the good works of such good people as himself the angels were thinking when they sang, "Peace on earth, among men good will." The gospel had been reborn, with a middle-aged businessman as its central figure. "Christ's spirit" had been adapted to "the changed conditions of this age."[25]

Social theorists may see in this the deep insecurities of the capitalist regime. Perhaps that is the deep explanation, but what showed itself on the surface was an empire of donations—Carnegie's benefactions to worthy causes throughout America—ascribing its foundation to Christ. The local shrine of the Carnegie religion, erected in 1906, is the beautifully proportioned public library that stands in the heart of Jackson, across from the First Methodist Church and within a short walk from the city's other old memorials of faith—a monument either to the secularization of Christianity or to the Christianization of secularism, depending on how you want to interpret it.

Between 1880 and 1930, the nation's population more than doubled, and Jackson's more than tripled, growing from about 16,000 to about 55,000 souls. The number of churches increased, as noted, but the size of churches and the number of "programs" they offered increased even more. Now there was something—some institutionalized religious connection—for everyone who might conceivably become interested in Christianity. Or so it was thought.

Jackson's First Methodist Church best exemplifies the big-church movement. Big churches needed big personalities to run them, and Frederick Spence, pastor of First Methodist from 1919 to 1943, was a big personality. Known for his "strong and virile pulpit messages" and his interest in "developing the church to meet . . . a growing and expanding life in the community," Spence "urged that the church must not become a one-day-a-week-and-prayer-meeting influence but must be a seven-day-a-week influence in the community." He sponsored innumerable activities: choirs, mission societies, charity groups, young people's groups, married people's groups, sports groups, little theater societies, movie nights, lecture series, music concerts, luncheons, teas, suppers, banquets, and an "Open Forum" to discuss "religious, social and economic problems and the part the church should play in their solution."[26]

All this meant organization, a vast web of volunteer officers and committees and a paid staff to keep track of them. Here, one might think, we are seeing a direct social influence of the business-obsessed 1920s: the church, having so much to manage, reached out to managers, to young men and women attracted by the boast that "its business [was] conducted as efficiently as any sound business . . . [T]here is no finer organized group to be found in the city."[27] Yet Spence himself was obstreperously liberal in religion and politics, he made no secret of disliking big business, and he was a terrible manager of money. None of these facts kept him from being accepted as the most eminent citizen of a town that by this time had become very conservative.[28]

First Methodist's success went far beyond the managerial class (which was far from the most conservative element of the community). From 1918 to 1933, membership more than doubled, reaching about 2,200, a very large number for a Protestant congregation. Members, their children, and other attenders of this church composed roughly one-twelfth of Jackson's total population. Not surprisingly, the local paper complimented Mr. Spence for his contribution to "the interests of the whole community."[29] Apparently the church did offer something for almost everyone, liberal or conservative, male or female, rich or poor.

To accommodate its growth and symbolize its success, First Methodist embarked on a construction program. It embedded its old brick building—which had been good enough, and expensive enough, when its sole function had been public worship—in a hive of classrooms, offices, meeting rooms, social rooms, and rooms for movies. One of its Victorian steeples disappeared; the other was shortened to blend with the church's suave new front. The style was still Gothic, but of a different kind. It was the smooth, sophisticated, late Gothic revival mode of the 1920s, all in decorative stone. The institutional emphasis had changed from soul saving to community building; the architectural emphasis, from primitive self-advertisement to the opulence that dares not shout its name. Again, personal leadership was the method behind the other methods: most members thought the new construction was "both needless and [financially] hopeless," but Spence pushed the project through, and the doubters were swamped by enthusiastic new adherents.[30]

Jackson's Catholic churches were also revolutionizing their appearance. The older parish, St. John's, covered its Gothic bricks with an impressive stone veneer. The newer parish, St. Mary Star of the Sea, replaced its brick church with a larger and much more splendid structure (1926)—all stone, Byzantine-Romanesque, with beautiful embellishments, including a stained-glass window designed by the pastor and depicting Jackson County soldiers arriving (center right) on a battlefield of the Great War. Lower right, and

FIGURE 3.3. *The World War I window, St. Mary Star of the Sea, Jackson, Michigan. Photo by Joseph Ho; used by permission.*

lower center, wounded soldiers look up to Christ, standing cruciform at the top of the window and flanked by angels bearing emblems of victory. At the lower left, a Sister of Charity tends a fallen nurse; above them, the Virgin raises her eyes to Christ, completing the connections among the soldiers, the church, and the martyred God. In the window's incarnational theology, Jesus is always with us, as fully present in the trenches of France as on the streets of Jackson.

This window, *Christ and the Battlefield,* is the principal mark left on Jackson's churches by the world struggle of 1914–1918. That vast social and economic storm passed over the local community, bequeathing no structural change or hint of one. The same might be said of World War II. At the end of that war, we are told by *It's a Wonderful Life* (1946), Americans went to church and "wept and prayed"—and that, apparently, was that. The film's conversion narrative has very little to do with the war, and neither did the subsequent shape of American Christianity, except for its enlargement with young attenders, products of the postwar baby boom.[31] Among the many parallels with earlier American history is the devastating diphtheria epidemic in eighteenth-century New England, which happens to have been strongest where neither the First Great Awakening nor any other religious disruption was taking place.[32] The antebellum Midwest was ravaged by dreadful appearances of malaria and cholera, but neither disease makes a significant appearance in narratives of the Second Great Awakening. As usual, the big news and the big religious movements barely spoke to one another on the street.

A much more important event for Christianity in Jackson, as in the rest of religious America, was the depression of the 1930s. Here was a social-economic cause with real effects: during the Great Depression, most of America's churches went broke. *His Marriage Wow* [sic], a Mack Sennett comedy of 1925, refers to a church that "was so old fashioned, it was clear of mortgages." In the 1930s, most churches were more modern; they had plenty of debts (they still do). As a result, some closed their doors; others turned off the heat, cut the minister's pay, or simply neglected to pay him anything at all. Many took out *second* mortgages. Almost all of them abandoned their building plans. Construction slowed at St. John the Divine, then halted at the end of the decade, before anything had been put in place to reconcile the Gothic nave, the Romanesque crossing, and the rudimentary transepts. Today, they remain much as they were when the money ran out. On the opposite coast, construction stopped on San Francisco's Episcopal cathedral, leaving a half-built concrete nave concluded by a wall of sheet metal. In Jackson, churches struggled to aid the poor, while dealing with their own financial problems. Even the Episcopal church had debts that were twice the size of its endowment.[33]

The Depression was the biggest catastrophe that ever happened to American churches, yet its permanent effects are hard to find. The proportion of people involved with the churches neither significantly declined nor significantly increased, although the slide from mainstream to evangelical Christianity continued, as it has in our own day.[34] Afterward, there was much less talk about a businesslike Christianity, but the influence of left-wing "Social Gospel" Christians showed no remarkable growth, perhaps because it had been so strong in the mainline churches even before the Depression—witness the liberal views of Reverend Spence. American Christianity absorbed the effects of social crisis and continued on its way, preoccupied with its own concerns. It might have made the same observation as the eccentric lady in *Citizen Kane* (1941), responding to a comment about how "the last ten years have been tough on a lotta people": "Ah, they haven't been tough on me. I just lost all my money."

The most significant development had already happened, inside the churches. It didn't reveal itself on maps. It didn't affect church architecture, at least not right away. It was a revolution from above, and it was effectively concealed from ordinary churchgoers. This revolutionary development was modernist theology.

In the late 1920s an enterprising scholar conducted a survey of religious opinion, not among church members but among ministers and seminary students. He sent questionnaires to Protestant pastors—eminently mainstream pastors[35]—in the Chicago area, and to seminary students at five institutions representing three major denominations. Five hundred ministers and 200 students responded—a significant number if you were concerned about opinion solely in the leading churches. The students, as a group, were even more mainstream than the pastors and of potentially higher professional status. Their schools were "of national importance and renown and the denominations recognized as of first importance in numbers and influence."[36]

The schools were left unnamed "in order not to embarrass" them.[37] Embarrass them? Why? Because the survey indicated that the mainstream had shifted its course away from the religious heartland. Elite pastors and seminarians no longer held the traditional beliefs of their denominations. And the seminarians had shifted so far that their affiliations could not be revealed.

Orthodox ideas were more apparent among the active ministers than among the students, but pastoral orthodoxy was much weaker than one would expect. One-fifth of Congregationalist ministers would not warrant their belief in a personal, morally perfect God; two-fifths didn't consider God omnipotent. Only three-quarters of the Methodists, the leading evangelicals of the nineteenth century, reported belief in the Trinity or in the idea that God is omnipotent. Only a quarter of them believed in the literal truth of the Bible's creation account, and barely half believed in miracles. Among the 500 ministerial respondents as a whole, the two beliefs just mentioned had sunk to 47 percent and 68 percent, respectively. Only 33 percent of the pastors denied that "evolution is consistent with belief in God as Creator"; only 38 percent thought the Bible was wholly free from legend or myth.

Turning to belief in Jesus's resurrection, which according to St. Paul is the touchstone of Christian faith:[38] if you were an Episcopalian or a Lutheran in the Chicago area, you could be sure that the message you heard on Easter would be preached without mental reservation; all the ministers in those denominations said they believed that the Resurrection had occurred. But if you attended another church, your chances were considerably smaller. The percentage of pastors professing a belief in the Resurrection differed greatly from one denomination to another: Evangelicals, 92 percent; Presbyterians, 86 percent; Baptists, 82 percent; Methodists, 74 percent; and Congregationalists, only 57 percent.

One often hears of the damage done to Christianity by the idea of biological evolution and by modern historical study of scripture (the so-called Higher Criticism). The institutional damage was not as obvious as one might expect. Seven decades after Darwin's *Origin of Species,* and about the same length of time since the Higher Criticism first gained popularity in America, leaders of the mainstream churches had assimilated modernist conclusions and were proceeding as usual. Seminary students had survived even more thorough acts of assimilation. Almost all of them, of whatever denomination, saw evolution as consistent with the idea of God as creator. Only 6 percent resisted the idea. Only 4 percent cherished the idea that the Bible is wholly free from legend or myth. As for the Resurrection, future ministers were only half as likely to believe in it as the ministers currently occupying a pulpit—42 percent as opposed to 84 percent. Thirty-one percent of the students positively did not believe; 27 percent confessed themselves unsure.

Such doubts and disbeliefs would probably have made a

highly unfavorable impression on the churchgoers who were funding such pastors and students. But the alienations, defections, and heresies were not proclaimed. A battle between "fundamentalists" and "modernists" might occasionally be reported in the press. Some took notice when Harry Emerson Fosdick published, to great acclaim in modernist ministerial circles, his sermon "Shall the Fundamentalists Win?" (1922)—as if, at that point, the fundamentalists had any chance of winning in the mainstream denominations. But for most mainstream congregations, the war always seemed to be happening somewhere else, in the next state, or New York City, or denominational headquarters. It seldom involved the local church. Except in the most liberal churches in the wealthiest and most tolerant communities—such as Riverside Church in New York, built for Fosdick by John D. Rockefeller Jr.—there was little attempt to emphasize departures from traditional theology.

Emphasis fell instead on the most reassuring aspects of the old faith. Virtually all the seminary students in the survey agreed with their predecessors in conceptualizing God as "Father"; and though only 11 percent (compared with more than half the active ministers) believed that heaven and hell are actual "locations," they were almost as sure as the active ministers (89 percent as opposed to 97 percent) that life continues after death. Only 21 percent thought that prayer could change "conditions in nature," but 82 percent believed that the Holy Spirit acts on and in "human lives."

One might charge these students with hypocrisy, with a willingness to minister to congregations gathered in accordance with beliefs that they themselves denied. Certainly there was a "deepened gulf between the clergy and the laity."[39] But the students were not demanding more of others than they demanded of themselves. Fully 85 percent affirmed that regardless of belief, "persons who love God and do justly with their fellow men are worthy of acceptance into the Christian Church." This conviction hardly proceeded from a desire to maintain the exclusive power of their own denominations—a common socioeconomic accusation against the clergy. No, only 16 percent believed that "in order to be a Christian it is necessary and essential to belong to the church"—any church.

Here (and not in the "monkey" trial) one sees the emerging shape of an issue that continues to divide and inspire American Christianity. It has been called the fundamentalist-modernist controversy, but the real question was always whether the mainstream churches could continue their dominance while moving away from teachings once viewed as crucial—the doctrinal measures with which they had begun. J. Gresham Machen, the greatest intellectual among the fundamentalists, put it in this way: "Rightly or wrongly, Christian experience has ordinarily been connected with one particular view of the origin of the Christian movement; where that view has been abandoned, the experience has ceased."[40]

When he wrote those words, Machen was a certified member of the mainstream Christian elite, a professor at the Princeton Seminary. But he had detected the fact that most members of the religious elite were no longer experiencing Christianity as ordinary people did. He could easily be accused of defining the Christian experience too narrowly and with too little regard for the diversity of methods that help to make it real. Yet the problem remained: Were the mainstream churches doing enough to inspire such an experience? Would big-church and modern-church activities continue helping people make the connection between potential and actual Christianity?

You can read the answer on the map of Jackson. After World War II, the mainstream churches maintained considerable popularity with families, especially the young families of the baby-boom era. Some even managed to expand and build. The Presbyterians left their Romanesque church and built a modern one on the fringe of downtown, near the elegant new Jewish house of worship. Other mainstream churches built big modern structures in Jackson's little freeway-oriented suburbs. Then came a demographic disaster. The baby boom ran its course, and so did Jackson's industries. In the five decades following 1960, Jackson, like many other communities in America, lost most of its industrial jobs and consequently much of its population. The downtown churches hung on, but with diminished membership. Yet Jackson's religious diversity continued to increase. The congregations that did best were evangelical Baptists and community churches advertising their firm possession of the orthodox religious experience to which Machen referred.

And Jackson's religious history is not unusual. The tendency wasn't confined to economically depressed communities. It could be seen nationwide. In 1940 four of the top mainstream Protestant denominations comprised, together, 22.4 percent of all church members in America, and four of the top evangelical denominations comprised 8.3 percent. In 2000 the figures were 9.6 and 15.7 percent, respectively.[41]

Every religious movement has a maximum reach. With the means at its disposal—its teachings and other measures—it can embrace only a certain proportion of religious experience; it can find and keep only a certain number of adherents. The mainstream churches had attained, at least temporarily, the limits of their methods, which had become increasingly undemanding and indistinct. They still offered a menu of choices, but the items looked very similar.

This did not imply that Christianity was dying or that, for Americans, God himself was dead, possibilities on which *Time* and *Newsweek* offered solemn comment.[42] Other churches were making converts, often from the mainstream churches themselves, using methods aimed at inspiring the kinds of experience from which the mainstream had originally flowed. Those *other* churches now showed themselves

boldly on the landscape. Today, Jackson and its close suburbs have about 120 churches, more than half of them evangelical. The great majority were created after 1970. Many of
these churches represent white southern Christianity, the
Christianity especially of people from western Kentucky
who came to Jackson when its industries were healthy. Many
others represent the Christianity of black immigrants from
the South. But by the late twentieth century, these southern "regional" Christianities had become fully indigenous
in Jackson and throughout the North and West. Defying the
classifications of cultural historians, "regional" religious
phenomena had become national religious phenomena.

The modern evangelical churches claimed to be revivals
of "traditional," "historic," and usually "primitive" Christianity. Yet they were as new as America's old-time churches
always are; they were the product of yet another revolution in
the "work" of religion, the "measures" of converting souls to
Christ. Later, this book will have much to say about contemporary religious measures. But in America, revival (a backward movement) and conversion (a forward movement) have
almost always gone together. There is biblical precedent. The
earliest books of the New Testament, the epistles of Paul,
insist that Christ's followers move forward—by reviving the
experiences they had when they were converted (in the case
of his initial readers, only a few years before).[43] Paul, the
master preacher, continually found new ways of instigating
reconversion, the re-creation of a Christian past, however
recent that past may have been.

Past and future, revival and conversion, restoration and
transformation: these are paradoxical companions, yet in
American culture, they usually inhabit the same locales.
They are volatile and disruptive pairs; their manners are
often terrible; they fight with each other and everyone else;
and although they often change their methods, they never
agree to quit. The great majority of Americans have always

regarded themselves as Christians, by heritage and upbring-
ing, almost by nature; nevertheless, they have spent hundreds
of years being both converted and revived. In the process,
they have revolutionized their churches and sometimes their
society, often in ways that might try even the patience of God.

How that happened, and kept on happening, is the subject
of the next chapter.

THE MAKING
OF REVIVAL

What does Christianity have to do with the San Francisco earthquake? Nothing. But in America, means can be found to turn any story into a drama of revival and conversion.

San Francisco (1936) is a movie about the disaster of 1906. Clark Gable plays a saloon owner who, despite his close friendship with a priest (Spencer Tracy), scorns all religion. After the earthquake, however, he finds his sweetheart (Jeanette MacDonald) in a refugee camp singing "Nearer, My God, to Thee" with other survivors. The scene affects him as the vision of Beatrice once affected Dante Alighieri. He tells the priest, "I want to thank God. What do I say?" "Just say what's in your heart," the priest replies. That, it seems, is the right approach. Gable kneels in the dirt and says, "Thanks, God. Thanks." Then he adds, in a rough approximation of "amen": "I really mean it."

With the reunion of the romantic couple, the movie is free to end. But the climax is yet to come. Somebody shouts, "The fire's out!" and somebody else cries, "We'll build a new San Francisco!" The refugees start walking back toward the city, and as they walk, they spontaneously begin to sing the message of the book of Revelation, as expressed in "The Battle Hymn of the Republic": "Mine eyes have seen the glory of the coming of the Lord." The Revelator, St. John the Divine, had seen God's city, the New Jerusalem, coming down from heaven.[1] Now, by a trick of special effects, the film's band of visionaries sees the New San Francisco, rising from the ruins of the old. In that glorious city, streetcars hurry along the streets, skyscrapers rise atop the hills, and the cables of a great bridge spring across the Golden Gate. It's the glory of the Lord as it actually appeared in the San Francisco of 1936, recorded in the film's last footage.[2]

This story of transformation and revival, small scale and large, individual and communal, has an outrageous power. The proof is the film's ability to recover from the moment when Gable says, "I really mean it." Every audience laughs at that, but somehow it doesn't damage the story. *San Francisco* is said to have made more money than any other movie of its year, and it was nominated for six Academy Awards, including the award for Best Writing (Original Story).

Conversion, transformation, revival, restoration—those are all good ways to resolve a plot. But faith is more than a plot idea. To feel its power, you have to "mean it" and keep on meaning it. Do you?

That's the question that has plagued American Christians right from the start. Puritan churches originally admitted no one to membership without evidence of a conversion experience. In search of the evidence, people probed their lives in spiritual journals, trying to make sure they were saved. Another kind of writing put the crucial question to the community at large. It was a species of sermon, sometimes called the "jeremiad," in which preachers warned, as Jeremiah had in Old Testament times, that God's people were losing their hold on God. Like the practice of inspecting one's own life to discover the signs of grace, it was an aid to reflection, a measure undertaken to convert or revive.

Other, more truly revolutionary measures might have been employed if the New England clergy had been less active in conserving the power of the institutional church. Enthusiastic reformers—Anne Hutchinson, Roger Williams—were driven out, and measures were taken to keep untransformed, merely hereditary adherents within the church, allowing them to be "halfway" members without presenting evidence of conversion. Even in these circumstances, however, there were signs of a large, though untapped, religious potential. Many people attended church every Sunday and had every social reason to claim conversion and become full members, but they had too much religious integrity to do so. People often declined to take communion, even when urged by their ministers, because they themselves weren't sure of their conversions.[3]

Ministers, too, might be unsure about whether they had been converted. Samuel Stoddard, who would become so prominent that he was called the Protestant pope, pastored a Massachusetts church for two years before he consented to be ordained. The problem was that he had enjoyed "no experimental [experiential] acquaintance with the Gospel." Then, suddenly, while administering communion, he "had a new and wonderful revelation" of God's love; after that "peculiar experience," he was fully "acquainted."[4]

Presumably, Stoddard's experience might have been enjoyed by thousands more, if the right measures had been taken. There was a smattering of local revivals from time to time, but a larger awakening didn't come until the 1730s. Why then? No one knew; no one knows. Observers saw the start of the Great Awakening as "strange and surprising": "We have not heard anything like it since the Reformation."[5] Some tried to explain it but failed. Jonathan Edwards, its principal American-born leader, studied the matter systematically. In his *Faithful Narrative of the Surprizing Work of God*, he describes one of its early beginnings, a dramatic upsurge of feeling within his congregation in Northampton, Massachusetts, in 1734–1735. When a notoriously worldly woman suddenly converted, others noticed it and started reflecting on their own spiritual condition; soon almost everyone in town was attending church or holding religious meetings at home. Edwards finds no earthly way of accounting for these sudden events. It wasn't as if sin and repentance had just been invented.

Edwards refused to attribute the revival to his own preaching, and he wasn't simply being modest. He was a forceful preacher, but he had been one for years before any revival broke out. He did, however, emphasize the presence of what might be called "contagion." As news of the Northampton revival spread to neighboring towns, revivals tended to begin there also. But the image of contagion, in which religion grows like an epidemic, omits the human, intentional element, the importance of choice and effort. When neighbors found that Northampton was enjoying a revival, some were earnest to have their own, and got it; for others, it happened independently—and every Christian seemed to be affected in an individual way.[6] Edwards was a person of scientific interests as well as a preacher, but he found that revivals were not a science; there was always a mystery about them.

Yet they had their own methods. They might even become an art. When George Whitefield arrived in America in 1739, he showed what could be done by a real revival artist. Again, "contagion" helped; some Americans had already participated in revivals; others had heard of them, and they had heard of Whitefield, too. They expected great things—too great for the many clergymen who saw the Awakening slipping out of institutional or, as they thought, intellectual control. Whitefield toured the colonies, developing the enthusiasm of enormous audiences. It was America's first mass movement, an example of what can occur when both the congregation and the preacher know what to do.

Of Whitefield, Benjamin Franklin said, "He had a loud and clear Voice, and articulated his Words & Sentences so perfectly that he might be heard and understood at a great Distance, especially as his Auditories [listeners], however numerous, observ'd the most exact Silence." Franklin believed that Whitefield's artistry was based on careful practice:

> By hearing him often I came to distinguish easily between Sermons newly compos'd, and those which he had often preach'd in the Course of his Travels. His Delivery of the latter was so improv'd by frequent Repetitions, that every Accent, every Emphasis, every Modulation of Voice, was so perfectly well turn'd and well plac'd, that without being interested in the Subject, one could not help being pleas'd with the Discourse, a Pleasure of much the same kind with that receiv'd from an excellent Piece of Musick.

According to Franklin, Whitefield's professional mistake was putting his words in writing. He was so much better at talking that "if he had never written any thing he would have left behind him a much more numerous and important Sect. And his Reputation might in that case have been still growing, even after his Death."[7]

Real damage might be done to a revival if its leaders didn't know where to stop, although that depended very much on the "auditories." Eighteenth-century Congregationalists and Presbyterians, who still expected an intellectual approach, would have been horrified by the techniques of Aimee Semple McPherson, who in the 1920s endeared herself to vast audiences by coming on stage dressed as a milkmaid, to represent the simplicity of the gospel message. And they would probably have been bored by the real simplicity of Billy Graham's Bible-school manner, which was highly congenial to stadium and television audiences in the mid-twentieth century. But a lapse from professionalism, however that changeable quality may be defined at the moment, is usually fatal to the revival process. From the Great Awakening to the era of the megachurch, congregations have often been seized with hysteria; people have wept and shouted and fallen to the ground, "slain by the Spirit"; but when preachers themselves become hysterical, it's almost always a sign that they have abandoned their art, and are about to be abandoned by their audience.

An early example is James Davenport, a young minister who lost his professionalism during the Great Awakening. Davenport went about New England churches screaming, "Come to Christ! Come to Christ!" and babbling extemporaneous sermons. Legally ejected from a humorless Connecticut, he turned up in Massachusetts, where his preaching "occasion[ed] great meltings, screamings, crying, swooning, and Fits" among some people, while scandalizing more. Again the law cracked down, but Davenport's popularity was rapidly diminishing anyway. Less than four years after he started, even he realized he had gone too far. He repented and went back to being a normal preacher. His outbreak of zeal—so over-the-top, so without the appropriate artistry—was regarded as one reason the general awakening ceased.[8]

A different audience attended the start of the Second Great Awakening in the Kentucky backcountry in 1801. Events at Cane Ridge began the popularity of the camp meeting, a place where people could gather by the hundreds or thousands, live out of their tents or wagons for a week or longer, and experience something more than a Sunday sermon. Like New Englanders, western settlers frequently wandered off on their own to wrestle with God; camp meetings provided a place where these spiritual adventures could be shared with masses of other people. At Cane Ridge, the call to conversion produced explosive results. The fields and woods turned into a giant religious marketplace where exhorters of many kinds preached to whoever would listen. Men and women, black and white, children and old people suddenly discovered their ability to be converted and to bring others to conversion. From far off, a sound could be heard "like the roar of Niagara."[9]

After Cane Ridge, camp meetings became a structural part of evangelical Christianity. The evidence can be found in church properties scattered across the American hinterland and in substantial resort communities where the heirs and assigns of the early evangelicals annually cultivate a gentrified spiritual life. The camp meeting is now an elderly landlord, the host of summer youth activities and self-discovery courses, but it was once a new way to God, discovered spontaneously and then developed by people who knew what they were doing. Evangelical fervor could be protracted if it was professionally managed. Someone had to organize a series of revival meetings; someone had to advertise them; someone had to show up to preach at them. Laymen might rise and deliver a message, but professionals were much more likely to have the right things to say.

Among the most detailed and candid accounts of early American revivalism are those presented by the professional evangelist Peter Cartwright (1785–1872), a Methodist missionary who roved the Midwest and the border states for over half a century, starting in 1803, soon after the Cane Ridge excitement. Cartwright's job was to make contacts, arrange meetings, and plan the particular sequence of singing, praying, and preaching that was most capable of inciting revival and conversion. If all went well, he could then "open the church"—help converts create a local congregation conformed to the Methodist discipline.

Cartwright had his share of "cold meetings"; he also had plenty of occasions "to steer the ship or guide the flock" when some of the members "ran wild." But under his guidance and that of other full-time evangelists, the whole western-frontier "country seemed all coming home to God."[10] The homecoming story was as old as the Prodigal Son, but innovative methods were now being used to facilitate the prodigal's "return"—in fact, transformation. Mass excitement, a direct appeal to immediate conversion, a careful choice of the best ways to approach particular audiences and, if possible, particular individuals—such measures almost always proved more effective than those of seminary-educated clergy, who had been taught (as many of today's mainstream clergy still are taught) how to hold a pulpit but not how to raise a crowd.

Ministers of the Second Great Awakening had a more practical, and often a more hazardous, education. They found, as Cartwright conceded, that the excesses following Cane Ridge were "hard to control."[11] So were attacks made on revival meetings by "infidels" trying to stop them. Today the removal of a cross from public land, or a high school principal's retaliation against a valedictorian determined to mention Jesus, is considered a newsworthy assault on Christianity. In an earlier America, basic Christianity was taught in every school, but private displays of religious enthusiasm, even those approved by a majority of the community, were often targets of violence and even terrorism. In the religious economy of Victorian America, the division of labor soon progressed to the point at which a strong man could earn a decent living as a chief of security (i.e., official warrior) at revival meetings.[12]

Those were the days when atheism had real muscle. But atheists were far from the only antagonists that new religious movements had to face. In the 1840s, American adventists found that merely preaching their opinions about the end of the world uncovered a wide vein of religious intolerance in statistically normal people. Adventists were mercilessly ridiculed, then violently attacked. In Ithaca, their meeting place was burned. In Boston and New York City their assemblies were closed by mobs. In Philadelphia the sheriff blamed the victims, forbidding adventist meetings because mobs had attacked them.[13]

But this history of religious violence in the United States starts much earlier. The record of a camp meeting that Cartwright helped to organize in southern Ohio in 1805 or 1806 shows what might be expected during the course of an evangelical service. This time, Cartwright says, there was a particularly large "collection of rabble and rowdies. They came drunk, and armed with dirks, clubs, knives, and horse-whips, and swore they would break up the meeting." The local magistrates were afraid to intervene; one of them, drunk, even fought with Cartwright to free an invader who had attacked him with a whip. Cartwright threw the inebriated official to the ground, jumped on him, and threatened to "pound him well." In the ensuing riot, Cartwright's forces beat their enemies and took thirty prisoners. So much for the Sunday morning service. On Sunday evening, the revival crowd was so dispirited that none of the preachers except Cartwright was willing to speak. As friends of the lowly Jesus, they felt a confused sense of guilt about the violence.

Cartwright did not. He was a professional who knew what to do. He stood up to preach, and the revival proceeded:

> The encampment was lighted up, the trumpet blown, I rose in the stand, and required every soul to leave the tents and come into the congregation. There was a general rush to the stand. I requested the brethren, if ever they prayed in all their lives, to pray now. My voice was strong and clear, and my preaching was more of an exhortation and encouragement than anything else. My text was, "The gates of hell shall not prevail." In about thirty minutes the power of God fell on the congregation in such a manner as is seldom seen; the people fell in every direction, right and left, front and rear. It was supposed that not less than three hundred

fell like dead men in mighty battle; and there was no need of calling mourners [people mourning for their sins and waiting to be converted], for they were strewed all over the camp-ground; loud wailings went up to heaven from sinners for mercy, and a general shout from Christians, so that the noise was heard afar off. Our meeting lasted all night, and Monday and Monday night; and when we closed on Tuesday, there were two hundred who had professed religion, and about that number joined the Church.[14]

Cartwright was wrong, on his own testimony, about the manner "seldom seen." The "power of God fell" month after month, year after year, during the many years he spent as a frontier preacher. So often did sinners collapse on the ground, struggle with God, and then "get happy," rising in the assurance of his grace, that one sympathizes with historians who suggest that it is misleading to discuss "the Great Awakening" and then "the Second Great Awakening"; people in America were *always* being awakened.

Revivals didn't happen, however, simply because people showed up. They happened when the appropriate measures were taken. As the preeminent historian of Cane Ridge has demonstrated, it is quite possible to write the history of that event without reliance on the idea of determining causes in the general social environment—the frontier context, the class structure, and so on. But it is not possible to write such a history without including the relevant religious measures and influences: a tradition of protracted communion services among Scotch-Irish immigrants; the example of some immediately preceding revivals; and excellent word-of-mouth advertising, which let people know that a startling experience might be available to them.[15] Once the revival started, preachers tried to develop the kind of appeals that would keep it going. Some of the appeals worked better than others, and some people in the audience were more susceptible than others; no one knew why, though it apparently had nothing to do with their social class. A remarkable number of those who received the Spirit discovered the capacity to be exhorters too. The shape of events was ultimately inexplicable, but it was certainly not just a mass hysteria.

A similar problem of explanation confronts us in the outpouring of the Holy Spirit at the Azusa Street meetings in Los Angeles a century later. Suddenly people were speaking in "tongues," in forms of language they hadn't learned and didn't understand—in the same way, it was believed, that people had spoken at the Feast of Pentecost. Azusa Street was the beginning of the Pentecostal movement, which today accounts for something like one-twelfth of the Protestant population of the United States and has developed many methods of pastoral leadership.[16] Yet even the Azusa Street meetings had a strong leader, Reverend William J. Seymour, who had influenced his little group of worshipers to pray for just such a thing to occur. That doesn't mean that it happened as an automatic response to his wishes. But much less does it mean, as some social historians imply, that it happened because Seymour was an African American who ministered to a group consisting of both blacks and whites. Revivals don't just spring forth from the social environment. As Charles Finney observed, revivals are most likely to happen when "*somebody* makes particular efforts for this end." There should be definite leaders, and prayers "*for a definite object*"—which there were at Azusa Street.[17]

Amid all the necessary religious measures, the element of mystery endured. Every revivalist knew that some audiences were cold, and there was nothing you could do about it. On the other hand, every revivalist had experiences that confirmed Alexander Pope's saying about authors who disobey the rules yet "snatch a grace beyond the reach of art."[18] A preacher might do everything wrong, yet see his meeting swept by the Spirit. Nevertheless, revival was clearly a business that could be learned. And technique wasn't something merely external, something easily distinguishable from the reality of religious inspiration. Technique could summon reality. It often did.

One of the most perceptive accounts of this relationship appears in Harold Frederic's novel *The Damnation of Theron Ware* (1896), a curious book that is simultaneously a satire and a realistic study of evangelical Protestantism and its enemies. At the center of the book is a conversation between a naïve young Methodist pastor and a veteran evangelist, Sister Soulsby, who describes the way in which she and her husband discovered their vocation. They had made some money in various, mostly shady, ways and were living in retirement when a revival came to town. They attended it every night, "at first," she says, "just to kill time":

> Then . . . we found we liked the noise and excitement and general racket of the thing. After it was all over each of us found that the other had been mighty near going up to the rail and joining the mourners. And another thing had occurred to each of us, too,—that is, what tremendous improvements there were possible in the way that amateur revivalist worked up his business. . . . Well, to make a long story short, we finally went into the thing ourselves.

But, asks the pastor, wasn't it just a sham? Were you ever sincerely converted, yourselves? "Oh, bless you, yes," Sister Soulsby says. "Not only once—dozens of times—I may say every time. We couldn't do good work if we weren't."[19]

It's a profound observation. Revivals require stagecraft, but if the stagecraft is good enough, it produces an authentic drama. This should be obvious; there's no reason, as Sister Soulsby said, to take offense at it. Perhaps there's no problem about admitting that authenticity doesn't happen automatically. Even in the Gospels, a man asking for a miracle says to Jesus, "Lord, I believe; *help* thou mine *unbelief.*"[20] This was no indication that the man didn't "mean it"—quite the opposite. And the miracle came.

Charles Finney (1792–1875), whose views I have quoted, was a person of great significance in the Second Great Awakening. His success in bringing revival from small-time western New York to New York City itself demonstrated that the movement could appeal to every part of America. But especially in his early days, Finney and other preachers often charged one another with insincerity. According to Finney, a clerical opponent confessed that he had "no more religion than your horse": "I do not believe what I preach; and . . . I told you I did not believe what I preached." The opponent tossed accusations back at Finney.[21] Yet a confession of natural "unbelief" wasn't necessarily unorthodox. Christianity had always preached the doctrine of the two selves: one self, which wants to believe and obey, observes that the other self does not, and considers what to do about that. Even St. Paul said this kind of thing about himself.[22] About the evangelists of Finney's generation, one authority has said, "All the devices to 'get up' a revival were frankly admitted, accompanied in every case by apparently sincere statements that all came from God."[23]

To the leading intellectual and institutional authorities of the Protestant churches, however, Finney looked like a violent revolutionary, and in some sense they were right. "Who is not aware," one asked, "that the Church has been almost revolutionized within four or five years, by means of such excitements? The Church has received into her bosom those who respect neither her doctrines or [sic] institutions, and must long feel the consequences of it."[24] Revivalism was the solvent of established order; that was the institutional objection. The doctrinal objection was that revivalism denied the omnipotence of God and the helplessness of sinners; it suggested that sinners could be moved, or tricked, into "converting" themselves.

Jonathan Edwards and George Whitefield, exponents of Calvinism, had believed that revivals would happen when God wanted them to happen. So did Finney. But none of these successful revivalists *acted* on the Calvinist principle of total dependence on Providence. In support of their cause, they used every measure that they themselves could think of. As time went on, it seemed clearer and clearer that although Finney was ordained a Presbyterian and was a Calvinist by heritage, he wasn't really a Calvinist after all.

Finney himself was far from thinking that people simply manufacture their own conversions, without the help of God. He devoted vast amounts of his *Lectures on Revivals of Religion* to the importance of prayer, and he didn't regard prayer as merely a way of working on one's own psychology. Yes, it was a method, a measure, an art, but it was an art by which people were authentically connected with God. At the beginning of his book, he characterizes religion as "something for man to do," but he adds, "Unless God interpose the influence of his Spirit, not a man on earth will ever obey the commands of God."[25]

The phrase "not a man on earth" applied to more than just infidels; it took in the church people and their ministers as well. And this is where reliance on God came together with an interest in new human "measures." In their normal state, as Finney perceived, Christians weren't very different from anybody else. Only a new "excitement" could shatter their indifference and stupidity. Once, in the days of Edwards and Whitefield, Calvinism had seemed new and exciting, because people had never heard it preached with conviction. Now, in Finney's time, it was just a doctrine that churchgoers hid behind, thinking that if God wanted them to be converted, he would do it himself. Any doctrine could grow old like this and lose its effect. Fortunately, however, Christianity had more than one available doctrine, more than one intellectual tool to work with. It had enough ideas to excite any audience:

"In one place, one set of truths, in another, another set. A minister must find out where they [the people] are, and preach accordingly."[26]

Suppose, Finney said, some preacher informed the farmers "that God is a sovereign, and will give them a crop only when it pleases him, and that for them to plow and plant and labor as if they expected to raise a crop is very wrong"; and suppose that the farmers believed it. "Why, they would starve the world to death." But in religion as in any other pursuit, "appropriate means" will produce worthwhile ends. Finney outlined all the appropriate means of revival, from ideas that should be emphasized in sermons to well-ventilated meetinghouses and pulpits kept free from preachers' tobacco juice. But the most important thing was to remember that the Church, the real Church, cannot exist unless enthusiasm is continually provoked. Even revival workers needed to be "reconverted" every "two or three weeks." Shockingly, however, some evangelical churches couldn't gear up to have revivals even "once in three years, to last three months at a time."[27]

One of Finney's many sarcastic critics charged that on his principles, "the house of God becomes transformed into a kind of religious laboratory" for the manufacture of emotions.[28] Finney himself was worried that the laboratory would continue in business but the results would be worthless. In an article written in 1845, ten years after the publication of his *Lectures*, he suggests that revivals have already "become so mechanical, there is so much policy and machinery, so much dependence upon means and measures, so much of man and so little of God," that their "character . . . has greatly changed."[29] Finney wanted revival to go on all the time, but he didn't want it to be something that just went on all the time. When the revolution was institutionalized, it would be killed.

And that is what appeared to happen. Long before Finney's death in 1875, revival had become a routine feature of evangelical churches. Western New York, where he had begun his career, had long justified a phrase that was partially attributable to him: it was a "burned-over district," a place where there had been so many evangelistic campaigns that there appeared to be nothing left for the Spirit to burn.[30] The same question arose about most other places in America: how many more revivals could there be? But estimating the untapped resources of religious experience is like estimating "world oil resources," which expand when people develop new ways of finding and exploiting them.

Evangelicals developed new ways. The Second Great Awakening, originally so primitive and apparently spontaneous, turned out to be exceptionally good at inventing new institutions. They gave it stability and permanence, thereby quenching some of its spirit, but they also extended its reach beyond the campground and the pine-board meetinghouse. Within the array of institutions were scores of colleges, hundreds of social-action groups, and tens of thousands of Sunday schools, singing schools, teachers' institutes, women's associations, businessmen's associations, workingmen's associations, charity associations, and missions of every shape and size. If you weren't interested in hearing a sermon, you might be interested in playing in the band or running a sewing class for young girls from the poorer part of town. Almost anything could connect you with the gospel spirit. And if something about the Methodists failed to make that connection, you could find it with the Campbellites, some varieties of Presbyterians, many varieties of Baptists, or any other group that appeared in America's vast directory of evangelical organizations. You could also start your own group and link it to like-minded others. Along this broad and responsive religious network, even an illiterate former slave, Sojourner Truth, could travel from New England to the Midwest and be recognized almost everywhere for her spectacular gift of exhortation.

Other new measures were technological in the strict sense

of that word. New printing methods allowed every evangelical group to publish its own journals and distribute them
cheaply, often by the hundreds of thousands. These journals
were more than internal means of communication; each was
a way of defining and advertising some distinctive approach
to God. Many were avidly controversial, uncovering anything
obscurely wrong with any form of Christianity but one, and
recommending that form to everyone justly dissatisfied with
the vanity, hypocrisy, oppression, or whatever else of the
Church in general. If your connection with Christianity was
weak, if you felt there was something lacking, there was an
organization and a journal just for you, whoever you were.

Tracts were even cheaper to produce than journals, and
these went out by the millions every year. So did volumes of
doctrine, controversy, personal experience, missionary experience, social reform, family advice, and edifying fiction, all
sold from house to house by "agents" or "colporteurs" working on commission. Sunday school hymnbooks, for which
there was a lively market, sold for only fifteen cents. Their
music could be played on home pianos and organs, now readily available (25,000 new pianos were sold in 1866 alone).[31]
Even more available were daily newspapers, cheap enough
for everyone, and eager to fill their pages with church material. The demand for sermons continued into the early twentieth century in major cities, and long after that in the hinterland. Orthodox views were not a criterion for publication, not
by a long shot; virtually every form of Christianity was welcome in the people's press.

Best of all, a national network of railroads and steamboats
allowed newspapers, journals, tracts, Sunday school literature, and preachers themselves to travel quickly from place
to place, establishing credibility by their national appeal.
Since the 1830s, building methods had been advancing as
fast as printing methods, so railroad ministers could have it
both ways: they could preach in a great metropolitan church,

built to their specifications, while maintaining their prestige by frequent travel on the lecture circuit, which could be very lucrative.

The evangelical and revival movement was by far the nation's leading source of entertainment. It could be scaled up to the level of a two-thousand-seat church or scaled down to the level of the front parlor (ideally equipped with a piano), and there was something in it to interest almost anyone. Once people were interested and entertained, they might become converted; and they often were. But there remained the mystery of the individual. You cannot reduce personalities to statistics, yet personality was the most important tool, as well as target, of the evangelical movement. For good or ill, the movement was shaped by a series of unusual individuals, each with a particular way of exploiting, or inventing, the tradition of American Christianity.

STARS THAT
RISE AND SET

Henry Ward Beecher (1813–1887) was one of those Victorians whom intellectuals of the next generation loved to hate. To them, he was the embodiment of the old-time religion, in all its emptiness and pomposity. He was a joke, a reason to laugh at an oppressive past.[1] The real joke, however, is that people in his own era denounced him as a dangerous innovator, a man whose life was far too liberated, and those people were closer to being right.

Beecher was the eighth child (the seventh was Harriet Beecher Stowe, of *Uncle Tom's Cabin*) born to Lyman Beecher, a Zeus-like figure on the heights of American Calvinism. Given Lyman's habit of hurling thunderbolts at the mortals beneath him, it is remarkable that Henry escaped with his identity intact. It wasn't easy. Channeled by his father into the Presbyterian ministry, he went off to raise religious fervor in the malarial Midwest. Results were mixed. He did, however, start to meet people, prosperous people who recognized his special talents.

Some of these people—wealthy eastern evangelicals, starting a church in Brooklyn, New York—invited Henry to come and take charge. Theoretically Congregational, the

FIGURE 5.1. *Beecher's building: Plymouth Church, Brooklyn. Author's collection.*

institution was named, in honor of the New England Puritans, Plymouth Church. Despite its revival name, Plymouth was the Church of Henry Ward Beecher, wrapped so tightly around him, spiritually and physically, that the church and the man were one. Plymouth was—and is—simply an auditorium, with seats for up to 3,000 people, embracing the speaker's platform. All eyes were focused on the preacher, with no large pillars or other obstructions to interrupt the sight lines. The minister stood in the midst of his people, screened by neither a pulpit nor any other religious object. There was no pretense of an "altar." The communion table was portable and could easily be put out of the way. Mourners' benches did not appear; Beecher would rather talk about anything but the threat of hell. Yet whatever he said, the amazingly precise acoustics allowed everyone to hear it distinctly.

These arrangements were a naked plea for public and personal attention, and they were successful. Plymouth Church was one of America's major tourist destinations. To it, Abraham Lincoln came repeatedly, and on one occasion had

trouble finding a seat. On Sundays visitors thronged the fer-
ries from Manhattan, hiked up the hill to Brooklyn Heights,
and waited impatiently for Plymouth's doors to open. When
people couldn't come to Beecher, Beecher came to them,
crisscrossing the country to deliver his message to packed
auditoriums and attentive reporters.

Beecher was a devourer of experience. He would read anything, talk to anyone, entertain almost any opinion. An ugly
man who looked a good deal like a frog, he still possessed
what the nineteenth century called magnetism. And he
became a great public speaker.

But what was his message? One of his themes was abolition. Finney had refused to admit slave owners to communion. The New England churches—to whose tables, strangely,
slave owners never applied—fulminated heartily against
them. Beecher dramatized the cause. He bought guns for
Kansas abolitionists, making Plymouth "the Church of the
Holy Rifles."[2] He held "slave auctions" at which his congregants purchased the freedom of enslaved people. Another
of his themes was women's rights; yet another, the theory of
evolution. He endorsed them both. He endorsed many theories and New Ideas. But his principal message was love, the
love that draws the soul to Christ, the love that emanates
from one individual soul to another.

Love was certainly not a discovery of Henry Ward Beecher;
everyone knew, as did St. Paul,[3] that love was the greatest
Christian virtue. But when Lyman Beecher visited his son's
revival services, he was disturbed that love was the only thing
he heard about. Few twenty-first-century churchgoers, even
the most "right-wing" megachurch evangelicals, would share
his surprise, much less his disappointment. Today, everyone
preaches "love." Henry Ward Beecher's biographer rightly
observes that today's "mainstream Christianity is so deeply
infused with the rhetoric of Christ's love that most Americans can imagine nothing else, and have no appreciation or

memory of the revolution wrought by Beecher and his peers" in the mid-nineteenth century.[4]

Twenty-first-century Christians might, however, reasonably expect Beecher's gospel of love to have included an emphasis on "family"—the working synonym for "love" in tens of thousands of American churches today. Even the nation's largest homosexual denomination, the Metropolitan Community Church, is a reliable supplier of discourse about the importance of marriage and the family (as progressively defined). But anyone who expected "family values" from Beecher would have been as disappointed as his father was when he missed any discussion of hell. According to Henry Ward Beecher, Jesus felt "that there were affinities and relationships far higher and wider than those constituted by the earthly necessities of family life." Jesus would probably have agreed. But Beecher pushed it further: "Not those who have your blood in their veins, but those who have your disposition in their soul, are your true kindred."[5] A disposition in the soul is not exactly the same as fellowship with Christ.

It likely came as no surprise, for people who reflected on Beecher's doctrines, when one of his assistants, Theodore Tilton, accused him of treating Tilton's wife, Elizabeth, as one of Beecher's own "true kindred." Tilton sued Beecher for alienating Elizabeth's affections. His complaint was filed in 1874, but the relationship had started long before; for years it had been discussed and lachrymosely debated among participants and friends, virtually all of whom believed, more or less, in Beecher's doctrine of love. Unfortunately for Beecher, these discussions and debates had often been put in writing, and now a vast store of documents was dumped into the newspapers.

It is impossible to determine exactly what had gone on. Something had happened; was it literally sex? Probably so, but when it comes to sexuality, nothing is too unlikely for Victorians to have done, or not to have done. The evidence, on all sides, was so extensive that the jury drowned in it. No verdict was reached. Back at Plymouth, an investigative committee cleared Beecher from blame, to overwhelming applause within the church. An accuser—another of Beecher's former friends—had to be rescued by police from outraged members of the congregation. Elizabeth Tilton was thrown out of the church when she changed her testimony and became, at last, an accuser herself. "If anyone wants any lying done send them to me," she later remarked.[6]

The episode horrified some and amused many, but the Victorians were not as stereotypical as their successors imagined: Beecher remained an influential public figure until the end of his long life. He deserves to be remembered. Stripped of their old-fashioned words and their topical references, the sermons he preached at Plymouth Church would be perfectly acceptable today in both liberal and evangelical venues, so long as someone interpolated references to "family" or "the disadvantaged" as the proper objects of Christian love. Among contemporary Protestants, his conception of socially transcendent affinities is still not considered useful.

Beecher was succeeded in his role as America's most famous evangelist by Dwight L. Moody (1837–1899), a much more orthodox preacher, and one with an even greater mastery of the "measures" that make the Church. As a young man in Chicago, Moody was inspired to devote himself to the needs of street people and others who weren't welcome in existing churches. Expanding his interests, he started his own mission, his own church, and then his own international evangelistic campaign.

When Moody died, in 1899, newspapers across the English-speaking world hailed him as the century's greatest exponent of Christianity. According to them, he had demonstrated the error of "the wise men who are telling us that Christianity is played out." Even in 1899, people were writing obituaries for Christianity; this, at least, is nothing new.

Moody had been more prescient than the pundits. Nevertheless, one may question the supposedly parallel assertion: Moody had shown that "the old-fashioned gospel message" had "lost none of its power." An old-fashioned message certainly wasn't the whole of it, as one can see by considering the simultaneous tributes to Moody's "genius for organization" and his development of "his method of evangelism" into "a system." It was the organization and the method that made Moody's message accessible to the hundred million people he was said to have spoken to.[7] "Old-fashioned" isn't the right phrase for that.

Moody's first international preaching tours were flops, perhaps because he hadn't done enough advance work, organizing his itinerary and lining up support from local clergy. Then he learned how to secure the attention that preachers get from local recognition and esteem and combine it with the advertising advantage of appearing to be new because you are moving from place to place. His 1873 campaign in the British Isles was hugely successful.[8] After that, he was famous for being famous. People flooded into his meetings because other people were flooding into his meetings. Once inside, they were prepared to be interested; being interested, they were prepared to be converted.

Yet this process couldn't have continued if Moody hadn't communicated something that people would have had a hard time finding elsewhere. What he offered was earnestness, clarity, and urgency, the sense that something special was going on, right then, and that everyone needed to decide what to make of it. Still more important, perhaps, was a means of communication that a lesser evangelist might have considered ancillary: the music program. This was as clear and straightforward as everything else about the Moody message.

Its leader was the great vocalist Ira Sankey. Moody had discovered his ability while Sankey was still working as a tax clerk. "What is your business?" Moody asked. "I am a

FIGURE 5.2. *Dwight L. Moody, confronting his audience (1876); Ira Sankey is the prominent figure second from the right. Source:* Harper's Weekly, *March 11, 1876.*

government officer," Sankey replied. "Well," said Moody, "you'll have to give it up." Sankey was on the platform when Moody asked for a song appropriate to a sermon he had just given. Instead of repeating a standard number, Sankey pulled out a newspaper clipping he had saved. It contained a religious poem by an obscure author. Sankey immediately composed, played, and sang the music appropriate to the poem. Thus he created the enduring hymn "The Ninety and Nine."[9] Moody and Sankey sponsored a book entitled *The Gospel Songs*, a collection of plain, pungent, doctrinally decisive, cheaply published, very singable, and very influential works. "These Moody-Sankey songs" were scorned by high-toned preachers, but they penetrated everywhere in England and America.

Moody not only preached; he also organized a Bible institute that, from its Gothic-decorated high-rise in Chicago, still operates as an important educational resource for evangelical America. Remarkably, however, he was always a lay volunteer, never an ordained minister. It has been claimed that he was so ignorant of theology he could not have passed an ordination exam, that it was almost impossible to tell from his sermons whether he was a Calvinist or not (he wasn't), and that he was an irresponsible rebel against institutional precedent and accountability: "There are no special rules for the unbiblical office of a 'revival preacher.'"[10] But Moody knew very well that he was a rebel and an eccentric and that he could never have succeeded so well if he hadn't been those things.

Moody was an inspiration for the next premier evangelist, Billy Sunday (1862–1935). In the eyes of the nicest people— teachers, intellectuals, social commentators, and the ministers and congregations of conservative churches—Sunday, a former professional baseball player, was the Platonic form of the vulgar religious demagogue. His admirers replied that if the critics would just visit one of his meetings, they would change their minds; they might not be converted to his kind of Christianity, but they would end up liking him. And this often happened. It was, as his followers said, one of the many "jokes" God plays on the "worldly-wise."[11] In plain terms, it showed that Sunday was smarter about his job than the seminaries and the settled ministers were about theirs.

An associate of Sunday divulged the awful truth: the

"bishops and board secretaries and distinguished preachers are really only local celebrities. Their names mean nothing in newspaper offices or to newspaper readers: there are not six clergymen in the United States with a really national reputation."[12] That may not have been true in the mid-nineteenth century, but it was true in the early twentieth, and it is true now. What attracts people to Christianity is so various, and is obtainable through so many channels, that few Christian leaders become important outside their own institutions. But if a single person is unconventional enough, and unconventional in just the right way, he or she can advertise Christianity to people who aren't connected with those established local circuits or aren't emotionally engaged by them. Billy Sunday knew this, and he had the commonsense view of religion that allowed him to profit by it.

By "commonsense" I don't mean "commonplace" or "traditional." Sunday insisted that he was preaching "the old-time religion," but his religion notably lacked the gravity, the doctrinal complexity, and the denominational enthusiasm that many ordinary preachers provided, Sabbath by Sabbath (usually without converting anyone).[13] Sunday's idiom was modern and colloquial, yet it was completely without the portentous, often mystifying modernism of the mainstream preachers. He had an intellectually dubious but emotionally formidable skill at collapsing and discarding all counterarguments to his teaching. Referring to Robert Ingersoll, the nation's leading unbeliever, who had produced a book called *Some Mistakes of Moses*, Sunday said, "Bob Ingersoll wasn't the first to find out that Moses made mistakes. God knew about it long before Ingersoll was born."[14]

Sunday was an inimitably vivid reteller of Bible stories. But the important thing was his skill at illuminating them with his audience's experience of the things they knew. After relating the story of Jesus's calling of Matthew ("Follow me") and Matthew's response ("He arose, and followed him"), Sunday said,

> You can be converted just as quickly as Matthew was. God says, "Let the wicked man forsake his way." The instant that is done, no matter if the man has been a life-long sinner, he is safe. There is no need of struggling for hours—or for days—do it now. Who are you struggling with? Not God. God's mind was made up long before the foundations of the earth were laid. The plan of salvation was made long before there was any sin in the world. Electricity existed long before there was any car wheel for it to drive. "Let the wicked man forsake his way." When? Within a month, within a week, within a day, within an hour? No! Now! The instant you yield, God's plan of salvation is thrown into gear. You will be saved before you know it, like a child being born.[15]

In a brisk sixty seconds, Sunday took his audience from wickedness to childlike innocence, from the mysteries of primordial providence to the mechanical certainties of electric vehicles, from the Bible to the gears connected to the lever in your hand, from Matthew's salvation to yours. Clearly the man knew what he was doing.

An associate summed it up: "His American birthright of plain common sense [as if all Americans had common sense] stands Sunday in stead of theological training. He is 'a practical man,' as mechanics say." Common sense meant practical thinking in all respects: "A Sunday evangelistic campaign is a marvel of organization. It spells efficiency at every turn and is a lesson to the communities which do Christian work in haphazard, hit-or-miss fashion."[16]

As Sister Soulsby said, "what tremendous improvements were possible"!

"Now—the servant of Naaman entered the hut of the Prophet Elisha and found him sitting perched upon a stool, writing on Papyrus, and he explained how Naaman had the leprosy —and the old prophet never got up, but just said, 'Tell him to bathe in the Jordan seven times—now BEAT IT! **BEAT IT!**'

—oo—

So the servant went back, and Naaman said, 'Well did you see him?'

And the servant said, 'Yes, but he's a queer old duck—he said for you to bathe in the Jordan seven times.'

—He held onto his nose and shut his eyes and down he went—in all over!

WELL—

Naaman thought he'd take a chance —so he went down to the river bank and got off his clothes and probably about the first thing he did was to stub his toe against a big rock! O-o-o-o-o-o-o!—

—And then—like as not —one of those big sand flies sat right down between his shoulder blades! We-e-e-e-e-e!!!

—But he went right ahead! First he stuck one toe in— and shivered—but finally—

—And then up he came and stamped and pounded and spluttered and got the water out of his ears—

—And nothing had happened except that his sores began to itch—but when he had dipped seven times—his flesh was made whole —

HIS LEPROSY **WAS HEALED!**

FIGURE 5.3. *Billy Sunday on the story of Naaman (2 Kings 5).* Source: *William T. Ellis,* "Billy" Sunday: The Man and His Message *(1914).*

FIGURE 5.4. *Billy Sunday on the imitation of Christ.* Source: *William T. Ellis, "Billy" Sunday: The Man and His Message (1914).*

Before visiting a community, Sunday insisted on being invited by local people and local churches that would put up the large sums of money required for adequate preparation. (He repaid their investments with the proceeds of the campaign.) Anticipating his coming, churches organized meetings in people's homes to pray for a revival. In Philadelphia more than 5,000 individual groups met twice a week. Street parades were organized; one in Scranton included 20,000 marching men. Transportation was arranged for "delegates" who lived in the countryside. "Delegations" were also "worked up" from community groups—miners, women's clubs, Boy Scouts, old soldiers, whomever—to attend Sunday's meetings at appointed times. Sunday had reflected on crowd psychology and was frank about his findings. His associate undoubtedly reflects his view of the "delegations": "The crowd spirit is appealed to by this method.... The work of making ready the delegation furnishes a topic for what is literally 'shop talk' among working men; and naturally each group zealously watches the effect of its appearance upon the great congregation. Delegations get a very good idea of what their neighbors think of them by the amount of applause with which they are greeted."[17]

First there was the applause, the excited self-recognition, the pleasure of people who were happy to get into a meeting place that often wasn't large enough for everyone who wanted to come. Then the music started—up to an hour of music, led by a huge choir drawn from the local churches. Prompted by "a variety of ingenious devices," the audience joined in singing old songs and new, but especially bright, happy songs. Sunday's message wasn't simply the threat of hell; more than anything, it was the happiness that anyone could achieve by fellowship with Jesus. He had learned much from the generous Beecher tradition: his was a message of love. In his campaigns, the favorite song was "Brighten the Corner Where You Are." So by the time Sunday took the stage, "the crowd

[had] been worked up into a glow and fervor"; it was clearly "receptive to his message."[18]

The message was conveyed in many more colors and tones than you could find in any normal discourse—comforting, scorning, threatening, chiding, calming, inspiring. Sunday believed that a progression of moods was essential to the purpose. He was most famous, however, for the "athleticism" of his preaching, which meant that he gestured dramatically, ran about the stage, got down on his hands and knees, "slid into base," and in general did anything he thought would project his themes.[19] If you wanted to, you could say it was all part of the act. But another word for "act" is "technique."

Sunday lavished concern on his preaching space. It couldn't be a conventional church or auditorium—too small. Besides, fixed seating would limit audience response, particularly when it was time for people to come up front and be saved. So he had special "tabernacles" built for his performances, huge wooden structures capable of holding 20,000 people. Worried about the volatility of crowds, he made sure that there were plenty of doors and fire extinguishers and that every wall would give way to a swift kick. And of course he worried about sound; he was speaking without a public address system. To minimize distracting noise, he banished all young children to a nearby nursery, and if anyone in the audience coughed, he stopped the service until the disturbance ceased. Not wanting to install a wooden floor, which would transmit every footfall in the crowd, but not wanting dirt either, he covered the ground with sawdust, hence the common expression for sudden conversion: "hitting the sawdust trail."

Sunday's campaigns would have been impossible without big publicity, and in that era the biggest publicity was made by newspapers. So Sunday cultivated reporters, invited them to his organizational meetings (no secrets about the man behind the curtain), gave them constant, colorful interviews, and provided sermons to fill their columns. The papers let people know that Sunday was controversial, that he was funny, that he was dynamic, that he was different from the ordinary preacher—that, in short, he was entertaining, and that he could connect with people who were not ordinarily entertained by religious services. And his methods were very successful, at least until the time when mass entertainment could be obtained more easily from the movie theater and the radio receiver than from Billy Sunday, and when the mainstream clergy became too modern and liberal to underwrite his campaigns. "The enthusiasm for the united work," said the leader of his music program, "was oozing out drop by drop."[20] Sunday's audience didn't vanish; he had struck a real vein, but the vein contracted. Other methods were needed.

Just as Sunday was the premier evangelist of the 1910–1920 period, so Aimee Semple McPherson was the premier evangelist of the 1920s. Sister Aimee, as she was always known, was a consummate organizer and self-publicizer, and she had a personality well worth publicizing. She did things that Sunday never did, and things he never could have done. In 1921, to advertise what turned out to be her breakthrough campaign—her preaching and healing services in San Diego— she flew over the city in an airplane, dropping handbills onto a surprised population. She preached in a police uniform: "Stop! You are breaking God's law!" She preached in Texas Guinan's speakeasy. And she freed herself from other people's churches.

McPherson (1890–1944) had been reared in the Salvation Army, had experienced Pentecostal spirit anointing, had gotten herself ordained by a Methodist church, and had courted the support of evangelical preachers; from the start, however, she ran her own show. With great foresight, she settled in southern California, a large and growing metropolitan area where she could create Christian theater good enough to compete with any movie palace. She would stay in one place,

FIGURE 5.5. *Aimee Semple McPherson healing a child at Balboa Park, San Diego, 1921; an audience of 30,000 stands just out of camera range. Courtesy of the San Diego History Center.*

but she would draw people to her. She built an enormous meetinghouse, Angelus Temple, next to Los Angeles's Echo Park. Around it she spun a network of nondenominational "lighthouses" (local churches) that she later turned into a denomination, the Church of the Foursquare Gospel.

Angelus Temple was the perfect medium for her ministry: a 5,000-seat auditorium with an ample stage; excellent acoustics; a huge, permanent choir; and a platoon of carpenters and costumers who were always on hand to produce the sets she designed for her performances—sermons conducted with the aid of motorcycles, live animals, scenes from the Garden of Eden (gorgeous, but no nudity), and anything else that would help Sister dazzle a crowd. She herself was dazzling. "She was just like an angel from heaven," remembered a prominent (and agnostic) scientist who saw her when he was a boy. "She taught me everything I know about teaching." Although she was best in person, she never neglected the newspapers: "She was a reporter's dream."[21]

An even better aphorist than Billy Sunday, Sister Aimee said that sermons started with the audience: "The recipe for rabbit stew is to catch the rabbit." And unlike many preachers in the mainstream denominations, she carefully identified which rabbits to hunt: "I'm after the passerby, the butterfly, the atheist, the society girl, the movie people and the sinner. . . . I love the christian [*sic*] people, but if I had to give up either the christian or sinner I'd give up the christian."[22]

At Angelus Temple, sinners were offered both new and seemingly old experiences. Painted on the underside of the dome was a blue sky with white clouds, so that worshipers could feel they had come to an old-fashioned camp meeting—an event that society girls, movie people, and other butterflies had probably never experienced but, as McPherson knew, could summon from the imaginary past that is America's old old-time religion.[23] On the temple roof were two steel towers, with an antenna stretched between them; Sister Aimee was an early and heavy investor in radio. It is unfortunate that she died too soon for wide-screen TV.

Many evangelical ministers, and such important laymen as William Jennings Bryan, thought that McPherson actually exemplified the old-time religion. As her own publicity put it, she "belong[ed] to the new order of things," but her ideas were "true to the 'faith of our fathers.'"[24] Ordinary people thought so too. That was quite an achievement, given her eccentricity, her early involvement in Pentecostalism (which evangelical Christians still frequently view with grave suspicion), and her "Hollywood technique," as her enemies accurately referred to it. Almost everyone acknowledged that the gospel must be presented in new ways, for new audiences; that was what Peter and Paul had done with the first gospel message. But methods and messages are hard to separate.

Did people go home from Angelus Temple worshiping Jesus or idolizing Sister Aimee? It would take a philosopher as acute as Thomas Aquinas to separate the substance of her message from the accidents of her methods.

Truly old-fashioned church people were not amused by the methods, or by her existence as a woman minister, or by her divorce, or by a peculiar episode that occurred in 1926, when she went to Santa Monica beach and . . . disappeared. Everyone thought she had drowned. Then, five weeks later, she turned up in Douglas, Arizona, telling a ridiculous story about having been kidnapped, taken to Mexico, and held for ransom. On her return to Los Angeles, a crowd of more than 100,000 welcomed her back. The district attorney was not so easily impressed by her story of providential deliverance. He charged her with obstruction of justice.

It was the biggest legal case of the 1920s, a decade of big legal cases. McPherson and her friends did everything possible to muddy the waters, and the charges were finally dropped. No one has ever figured out what happened after her trip to the beach, although most students of the event have concluded that she ran away with a lover, her radio engineer.[25]

McPherson's religious movement survived this scandal and later, less serious ones. She had found her audience, which had never been anyone else's audience, exactly. One cannot account for this phenomenon by noting that many of her followers were lower middle class, or that two-thirds of them were women.[26] The same can be said about other preachers' churches, perhaps most of them. Sister's people were simply the individuals who were reached by her. And if she was successful in reinvigorating their feeling for the old-time religion, as some believe,[27] her efforts weren't something that appealed exclusively to one American social class. Today the Church of the Foursquare Gospel counts 250,000 members in this country and 8 million in the world.[28]

By the time McPherson died, however, the relationship between evangelism and the techniques it used was changing again. Many people expected, or feared, that radio and television would make evangelical voices more commanding than ever before. Generally speaking, these people were wrong. As radio advanced, large-scale evangelism tended to fade. A distinctive doctrine, or a distinctive personality, gifted with a special sensitivity to some share of the market, could keep it alive. McPherson did. But even her attractions faded. She wasn't the same on radio. Most in-person evangelists found it harder to attract an audience once other sources of entertainment could be enjoyed just by staying home and turning the dial. Television completed the process. Across the nation, lodge halls emptied, lecture series folded, amateur theatricals disappeared, and Christian congregations discontinued their Wednesday night prayer meetings. "Revivals" went on as a routinized function of many local churches, but people who needed conversion were unlikely to resist the charms of ABC, NBC, and CBS and turn up at the Special Service.

The only great evangelistic success of the network television era was Billy Graham. His crusade in supposedly pagan New York (1957) was so successful that ABC televised it nationally. It was a hit. "From that point on," according to a friendly critic, "his crusades would tend more and more simply to provide the stagework, the settings, the props, for his television productions."[29] Graham's earnest yet serene approach recommended him to the widest conceivable audience, something very important in the days before cable TV, when national niche markets barely existed. Contrary to some expectations, television was remarkably resistant to the dynamic personal connection that the great evangelists had once achieved, even in gatherings of thousands. It's hard to make emotional demands on an audience that is watching you perform inside a little plastic box.

Graham offered a larger, though thinner, experience. He

followed the example of Moody and Sunday; he worked with local churches to attract a crowd, but his crowds were bigger than any his predecessors could have managed in the days before public address systems. A baseball stadium filled with people can look very impressive on TV. Yet Graham had the good sense not to issue audacious challenges to his audience, as many of his predecessors had done with theirs. His listeners hadn't stood in line to get into his tent; they had walked comfortably into a capacious sports venue or tuned in on TV; less could be expected of them. He provided songs (with the mellifluous George Beverly Shea filling the Ira Sankey position); delivered an inoffensive, generically evangelical sermon; and invited listeners to make "a decision for Christ." At the typical Graham revival, whole sections of the audience stood up and walked toward the speaker's stand as soon as the invitation was made. These weren't new converts; they were loyal church members, happy to "renew their commitment."

A close student of early revivalism points to the irony "that, much later, American evangelicals would identify [its] rituals as part of the 'old-time religion,' when in fact almost every technique involved innovations."[30] Graham worked well with that sense of old-timeness, and seemed to renew it. But revivals had come a long way from the early years, when leading clergymen demanded that their colleagues "thrust the nail of terror into sleeping souls!" and Jonathan Edwards had to stop in the middle of his sermon because the congregation's "shrieks & crys" were so "piercing & Amazing."[31]

Few people expected that evangelism would ever become strange and colorful again. But it did. The little plastic box seems larger when you have a wide array of choices and there's something that *you* especially want to see. When only a handful of TV stations were available in any given area and only a few hours were devoted to religious programming, it was hard to experiment with what people wanted to view. By the 1980s, however, the market had been freed by deregulation and cable TV. Now William James's varieties of religious experience could be fairly addressed.

The results were surprisingly—to many people shockingly—diverse. The calm center of the electronic church continued to exist: Billy Graham, joined by Bible teachers with rationalist lecture styles (Herbert W. Armstrong) and sunny motivational speakers such as Robert Schuller of the Crystal Cathedral, who preached a conversion to optimism, happiness, and personal "power." But coming in from the wings were more religious personalities than you could have imagined: faith healers, cult leaders, exponents of the "name it and claim it" school of spiritual achievement (known to rival evangelists as the "blab it and grab it" school), soft-rock Pentecostals blessed with a sense of humor (Kenneth Copeland), raging scourges of loose living (Jimmy Swaggart), friendly companions of retired persons and women in the home (Jim and Tammy Faye Bakker), and other persons with an odd, niche-sensitive charisma (Gene Scott).

People often associate televangelism with the few TV personalities, such as Pat Robertson, who married religion with politics. And people who object to that marriage often overestimate the impact of both political and religious programming. To use Marshall McLuhan's terminology (though not in the way he meant it): television is a "cool medium." Watching a TV preacher sitting on a couch chatting with guests and offering political comments, or even ranting beneath a spotlight, isn't the same as attending a church service or a political rally. It's easy to drift to another channel. But Robertson's show, and Jerry Falwell's televised sermons, and other shows like them did have an important effect: they alerted the large numbers of people who were out of sympathy with the modern liberal political consensus that other people were out of sympathy too. Television (once freed from the hegemony of the three networks) and its successor, the Internet, were methods of assembling political-affinity groups that had been latent within the standard churches and parties. These groups—such as Falwell's "Moral Majority"—were dynamically political yet traditionally religious.

Or were supposed to be. "Morality," to this majority, was no longer a restrictively "Christian" ethic. It was a default morality thought to be possessed by everyone who had not been corrupted by modern liberal relativism. Its advocates, dubbed by their enemies "the religious Right," reached out to people of every faith and achieved many converts, including Roman Catholics. This was a new thing for a movement born among evangelicals. The movement's agenda was also new, since it responded to new motions in the modern liberal society it opposed: court decisions about abortion, advanced ideas about sexual morality, secularism in the public schools, social regulation by a soulless state.

Yet, as chapter 6 will illustrate, there was nothing new about religious involvements in politics, nothing whatever. The revolutionary thing was the defining moral concept of this particular involvement. The central idea was "family values"—an idea, or at least a phrase, that sounds traditional but is surely not. It had never been a leading emphasis of American Christianity.

"Family values" appear nowhere in the Bible. Families do; values do; but most Christians who believe that "family" designates a special type of religious "value" would be hard-pressed to name even one exemplary Bible family, besides Mary, Joseph, and the Christ child. A prominent scholar once remarked that if you want to find a happy family in the Bible, the best example would be Ahab and Jezebel.[32] The old American evangelists could take the family or leave it alone. Peter Cartwright brooked no interference from converts' meddling relatives; if they made trouble in his meetings, he wrestled them away—so much for family values.[33] Later in the nineteenth century, urban missions posted signs saying, "Have You Written Mother?" next to signs denouncing alcohol, and Christian novelists invented exemplary children who never tired of confronting moral problems. The standouts were Martha Finley's Elsie and Jacob Abbott's Rollo, each the hero of many books. By making children the moral detectives, however, such books emphasized the fact that sin can be found everywhere, even in the best of homes, or people. When Rollo, who is a very nice little boy, gets grumpy because it's raining, his kindly father explains to him that by his "wicked repinings" he is sinning in six different ways.[34]

But the favorite fiction of evangelical Christians continued to be John Bunyan's *Pilgrim's Progress* (1678), which opens with the protagonist abandoning his attentive family. "Life, Life, Eternal Life!" the pilgrim cries, as he flees from his wife and children. The scene was not without precedent. Jesus himself said, "A man's foes shall be they of his own household. He that loveth father or mother more than me is not worthy of me: and he that loveth son or daughter more than me is not worthy of me."[35] Despite this teaching, the politicized evangelicals of the late twentieth century created a religion of the family, sometimes reorienting their churches from an emphasis on conversion—an individual, often ecstatic event, as likely to undermine as to solidify the family structure—to an emphasis on another kind of transformation, the creation of successful families and family-like communities.

The cultivation of family values happens almost everywhere in current Christianity, but perhaps most systematically among the megachurches, today's most visible inheritors of the evangelistic and revival tradition. Megachurches, hundreds of which have been built in America during the past thirty years, are impossible to define, except by saying that each is very big (with thousands of adherents) and very focused on the mission of reviving and converting what are often called "broken lives" and "broken relationships." Such a church may have some affiliation with a traditional denomination; more often it is the stand-alone creation of a charismatic individual, much like an old-time evangelist, or of a "fellowship" with a distinctive method of "planting" churches. As you might with a conventional church, you go to a megachurch to hear the Word and listen to the music, though now the effect is enhanced by rock bands, big-screen video displays, and other appliances of contemporary entertainment. By now, it isn't just teenagers who like these things; it's their parents, too.

Megachurch values—"family" and otherwise—are assumed to be traditional, yet to really traditional Christians, their presentation looks and sounds like an attempt to rival the superficial excitement of the modern world. A friendlier interpretation would mention both rivalry and replacement; it would detect the underlying idea of a modern but opposing world, welcoming everyone but especially people who either are intimidated by traditional churches or suspect that these institutions are actually fixtures of *this world*. To these men and women and their families, the megachurch provides both the large-scale, anonymous personalism of the revival meeting, in which there is always a message for *you*, no matter how many other people turned out for the service, and the small-scale, "Hello, Stephen!" personalism of weekly Bible studies, home-based fellowship sessions, breakfast groups, substance-abuse groups, kids' groups, teens' groups, women's groups, men's groups, singles' groups (groups for people who don't want to be single), and yes, in many cases, social- (i.e., political-) action groups, all of which the megachurch offers and its megastaff coordinates.

Some megachurches, especially those in African American communities, are militantly "progressive" in politics; more are militantly "conservative"; a few are socially conscious but militantly nonpolitical.[36] All attempt to provide a "motivational worship experience." But their major, continuing concern is the development of the group, the family, and the quasi or substitute church family. This concern is reflected in the thousands of evangelical congregations and fellowships that are not large enough to be "mega" but that organize their worship and group life in similar ways.

For over a century, mainstream churches had been offering a wide range of group attractions. They were acutely aware of their responsibilities as pillars of the community. While the revivalists were saving individual souls, mainstream churches were cultivating social consciousness. They apparently possessed every professional means of dealing with the social problems of the 1960s and its unceasing aftermath. But they didn't. The fellowships and the megachurches then devised their own means. They are intensely social, but the society they try to create juts out sharply from the mainstream, where divorce, abortion, drugs, and other means of flight from family values have become routine, obviously undeterred by the mainstream's old-time religion.

The megachurch attempts to combine two things that had seemed very different: the hive of earnest organizations constructed by the big-church movement after evangelical fervor waned within the mainline denominations, and the evangelical fervor itself, the radical spirit of separatism that had been preserved in off-brand churches until it spread to the counter-countercultural movements of the 1970s. This is curious, and it may not last: both modern media and modern "family values" seem to militate against an emergence of the great, commanding personalities that can extend the interest of a popular movement. At the moment, however, megachurches are a successful exposition of a paradoxical American idea: everything can be revived and, once revived, can be transformed into something radically new.

THE LOW WALL
OF SEPARATION

In 1787 James Madison, arguing for ratification of the Constitution, identified the benefits of a diversity of state governments:

A religious sect, may degenerate into a political faction in a part of the Confederacy; but the variety of sects dispersed over the entire face of it, must secure the national Councils against any danger from that source: a rage for paper money, for an abolition of debts, for an equal division of property, or for any other improper or wicked project, will be less apt to pervade the whole body of the Union, than a particular member of it; in the same proportion as such a malady is more likely to taint a particular county or district, than an entire State.[1]

The passage neatly represents its historical moment. Madison knew that Americans are vulnerable to sudden innovations, to "rages," religious as well as political and economic. Yet he was far from abandoning religious language. To say that something isn't just improper but *wicked* is almost as clear an appeal to religious feeling as the idea in the

Declaration of Independence that people "are endowed by their Creator with certain unalienable rights."

Madison knew very well that several states still possessed established churches. Connecticut and Massachusetts would keep them until 1818 and 1833, respectively. He was also familiar with the leading role that ministers of two denominations—Congregational and Presbyterian—had played in agitating for the Revolution. But Madison's resonant word for religion-in-politics is "degenerate": a sect may *degenerate* into a political faction. For him, the most important thing isn't to guarantee a divorce between church and state; it's to distinguish which is which. If you can't tell the difference between a church (a "sect") and a political party (a "faction"), then you present a political danger. Your religion has *degenerated* into politics.

In strict terms, the danger Madison identified has seldom appeared in America. No church has ever become a political party, and there has been only one instance in which a state, or statelike entity, was the same as a church. That happened in the mid-nineteenth century when the Mormons attempted to create an American theocracy in Utah. The attempt failed because the federal government refused to recognize it and, at one point, sent soldiers to suppress it.

Nobody could maintain that sects degenerated into factions during the period directly following the American Revolution. To use a favorite twenty-first-century term, this was a time when religion was being privatized. Individual states were cutting churches adrift from government, and until the Second Great Awakening grew strong in the 1820s, no great religious issues shook the nation as a whole. In the days before cheap communications, it was hard to turn any cause into a national movement. Christianity was a background consideration in politics.

Yet you could still see it clearly if you looked. The Northwest Ordinance, passed by Congress in the same year in which Madison made his comment about politics and religion, provided a political organization for the soon to be mighty provinces north of the Ohio and east of the Mississippi. In this document, "religion"—which for almost everyone in America meant the Christian, and specifically the Protestant, religion—is pictured as the root and fruit of social well-being: "Religion, morality, and knowledge, being necessary to good government and the happiness of mankind, schools and the means of education shall forever be encouraged." There was no idea of keeping religion out of the schools.

It was during the early years of the Republic that Thomas Jefferson made his now-famous remark about the Constitution's "wall of separation between Church & State." At the time, the comment went virtually unnoticed. Three years later, in his second inaugural address, Jefferson himself expounded a theory of God's providential relationship to America that would gratify any member of today's religious Right. He confessed his need for "the favor of that Being in whose hands we are, who led our forefathers, as Israel of old, from their native land, and planted them in a country flowing with all the necessaries and comforts of life; who has covered our infancy with his providence, and our riper years with his wisdom and power."[2]

"Church & State" was one thing; a generic but emphatic Christianity was another. In early America, religion was a constant influence on the attitudes and practices that made the state. It exercised an unembarrassed and uncontested influence on the authority that local governments wielded over daily life. This influence was often inconvenient. When President Washington toured New England in 1789, he found himself marooned in an obscure village where he had reason to regret his constituents' wealth of religious conviction: "It being contrary to law and disagreeable to the People of this State (Connecticut) to travel on the Sabbath day—and my

horses, after passing through such intolerable roads, wanting rest, I stayed at Perkins' tavern (which, by the bye, is not
a good one,) all day—and a meeting-house being within few
rods of the door, I attended morning and evening service, and
heard very lame discourses from a Mr. Pond."[3]

In America, there were hundreds of Mr. Ponds, but their
restrictive effect on how other people spent their Sundays was a cause of annoyance, not of public controversy. It
wasn't until the 1820s that the community's commonplace
enforcement of religious values became an issue—because of
the Sabbath. The same technological changes that speeded
travel and spread the Awakening also damaged traditional
assumptions about the relationship between social authority and Christian customs. Many old believers were shocked
to find that boats on the new Erie Canal kept going on Sundays. Then they noticed that the U.S. mail kept going too.
They petitioned the federal government, but without success.
They tried running their own, Sabbath-respecting boats on
the canal; these also failed. Reluctantly, they adapted themselves to new conditions. Yet in many parts of America, Sunday closing laws for retail stores prevailed until the 1960s. In
many places it is still illegal to sell intoxicating beverages on
Sunday mornings. The idea is that you should be in church.

What you should not be doing is gambling, cavorting with
prostitutes, viewing pornography, or any of those other things
that have until recently been considered obviously legitimate
targets of state power. Some of them were labeled "public
nuisances," but most were so anathematized by Christianity that no other explanation is needed to explain the laws
against them. The laws were based on religious beliefs that
long preceded the existence of the United States.

Nineteenth-century evangelicals were frustrated by the
obstacles to preserving an old-time Sabbath. Yet it was in
the same period that they started to develop more ambitious ideas about their own relationship to state power.

These ideas began as the opinions of a small minority, opinions about what individual Christians should *not* do. They soon changed into judgments about what Christians (and Christian churches) *should* do, then into demands about what the state *must* do to enforce Christian ideas. The two great Protestant Christian crusades were the abolition of slavery and the prohibition of alcohol. Today, few people see any connection between them; then, few people missed the evangelical link.

The speed with which both crusades developed illustrates the volatility of Christianity in America. In the 1780s, the Methodists, then a tiny sect, exhorted their members against slaveholding. By 1844, when they had become the largest denomination in America, they were quarreling bitterly among themselves about every aspect of the question. In that year they split into two denominations, northern and southern, over the matter of a slaveholding bishop. By 1850 the Baptists had split in the same way, and the Presbyterians were coming apart in several directions. These events were considered so serious that John C. Calhoun, of all divisive people, lamented that "the strong ties which held each denomination together" were now snapping.[4] For many northern religious leaders, the goal wasn't just stopping slaveholding by members of their local churches; it was stopping slaveholding by anyone.

Religion was not a logically necessary part of the abolition movement. Of all the causes that have agitated America, this was the one most likely to have evolved, deductively and incrementally, within a political order in which individual rights were officially enshrined. Yet religion was necessary to the movement's prophetic urgency. When Sojourner Truth traversed the northern states advocating abolition and embodying women's equality, she wasn't preaching the gospel of Jefferson; she was preaching the gospel of Christ. When Julia Ward Howe wrote her abolition battle song, she was relying on scripture and giving a revolutionary turn to it: "Let the Hero, born of woman, crush the serpent with his heel, / Since God is marching on."[5] The hero is Christ at his militant second coming; the serpent is slavery.

Evangelical feeling wasn't the whole story. Howe herself wasn't an evangelical, though she could write like one. Northern unitarians were even more opposed to slavery than northern evangelicals. And while some southern evangelicals, such as Peter Cartwright, migrated north because they couldn't stand to live among slaveholders,[6] most proved more willing to break up their denominations than to sanction abolition. Yet the antislavery movement became large and fervent when a strong minority of church people generalized their personal revival and conversion experiences into a desire for revival and conversion of the Republic as a whole.

It was similar people—usually, in fact, the same people—who provided the impetus for the "temperance" and then the prohibition movement. This is one predictable thing in church history: if you find someone who was involved in abolition, that person will likely have been involved in "temperance" as well. And for the North, it is almost certain that anyone involved in "temperance" will also have been opposed to slavery, if not an outright abolitionist. The religious connections transcended all social, economic, and denominational differences.

The question is how to explain the mighty prohibition movement, even on Christian grounds. Granted, the saloon could be identified, and hated, as competition with the church. In 1881 there were forty-six saloons in Jackson, Michigan, but only fourteen churches. And granted, there were good practical reasons for worrying about the drinking habits of Americans. In the 1820s, they were drinking a lot more alcohol than was good for them: people fifteen years of age or older were consuming on average about two and a half times more than they would be 150 years later. Whiskey, cider, and rum were among Americans' least expensive and undoubtedly most pleasant forms of recreation. American water was generally polluted, and American food—heavy on salt pork and fried bread—was so nauseating that something tasty was needed to wash it down. Americans found it in vast quantities.[7]

The odd thing is the sudden growth, the wide support, and the persistent strength of a movement, especially a religious movement, for outright prohibition of alcoholic beverages. It had nothing to do with any traditional form of Christianity. Communion in bread and wine is the central Christian rite. In the early Republic, hard liquor was a normal accompaniment of church parties and celebrations. Churches and taverns were often located next to each other, to their mutual advantage. Early preachers liked their rum and whiskey; they were shocked when moral revolutionaries told them there was something wrong with drinking customs that were "almost universally" enjoyed by Christian ministers. Preachers were sometimes paid by their congregations with gallons of liquor, just as colonial ministers had been paid with tobacco.[8]

Before 1800 virtually no one believed that the Bible was opposed to drinking. Drunkenness, yes. Alcohol, no. But once people in the evangelical churches began to find inspiration in the idea of abstinence, a biblical explanation was created: the Bible uses a variety of terms for wine, and the crucial passages imply nothing more than grape juice. To believe that, one must believe that when the Bible praises "wine that maketh glad the heart of man," it really means that grape juice makes you happy. The Bible also records people's surprise that the good wine Jesus made from water, at the wedding feast of Cana, had been saved for last. Does this mean that the most potent *grape juice* was usually served immediately? It is remarkable that such biblical objections meant so little to Bible-quarrying evangelicals.[9]

The serious campaign against alcohol was started by America's best-known physician, Benjamin Rush, who in 1788 began circulating a pamphlet (consisting mainly of quack science) advocating temperance. It attracted attention from other busybodies, but nothing much happened until the second decade of the nineteenth century, when Lyman Beecher, disgusted by the joyful though moderate drinking of his clerical colleagues, took up the cause. From the start, this was a revolution from above. Many Christians in the early temperance coalitions insisted that the goal must actually be temperance, not abstinence, but ardent preachers and other professional publicists insisted that nobody could take one drink and stop; therefore, abstinence must be demanded. At that point, many people, especially theological conservatives, left the movement, identifying it as an attempt to force the views of its leaders onto everyone else.[10]

But "temperance" was an enormous success. By 1845 the nation's per-capita liquor consumption was only a quarter of what it had been in 1830,[11] probably because of intense evangelical propaganda. To people concerned primarily about the bad effects of hard liquor, that sounded like victory. For professional agitators, it wasn't nearly enough. They responded by trying to drive liquor completely out of America. They promoted restrictive licensing laws and then simple prohibition.

Another group of moderates seceded, but the campaign continued. It conquered all the mainstream Protestant churches except the Episcopalian. It mobilized both "liberals" and "conservatives." It occupied the Sunday schools, the camp meetings, the hymnals, the religious journals, the lecture circuits, the seminaries, the inner-city missions, the workingmen's associations, the Young Men's Christian Association (originally something more than a place to take a swim)—all the institutional means of attraction, conversion, and retention used by the evangelical churches. On both the state and the national level, its leaders established political pressure groups led by professional operatives who bullied, threatened, and dictated to legislators. Beginning with Maine in 1851, it achieved prohibition in one state after another. When the limits of state and local action were reached, it intensified its campaign for national prohibition. In 1917 it induced a pusillanimous president to order various types of prohibition as a wartime measure, necessary to conserve agricultural supplies. Finally it procured a constitutional amendment prohibiting intoxicating beverages. Then, when that amendment was repealed, after a mere thirteen years of failure . . . the movement went away. A chronic component of American Protestantism died as suddenly and as easily as a great social movement ever has.

Religious historians have not been much concerned with explaining this sudden cessation, perhaps because no intellectual or social-economic explanation appears to be available. It's a good example of the unpredictability of American religious feeling, of the way in which particular means of evoking religious experience exhaust their potential and are abandoned. First the forces of temperance achieved their goal; then came doubts about whether the goal had been worth the work. The response was, Let it go. The underlying antipathy to alcohol remained, even in mainline Protestant churches (most Catholics had never flirted with prohibition), but the intensity had departed.

Much less effort has been devoted to explaining the evaporation of the temperance movement than to explaining its origins. In that case the smoking gun is ordinarily found in the hand of the middle class. The movement's real, though largely unexpressed, motivation is said to have been the desire of the urban middle class to defend itself against rapacious plutocrats, bearing down from above, and an industrial proletariat, swarming up from below.[12] If you accept this theory, you don't need religion to explain a religious phenomenon; all you need is a theory of social class. But when you read the histories of frontier evangelists (Cartwright's is one example), you see that the ideal of temperance dawned as easily above the desolate prairies of Illinois as it did above the factory chimneys of New England. One could see the light of temperance without ever having encountered a factory, a proletarian, or a person who was actually rich.

It is true that some leading prohibitionists were inspired more by strictly political or social concerns than by religious ones; Frances Willard, the great proponent of women's rights as well as a variety of socialist and populist causes, is probably an example.[13] But when prohibitionists criticized the Church, as they frequently did, the attack was much less likely to be motivated by their own lack of religious feeling than by their impression that the Church itself lacked "genuine soul hunger." In other words, the churches weren't religious enough.[14]

Nevertheless, a statistical study of 616 leading prohibitionists shows that 37 percent of them were members of the clergy. The next-largest categories were businessmen (17 percent) and lawyers (16 percent), immediately followed by social workers (9 percent) and, at a great distance, physicians (1.5 percent).[15] If prohibition was "really" a political or social cause, and only secondarily a religious one, it is strange that the political class, the lawyers, should form such a small proportion of its leadership, and that the social leaders of a thousand American towns, the businessmen and doctors, should make a relatively small showing too. Businessmen, after all, should be devoted to defending the middle class, and physicians should be well acquainted with the evil effects of whiskey. But even when the businessmen and the doctors are added to the lawyers, they don't come up to the preachers.

As its enemies charged, the temperance movement showed every characteristic of a spiritual revolution conducted from above. It is harder to define the leadership of the antislavery movement—or to be more accurate, the conflict over slavery, since there was also fervent activism on the pro-slavery side. According to a religious historian not known for overstatement, the proslavery movement that developed after 1830 was a "revolution."[16] The conflict embraced many types of struggles in many arenas, but its quick growth and high intensity within the churches cannot be attributed to a generally outraged laity or even to the influence of humble local clergy. Discussing one aspect of the slavery dispute, the sundering of the Methodist Church on a north-south line, Cartwright asked, "If these secessions had been left to the voice of our members, would they ever have taken place? No, verily, no, will be the answer of every intelligent man, woman, and child."[17] The responsible parties, in his view, were the leaders, north and south: the bishops, the prominent speak-ers, and the editors of church papers. They were in charge of the means of communication, and they used them to change the church by continually reminding it of their own agenda.

Cartwright, who was well positioned to study the offi-cial class within his church, was witnessing something more than the collision between abolition and antiabolition movements. He was observing the start of national religious politics. As they matured, evangelical institutions naturally developed their own leaders and constituencies. Their fund-ing was increasingly national, and so was their leadership. Gradually it concentrated itself in what may be called the political and social policy–making circuits of the big denomi-nations. The Civil War intervened before the abolition move-ment had a chance to develop professional lobbying organi-zations. It was the long crusade for prohibition that educated Christian social activists in all the ways by which politics can be influenced.

Unfortunately, organization and specialization did not promote education in other respects. For the prohibition-ist elite, evidence and science consisted chiefly of earnest speculations about social well-being. This was often true as well about the church movement that grew up alongside the national movement for prohibition, and with many of the same personnel—the Social Gospel movement.

That name is normally used for a movement, most active in the 1890–1930 period, associated with various socialist and progressive ideas, for which it endeavored to find a religious basis. The label comes from a book, *A Theology for the Social Gospel* (1917), written by a Baptist pastor and social worker, Walter Rauschenbusch. The book contains many memorable phrases, but by 1917 there was nothing remarkable about its themes. Like most other polemics, it is a tissue of assertions looking (though not very hard) for evidence. It assumes that a "social gospel" already exists. It assumes that readers understand that capitalism, a system in which people work "primarily for profit," is the root of all social evils and is thoroughly anti-Christian—an "unsaved organization." It also assumes that readers will readily accept the idea that the church's responsibility is to "Christianize" society.[18] The specific means of transformation are left unstated, but it is obvious that massive state power will have to be invoked to convert a profit-motivated society into one inspired by the concept of "cooperation." Again, there is the sense that everyone in the audience already knows and accepts these ideas, whatever precisely they may imply.

In 1912 Theodore Roosevelt had used the social gospel idea to Christianize his Progressive Party campaign for the presidency. Speaking in a manner that, if he were running today, would place him on a fringe of the radical Right, Roosevelt intoned: "We stand at Armageddon, and we battle for the Lord."[19] Such speeches earned him the ridicule of conservatives, though by that time neither the revolutionary phrases nor the basic ideas were new. The ideal of "the cooperative society" had been intellectually and politically fashionable for at least three decades before the Social Gospel achieved its name. It was not immediately accepted in religious circles, but the general notion of Christianizing the nation by removing its social evils had already enjoyed a long history. It had been prominent in the days of sabbatarianism and then of abolition; it was still potent within the prohibition movement. It may not have drawn many people into church, but it was certainly a way of keeping them there, especially if they were people for whom the drama of individual conversion, lost amid the proliferating activities of the mainstream churches, no longer provided a source of identity and significance. When one reads the life stories of Social Gospel workers, one often meets people who, like Rauschenbusch himself, suffered crises of faith about the churches' incapacity to solve the problem of poverty but were then transformed by a personal encounter with the newer, social version of the salvation story. As Rauschenbusch put it, "The individual is saved, if at all, by membership in a community which has salvation." That community was the Church—but only if it was working for "social redemption" in the modern, "scientific unfolding" of "organized righteousness," the "commonwealth of co-operative labour" that he identified with "the Kingdom of God."[20]

Regardless of its motives or ideals, this kind of appeal would have shocked even the most aggressive of the old-time Christian reformers. They had believed that salvation is an individual response to individual sins and cannot wait for something to happen in society at large. But if maintaining a sense of challenge is essential to maintaining a religious movement, the Social Gospel offered the ultimate challenge: it suggested that you can't be saved until all the rest of society has been saved.

Neither Rauschenbusch nor any of his contemporaries imparted a clear meaning to this new idea of salvation. After all, how could you tell when social salvation had been achieved, or what projects were likely to achieve it? But while the language of the Social Gospel couldn't be taken literally, its urgency could be and was. The general idea of a social gospel elicited an intensified commitment to Christ among Protestants who labored in missions to the poor, among Catholics who served in Dorothy Day's Catholic Worker movement, and among those Protestants and Catholics who went to prison rather than cooperate with the war efforts of 1917–1918 and 1940–1945.

Yet these were individual acts, performed in limited contexts. America as a whole could not be "Christianized" without professional political action. Following the lead of the already professionalized prohibition movement, with its boards and committees and front groups, Social Gospel Christians turned to action taken by central offices in coordination or competition with other central offices. The big denominations all created research and lobbying organizations, run by specialists, to advance their political and social aims. In 1908 they formed a central organization of central organizations, the Federal (later National) Council of Churches of Christ in America. Its secondary purpose was to advertise the unity of the Body of Christ (although it omitted both the Catholics and the conservative evangelicals—in short, most American Christians); its primary purpose was to Christianize America's political economy by "institutionalizing the Social Gospel."[21]

Historians used to suggest that the Social Gospel just went away, perhaps in the purportedly conservative 1920s. Many have now reexamined that view. The movement hadn't left; it had merely institutionalized itself in the mainstream churches. Its reach and penetration can be seen in a manifesto adopted by the Federal Council of Churches (FCC) in 1932.[22] This statement is the kind of document that always gets forgotten, both by traditionalists longing for their grandparents' day, when the churches didn't "meddle in politics," and by progressives longing for *their* grandparents' day, when church people worked to achieve modest but noble aims, such as Social Security and an end to Jim Crow.

Both parties would be surprised by the carefully considered and loudly proclaimed ideas of the churches, in the FCC assembled. The nation's most grievous social problem, the oppression of African Americans, is mentioned only euphemistically in a general wish for "justice, opportunity and equal rights for all; mutual good-will and cooperation." But no such restraint is manifested on the economic front. The churches demand nothing less than a complete transformation of the country's economic life, which is now to be governed by "the Christian principle of social well-being." This means that all Americans, "employees and employers alike," must "work for the public good"; that there must be "social planning and control" of the entire financial system; and that "the profit motive" must be "subordinat[ed]" to what is called "the creative and cooperative spirit." Yet even these demands, it was found, did not go far enough. In 1933 the FCC expanded its statement, declaring that "the Christian conscience can be satisfied with nothing less than the complete substitution of motives of mutual helpfulness and good will for the motive of private gain."[23]

No bloc of churches had ever issued more strident commands. Neither President Roosevelt nor the members of America's local churches were contemplating the extinction of the profit motive. Here was another revolution conducted on the spiritual heights: the Christian conscience had been consulted by headquarters staff, and its concerns had been found equivalent to those of headquarters staff. The connection with the Social Gospel is evident. Not so certain is the place of this version of the gospel on the now familiar Left-Right spectrum. Social Gospel Christians had no trouble nailing both "conservative" and "liberal" planks to their platform. In 1933 the FCC was still demanding a government prohibition of alcohol—or as the FCC put it, "protection of the individual and society from the social, economic and moral waste of any traffic in intoxicants and habit-forming drugs." The ideas of the FCC may seem a curious assemblage of left-wing and right-wing nostrums, but to church leaders, they were mere Christianity.

Much the same can be said about the social programs advocated by the FCC, its constituent denominations, and mainstream church associations during the following thirty years. The FCC and the Northern Baptists—to cite one denomination—combined agitation against liquor advertisements with agitation against compulsory military training in peacetime and for strong government action in the housing field.[24] True, most of the mainstream churches' social advocacy can fairly be characterized as left-wing. The FCC, ever ready with opinions, demanded federal involvement to remedy the "crisis in education," urged member churches to be "unequivocal in giving guidance to the Nation in the program of broad social welfare," advocated aid to Europe as long as it was not an expression of "self interest," and supported international trade as long as it wasn't conducted on behalf of anything except the "general interest" of the world. (One may wonder how many local churchgoers were insisting that the nation be governed on these principles.) But the idea underlying most church involvements in the social field was the expansive principle enunciated in 1949 by a prominent spokesman for the Congregationalists explaining why he was advising Congress to extend Social Security: "The church cannot be the church and remain silent when people are involved."[25] Taken seriously, as the speaker was taking it, this means that the church can never be silent about anything.

Big church was hectoring big government and insisting on its right to do so. And by 1950, big church lobbies had moved into Washington in a big way. Most came in the 1930s and 1940s; the Methodists got there earlier. Their Board of

Temperance, an antiliquor, antidrug, antipornography, anti-lottery, and anti any other form of gambling organization, arrived in 1916. It continued after the death of prohibition, operating from the Methodist Building, which was conveniently situated across from the Capitol. This denomination's political undertakings were not limited to America. It had another lobby group, this one headquartered at Dupont Circle, to look after foreign missions and foreign affairs in general. In 1947 its Washington secretary modestly characterized his work as "Christianizing international relations." Methodist representatives roamed the world, visiting government officials in Europe and many non-Christian nations, chiefly Muslim.[26]

Church officials were aware that "lobbying" was a bad word and tried to get away from it. Around 1950 the secretary of the Washington office of the Division of Public Relations of the National Lutheran Council told an interviewer that "in accordance with the traditional position of the Lutheran Church," he was not what you would call a lobbyist. Still, he said, it was "the church's responsibility to participate in the shaping of public sentiment," which meant that it had a responsibility to operate a political "public relations" office, or lobby.[27]

The Protestants weren't alone. From its ten-story building on Massachusetts Avenue, the National Catholic Welfare Conference ran an array of programs concerned with everything from labor unions to international peace. It was particularly concerned with government action that might help or hinder Catholic schools or hospitals. The conference was aggressive and blunt. In 1948 its secretary, who was urging Congress to vote appropriations for housing, was asked by a Representative what "warrant" he found in the New Testament for spending tax money on the church's charitable purposes. The secretary referred to general New Testament ideas about helping the poor. The congressman pressed the question. "Through the State?" he asked. Yes, the monsignor replied; the state should "encourage" the church, and when the church had spent its own money, the state had a responsibility to spend the money of "the citizenry as a whole" on projects favored by the church.[28]

Opposition to church involvement in politics tended to be severely constitutional (civil libertarians building and rebuilding the "wall of separation between church and state") or severely sectarian (Protestants maintaining that public money should not buy textbooks or bus rides for students in Catholic schools). Conservative and evangelical churches formed associations to counter the FCC and its political interventions, but they received virtually no attention from the national media. One of them, the National Association of Evangelicals, was formed in 1942 as a home for churches that did not agree with the religious modernism of the FCC or its emphasis on political action. The association, which now claims forty denominations among its membership, grew slowly and did not establish a distinct political profile until the 1980s. Then its public blessing was sought, and found, by Republican presidents. Its path veered from opposition to politics to the embrace of politics in a conservative form.

For many years, however, the mainline (now the generally modern liberal) denominations held the national stage alone, and were determined to keep holding it. Disturbed to find that the new medium of radio tolerated the participation of off-brand Christians and that the most popular religious shows were the "Old-Fashioned Revival Hour" and programs by the Seventh-day Adventists and the conservative Lutheran Church, Missouri Synod, the Federal Council of Churches devoted its best efforts to driving these competitors from the air. It successfully pressured the networks to give its members free time, while banning even paid broadcasts by other religious groups. It pressured the one network (Mutual) that allowed paid religious broadcasting to restrict this "racket" severely. When television came along, the National Council of Churches (NCC) repeated the performance of the Federal Council of Churches, keeping evangelicals out of network broadcasts and pressuring local stations to ban them.[29]

This campaign, like prohibition, succeeded only partially and temporarily. Evangelicals took advantage of the local stations' need for funds and got them to accept paid radio and TV programs that in many cases were syndicated nationwide. In the late twentieth century, when the network cartels were broken by FM radio and cable TV, and regulations about paid on-air "public service" content became more pliable, NCC-style programming suddenly became hard to find. The mainstream audience was no longer the same as the mainstream churches.

At midcentury an analyst of religious life, Herbert W. Schneider, concluded that the Social Gospel movement had not ended; it had simply become more involved in the "practical work of the churches": "The basic aims and efforts of Christianizing society are more deeply rooted than ever. . . . The focus of concern has been shifted from saving souls to saving society, from reliance on supernatural grace and mercy to working for social 'redemption' by economic and political measures, from religious revivals to social reconstruction, from moral platitudes to moral criticism."[30]

Schneider was a thoughtful observer, but his analysis of religious trends was as fallible as such analyses usually are. Given the volatility of American Christianity, it's hard to see how he could have been completely right, whatever he said. He was right about the persistence of the Social Gospel—of the assumption that the Church's mission is to redeem society by political means—but his statements are full of unconscious ironies. By the 1980s, the idea that the churches' job is to Christianize society would be openly avowed by only the most extreme religious activists, and least of all by the liberal bureaucrats whom Schneider depicts as running the "practical work" of the mainstream churches. Meanwhile, the job of applying Christian principles to economics and politics had been taken up by conservatives as well as liberals, and politicians were attributing both their victories and their defeats to the influence of the religious Right, with barely a nod to a religious Left.

Politicians may not be as canny as they think they are. In America, crucial elections tend to be won by small margins, and citizens tend to define themselves and their politics in a variety of ways. A union member who ordinarily votes for liberal Democrats may simultaneously vote against a gay-marriage referendum; a dedicated social democrat may simultaneously be a theologically conservative Roman Catholic, determined to end abortion. If agitation by the religious Right produces 3 percent of the vote, that will constitute a "margin of victory" in many elections and will be used to garner contributions by both the winning and the losing sides. Yet the vote total will embrace many other 3 percent segments, including the ever-present 3 percent (or more) that represents hardcore opposition to religion in politics. And no one should discount the continued influence of religious people on the left. Religious leaders have headed the endorsement lists for every important liberal cause of the past fifty years, from the battle over Vietnam to the battles over abortion and gay rights, and even to the Occupy crusade (2011), which was actively supported by many mainstream clergy. Sometimes a literate politician even goes so far as to identify the influence of the Social Gospel on his or her own intellectual development; George McGovern is one example, and President Obama is another.[31]

As for the religious Right, there should be no doubt that its influence, though great, has been oversold. In 1979 Jerry Falwell, a Baptist minister, organized the coalition known as the "Moral Majority." That was the first evidence detected by the national media, slow to report significant religious developments, that there was a massive rebellion among conservative Christians against modern liberal religion and politics. For the rest of his life, Falwell was an influence on the Republican Party, and he was not hesitant about advertising that fact. But the attempt to reduce Americans' connections with Christianity—or politics, either—to a concern with a unified and "traditional" set of ideas was based on false assumptions.

Like all large groupings of Americans, the religious Right gained influence more from its diversity than from its unity. It was not a revolt just of fundamentalists or people whom newspapers call fundamentalists. It was a revolt of Roman Catholics against the Supreme Court's licensing of abortion and of evangelicals (many of whom believed that the pope was literally the Antichrist) against the courts' prohibition of religion in the public schools—a prohibition that Catholics had traditionally supported. The religious Right included millenarians demanding greater support for Israel, because Israel figures in Bible prophecy, and Calvinists who thought it heretical to give religious respect to "national Israel" but were incensed at their own country's drift into moral permissiveness. Much of the political leadership of the religious Right, and virtually all its legal and research assistance, came from men and women who combined traditional ideas about the state's responsibility in the moral sphere with essentially libertarian ideas about the limitation of state power in other spheres.

Beneath the agitation about displaying the Ten Commandments on courthouse lawns ("where they have always been") and the idealization of President Washington as a Christian hero, this was another messy revolution in American religion, one that tried to combine the new with the old, insisting that progress was merely restoration. Its messiness allowed it to connect with more people than a neatly packaged, closely supervised movement could have done. The messiness reflected Americans' diverse self-identifications. It also prevented the revolution from completing its agenda, however that might have been construed by the various participants. Like most other American revolutions, it had a partial success, subject to revision. It revealed the fact that there are many millions of people in America who believe devoutly that God exists and has a purpose for their lives, a purpose that has much to do with maintaining American traditions in religion and politics but much less to do with voting Republican or even going to church.

Leaders of the religious Right suffered from the same difficulty as leaders of the religious Left. As Finke and Stark have argued, people's commitment to their religion depends in part on the religion's critical "tension" with the social environment; a religion that lacks clear boundaries and challenges is in trouble.[32] Political engagements tend strongly to reduce the tensions. Preachers may picture themselves as speaking truth to power when they promote political causes, but theirs is usually quite a safe project. The religious activism of the past thirty years has often meant little more than gathering an audience so that social liberalism can be preached to social liberals, and social conservatism, to social conservatives.

But there was at least one political and religious movement that developed in more challenging ways: the civil rights revolution led by Reverend Martin Luther King Jr. If anything shows that the individual is the wild card in American religious history, this is it. Like the abolition of slavery, the eventual achievement of full civil equality by black Americans could have been predicted from America's classical-liberal principles. The fact that leadership came in large part from the African American churches might have been predictable as well. But the method by which it was achieved, nonviolent action, wasn't at all predictable. And here one must consider King's own intellectual revolution, his creative reinterpretation of both the New Testament and the Social Gospel movement.

King believed that the New Testament mandated not only political action but also a "nonconformity" that was radically different from Social Gospel politicking or bureaucratized good works. It called for personal chastening, revival, and conversion. King quoted St. Paul: "Be ye transformed by the renewing of your mind." He turned the allusion into a demand for action: "This experience, which Jesus spoke of as the new birth, is essential if we are to be transformed nonconformists and freed from the cold hardheartedness and self-righteousness so often characteristic of nonconformity. Someone has said, 'I love reforms but I hate reformers.' A reformer may be an untransformed nonconformist whose rebellion against the evils of society has left him annoyingly rigid and unreasonably impatient."[33]

These thoughts formed the internal basis of King's American nonviolence. Fervent yet disciplined and reflective, nonviolence allowed for personal as well as social "redemption." And it worked much better than anyone would have predicted. King brought the Social Gospel back to the Bible and forward to a movement that discovered spiritual resources many Americans never knew they had.

MILLIONS NOW LIVING
WILL NEVER DIE

M any of our neighbors are intellectual revolutionaries in the most drastic way: they believe that life as we know it is about to end. Some believe that Christ will soon appear and remove, or "rapture," his followers to heaven. Some believe that he has already come and is preparing to initiate a glorious millennium in which humanity will enjoy the gift of everlasting life. A few still believe, as did many in the nineteenth century, that by their own good works, they themselves are preparing Christ's kingdom, and that after its establishment Christ will return to crown their efforts.

These beliefs may be shocking to readers of the ordinary media, but they have been prominent in America for much of its history. In 1835 Charles Finney declared, "If the church will do all her duty, the millennium may come in this country in three years."[1] At many times in the nineteenth and twentieth centuries, large numbers of Americans expected God to bring the present world to its end. In 2011 billboards appeared across the country announcing that the Rapture would occur on May 21, with the complete annihilation of the physical world to follow five months later. The nonfulfillment of that prophecy produced further prophecies, based on the conviction that the basic chronology "had to be correct."

To most observers, visions of the end—though embraced by millions of people who are demographically indistinguishable from their fellow Americans—are figments of disordered imaginations, manifestations of religious mania. But no matter what fantastic pictures it paints, or how wrong it turns out to be, the discourse of American millenarians is typically calm, sober, even bloodless. It is the discourse of people using logic to discover meaningful patterns in scripture and history. It is the perennial revolt of reason, which always seeks a fresh examination of the evidence, against the established certainties of the mainstream churches, whatever those may be.

That is the way in which America's first great millennial movement began. William Miller (1782–1849), who started it, had imbibed religious skepticism from the intellectual leaders of his little town. But somehow he wasn't satisfied. He began his own study of the Bible, governed solely by his own reason.[2] To his surprise, he discovered that when studied in accordance with the most rational rules of interpretation he could identify, the Bible revealed a coherent historical explanation of the world, an explanation that could be confirmed by the facts in secular histories. The Bible's numbers and symbols, he concluded, pointed unerringly to the final realization of God's plan: the second coming of Christ and the rapture of his saints. Miller found a reason for believing in the God of the Bible; he also found an exciting connection between the thinking individual and God's plan for the cosmos.

For Miller, the most important set of Bible prophecies appeared in the book of Daniel, which predicts that God's temple will be given over to "transgression" until 2,300 days have passed; "then shall the sanctuary be cleansed." Following a hint from Numbers 14:34 and Ezekiel 4:6, Miller took

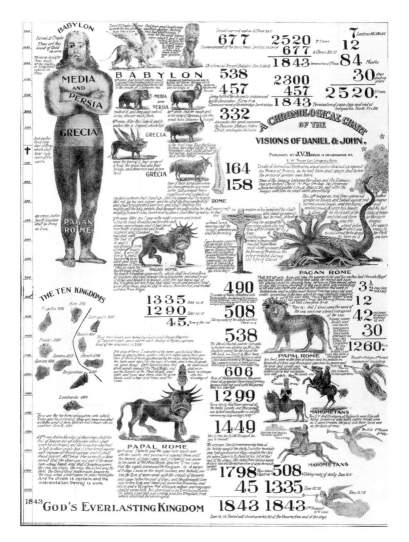

FIGURE 7.1. A chart used by the Millerite movement, with Bible numbers and Bible symbols, including Nebuchadnezzar's image with head of gold and feet of clay (Daniel 2), all leading to the year 1843. Courtesy of Andrews University, Center for Adventist Research.

"a day for a year" and calculated 2,300 years from the decree of Artaxerxes authorizing the restoration of God's sanctuary in Jerusalem to the cleansing of impure religion in a final judgment. The result was the year 1843. Miller modestly predicted that the end would come either that year or (in case he had been slightly wrong about his starting date) the next one.[3]

He took a long time to announce his discovery. He wanted to be sure; besides, he was nervous about speaking before skeptical audiences.[4] But once the great announcement was made, his evidence gained him followers eager to publicize his findings. They printed hundreds of thousands of pamphlets. They started newspapers. They held meetings in a giant tent that could be moved from town to town, attracting attention wherever it went. They made charts presenting his explanation of history in startlingly graphic form. Above all, they appealed to Americans' belief in practical, quantifying reason, in what can be added and subtracted. The assurance that the Bible's message could be reduced to numbers, and the numbers could be checked against one another and against fact, had an irresistible attraction for many people who had wanted to believe but couldn't.

Then came 1844, the year of the Great Disappointment. Most of Miller's audience melted away, and even he observed that something must have gone wrong somewhere. But some of his followers continued to find his vision, and even his numbers, convincing. One group, including a middle-aged farmer, Hiram Edson, and two young people, Ellen White and her husband, James, was persuaded that the cleansing of the sanctuary had actually begun in 1844 but occurred invisibly, when Christ entered the innermost *heavenly* sanctuary to conduct an "investigative judgment" of humanity. Having thus defended Miller's claims by giving them a new interpretation, these people were prepared to accept other sources of inspiration, such as Ellen White's own prophetic visions. But the formative concept was the idea that what has once been rationally established must always be true; the Christian's obligation is to discover its real meaning. The result of this conviction was the Seventh-day Adventist Church, which today numbers about 16 million members worldwide.

The Seventh-day Adventists continue to expect the second coming of Christ, although they point to no dates. But what about the first part of their name, "Seventh-day"? That refers to their belief that the Sabbath should be observed according to the Old Testament calendar, on the seventh day of the week, Saturday. Their early leaders were convinced of this by the arguments of the small Seventh Day Baptist sect. From other sources they acquired an interest in vegetarianism and similar health-related measures. There were more ideas: "soul sleep"—the doctrine that there is no immortal soul, that when people die, they are dead, unconscious, unless God decides to give them eternal life—and "annihilationism," the doctrine that the wicked will simply be annihilated, not sent to an eternal hell.

None of that had anything to do with the second coming of Christ, but all of it could be supported rationally. The health part seems particularly reasonable given the repulsive feeding habits of the nineteenth century. Seventh-day Adventists faced strong disapproval from small-town America, where people closed the shop on Sunday, went to church, then ate an enormous, meat-filled dinner. But the Adventists' eccentrically rationalist procedures enabled them to escape the curse of the Universalists. Not only did they have a kind of reason on their side, but they faced the constantly invigorating challenges that result from holding a variety of unpopular beliefs, not just one.

And they were not the only adventist survivors. The most colorful proponents of the Second Coming, soul sleep, annihilationism, and the general idea that scripture, rationally analyzed, is always productive of "new light" were the adventists now known as Jehovah's Witnesses, originally and more humbly known as Bible Students.[5]

The denomination began in the 1870s when a young man in the men's clothing business, Charles Taze Russell (1852–1916), discovered the teachings of certain radical adventist rationalists. Impressed by their logic, he followed the example of everyone else who had a religious idea: he started a journal. His was *Zion's Watch Tower and Herald of Christ's Presence*, which would, in the twentieth century, attain the largest print run of any religious magazine in the world. Drawing on revised analyses of prophetic numbers, Russell became convinced that the Second Coming had occurred, invisibly, in 1874. He anticipated the Rapture for 1881. Then other years became important, especially 1914, which he associated with the battle of Armageddon—a chaotic war of labor against capital, "the anarchy of the world"—and the beginning of Christ's millennial rule.[6] Russell's works were widely disseminated; his sermons appeared in thousands of newspapers; he was known to all.

When 1914 arrived in company with the Great War, Russell's followers considered him vindicated, despite the fact that the war was not exactly what he had looked forward to. He died in 1916, leaving his disciples to rationalize the best they could. Eventually they decided that the Second Coming had occurred (invisibly) in 1914, not 1874, and that the millennium would begin shortly.

Russell was a small, studious man, most concerned that his followers be "fully consecrated" to God's work. When he married, he and his wife agreed not to have sex, and they didn't; that would have distracted them. His was a genteel movement, centered on meetings of "the friends" for discussions of his refined eschatology. His successor as president of the Watch Tower Society took it in a different direction.

Joseph F. Rutherford (1869–1942), always called Judge

Rutherford because he had served on a handful of occasions as a temporary judge in Missouri, was a big, outspoken, angry, often drunk demagogue. An attorney for the Watch Tower Society, Rutherford conducted a revolution from above, purging all opposition and revising Russell's teachings until little remained except an expectation of the end time, a belief in the significance of 1914, and a rationalism that excluded most orthodox Christian beliefs.

In 1918 Rutherford invented one of the greatest advertising slogans in American history: "The World Has Ended— Millions Now Living Will Never Die." His thesis was that God had begun a new order ruled by Christ; all that was left for God to do was to liquidate the old order and return the earth to a deathless paradise. Rutherford predicted that this would begin in 1925. When it didn't, he went right on anyway, despite the loss of three-quarters of the Watch Tower Society's adherents.[7] He was discovering that a certain kind of rationalism could keep a core constituency loyal, no matter what.

In a long series of monanymic books (*Light, Prophecy, Government, Riches,* etc.) printed in millions of copies, Rutherford kept proving, by dry exposition of scripture, that apocalypse was very near, but he also kept creating new excitements and challenges. He renamed his denomination Jehovah's Witnesses, a term appropriate to its function as a "witness" against the world. He insisted that all governments and religions (except his own, which he called the Theocracy) were operated by the devil and were about to be destroyed at Armageddon, now pictured as God's assault on non-Witness humanity. He sent his disciples out on Sunday mornings to picket churches with signs reading "Religion Is a Snare and a Racket." He instructed them to gain access to corporate leaders by greeting their staffs with the commanding statement, "I am from Judge Rutherford; I have important business."[8] He rented sports palaces for religious rallies

FIGURE 7.2. *Judge Rutherford, who is said to have looked more like a judge than any real judge could have looked. Author's collection.*

and addressed crowds bigger than Billy Sunday's. He built a beautiful mission-revival home in San Diego, called it Beth Sarim ("House of Princes"), and deeded it, with great fanfare, to David, Gideon, Samson, and the other ancient worthies who, he said, would soon be resurrected and would govern the world from that Palestine-like place. Meanwhile, he lived in Beth Sarim and welcomed the press to come and take pictures of him doing so.

These campaigns had narrow but intense effects. Most people knew about Rutherford, and tried to ignore him. A few, however, were attracted to his special combination of rationalism, millenarianism, and hard-core political and religious vilification. When he died, he was still suggesting that the end was imminent, only a few months away. His last book, *Children* (1941), enjoins young followers not to marry: there isn't enough time.

Such methods were effective in some ways, but self-limiting. Rutherford died with about 60,000 active adherents in America, about the same number he had started with. His successors engineered another revolution. Without sacrificing his essential ideas, they replaced a demagogic, hard-sell approach with corporate management and the soft sell. Their literature no longer proffered cartoons of priests and ministers conniving with Satan, or Hitler at the least; it showed happy, multiethnic Witnesses enjoying the "paradise earth" that would follow Armageddon. The Witnesses held enormous rallies—one of them, in 1958, assembling 250,000 people—but they were anxious not to cause any disturbance. Their main purpose, it appeared, was to "give a good witness" to their cleanliness and order. They were no longer the rambunctious Theocracy; they were the sweetly reasonable, mildly suburban "New World Society" (as the group often called itself).

This approach proved attractive. By 1968 there were about 1.2 million active Witnesses in the world. Then, suddenly, the corporate leadership reverted to its original Millerite tendencies. It couldn't resist making one more specific prediction of the end of the world. It discovered that Bible chronology clearly pointed to 1975 as the important date. This insight roused the Witnesses to a frenzy of proselytism.

By the end of 1975 they had increased their numbers by about 84 percent.[9]

At first, when the millennium didn't arrive, the leadership tried not to comment. Then it suggested that ordinary Witnesses had reached premature conclusions. By 1979, when more responsible statements were made, the Witnesses were losing rather than gaining members (down 3 percent in the United States during 1978); their teachings and their way of teaching no longer seemed entirely rational. The numbers eventually stabilized and then crept upward—largely, it appears, because the Witnesses' revolving door kept moving, taking in new members, especially children, who hadn't been aware of 1975, while dispensing with the disappointed. The Witnesses continued, though with a much lower profile. Their current selling points are family values, an ethnically diverse membership, and (as always) doctrinal clarity and rationalism. At present these appear inadequate to cope with the clarity, rationality, and long memory of the Internet, which allows potential converts to go online and discover the Witnesses' history of prophetic failure, with devastating effects on the church's ability to find and keep adherents.[10] Alive, though no longer dynamic, the Witnesses require some new model of ministry but so far have not been able to find it.

The most popular end time oracles of the 1970s, however, weren't those of the Witnesses; they were those of *The Late Great Planet Earth* (1970), a book by an evangelical Christian named Hal Lindsey. Lindsey had been a staff member for the interdenominational Campus Crusade for Christ and became a fixture on the interdenominational Trinity Broadcasting cable TV network. His book was published by Zondervan, a major conservative Christian firm. The cover of the 1977 printing proclaims, "More Than 9,800,000 in print!" That printing advertises a movie, released in 1979, with the same title as the book. It was narrated by Orson Welles, included interviews with famous scientists, and grossed $19,500,000.[11]

The content of this film is well described by the 1977 "Preface to the Movie Edition," which seems to have been written by the journalist who had helped Lindsey get his speculations on paper:

> The world is in the grip of famine . . . energy supplies are running out . . . strange new diseases erupting without means of control . . . the population growing beyond manageable proportions . . . frustrated people everywhere turning to riot, rebellion, and terrorism . . . the air becoming foul with pollution . . . genetic experiments raising disturbing moral questions . . . earthquakes, floods, and unbelievably cold winters pointing to a growing imbalance in nature, perhaps even to a new Ice Age . . . people turning to bizarre religious cults . . . and, with the spread of nuclear weapons, the threat of holocaust hanging over us like a lengthening shadow.[12]

The interviews with scientists were not irrelevant. The book itself makes every effort to escape from a traditional Christian atmosphere and attract a popular-science, modern-marvels audience. These people, it assumes, are seeking "awesome information" about the Rapture, which is "the living end," the "ultimate trip." But the thrills are supposed to come from the products of scientific reason, from demography, economics, meteorology, genetics, and epidemiology, not from "bizarre religious cults." Evidently, Lindsey intends his audience to be young people. He writes, "We have been described as the 'searching generation.' We need so many answers— answers to the larger problems of the world, answers to the conditions in our nation, and most of all, answers for ourselves."[13]

That statement was an act of ventriloquism; Lindsey was forty years old when he completed the book. The "problems" are those that anyone might have encountered in the middlebrow, secular, scientistic media of the time. The prophecies are cast in the same mold. The book of Daniel is said to foretell the European Common Market; the book of Revelation is said to describe "an all-out attack of ballistic missiles."[14] Lindsey's apocalyptic timeline, deduced from a new reading of Bible passages that are always susceptible to new readings, goes like this: first the formation of the state of Israel (done!); then the Rapture (soon!); then the Great Tribulation, involving wars among Israel, the Arabs, China, the Soviet Union, and Western Europe (at least!); and then Christ's second coming, followed by the millennium (finally!).

According to Lindsey, the Second Coming had to occur "within forty years or so of 1948," and a lot had to happen before that happened.[15] Yet while time inexorably falsified his ideas, he showed no sign of giving up. He published more books, making more predictions about the 1980s and then the 1990s. The 2012 New Year's message on his website said, "The world still needs to hear the message that time is short and Jesus is coming soon."[16] But it was too late: the soul of millenarianism is rationalism, and the soul of rationalism is the ability to substantiate one's claims with some kind of evidence. Lindsey's books faded into the obscurity occupied by unchecked population growth, global cooling, and other scientifically derived fantasies.

Yet the interest in apocalypse remained, together with the reawakened knowledge that scripture predicts it and the ambient expectation that it is going to take place soon. So what would it be like for *you* to live in the world that end time speculators forecast? An answer was provided by fantasy fiction, particularly by the long and popular series of *Left Behind* novels (1995–2007). These books, by Tim LaHaye and Jerry B. Jenkins, have been accompanied by many ancillary products—including films, video games, comic books, spin-off novels, and so on. They tell the story of a group of non-Christians and nominal Christians who survive the sudden disappearance of their true-Christian, converted, born-again friends and relatives. By patient reasoning on the scriptural evidence, the survivors figure things out: prophecy is being fulfilled; the Rapture has occurred. Knowing, now, that this all makes sense, the left-behinds are of course converted; their souls are saved. But meanwhile, the world is hurtling past one apocalyptic Sign after another as the Antichrist (a one-world politician, very big with the United Nations) begins his work. Our newly converted friends form a committee to fight the encroaching evil, and exciting events ensue.

It is significant that the little band of adventurers forms amid long dialogues about commonplace disappointments, insecurities, and family problems, the stuff of modern church discussion groups and counseling sessions. The atmosphere is identical to that of a group Bible study in an evangelical church. And that's what *Left Behind* is really about; it's a dramatization of the ordinary thoughts and feelings of evangelical churchgoers. Seen from that vantage point, the end times aren't much different from the present, except that the ordinary Christians who appear in the stories occupy the center stage of world history. Not only do they see what is happening (anyone can do that), but they *know what it means*. As the book of Daniel says about the "time of the end," "None of the wicked shall understand; but the wise shall understand" (Daniel 12:9–10). *Left Behind* is a way of assuring you, if you are an evangelical Christian or thinking about becoming one, that you haven't actually been left behind.

End time prophecy keeps the basic, traditional picture of Bible history while showing modern Christians their own relationship to interesting stories that they might not have noticed before. You can see this in an end time picture dating back to 1889 (figure 7.3). On the upper left is the glory of God in his city, thronged by attending angels (Revelation 5:11); below is the history of the world from the Garden of Eden (Genesis 2–3) to the worship of the golden calf (Exodus 32) to

FIGURE 7.3. *The universal story. Courtesy of Andrews University, Center for Adventist Research.*

the succession of earthly kingdoms, represented by a solemn progress of prophetic beasts (bottom middle) from the book of Daniel (chapters 7–8). On the right is the modern world, the era of railroads and riverboats and modern people smoking and dancing and drinking in bars and worshiping the end time beasts of the New Testament apocalypse (Revelation 12–13). Who would not be interested to discover that, in the pleasant environs of Albany or Indianapolis, this is the drama that is actually going on? Who would not want to join the pilgrims in the center of the picture, losing their sins at the foot of the Cross—the center of history, though unnoticed by most of the world? At last, as William Miller wrote, these "children of the kingdom," once "perplexed," will be welcomed on high (upper center of the picture), there to be "comforted, glorified, justified, exalted, and not a dog to move his tongue."[17]

Self-dramatization has often been Americans' access to religious experience. As previously noted, even Jefferson found a place for Americans in the Bible's providential history. People participating in end time traditions have always found a prominent place for themselves in the prophecies they interpret. They have never discovered that the end is coming 435 years from now; they have consistently discovered that it is coming in their own time. And they have considered it their duty to specify their own significance. Judge Rutherford proved from the Bible that the spotlight of history shone on everything his followers did. He established, for instance, that the resolutions passed at Watch Tower conventions in the 1920s were the seven vials and seven trumpets of the book of Revelation.[18] A more advanced form of self-dramatization appears in the first *Left Behind* book, which seeks to inspire *faith* in Bible prophecy by showing, in elaborate detail, that prophecy is corroborated by *fictional* events, which are nevertheless imagined as if they were *really* happening—to you, right now.

But what if you're wrong? What happens if you aren't one of "the wise" who "understand"? What happens when your expectations, however rational they may have seemed, are cruelly disappointed?

Analysts of religion, as well as religious people, usually expect a single, sufficient answer to such questions. The most influential response is still *When Prophecy Fails* (1956), an engaging social-psychological study of a group of suburban Chicagoites who expected beings from outer space to rescue them from an impending apocalypse.[19] When the flying saucers didn't come, the group dissolved. But it didn't dissolve right away. At first, threats to the faith inspired an increased zeal to advocate it. The immediate presence of fellow believers helped some members of the group to keep believing for several months. Even after that, a few people continued treading the astral trail, joining or forming other spiritual groups. The authors of *When Prophecy Fails* emphasize disappointed believers' attempts to fight off "cognitive dissonance" by denying or reinterpreting evidence that is contrary to their beliefs. They respect reason; they just don't use it very well.

This makes sense. But was the flying-saucer group a good test case? Probably not. It was neither a large religious movement nor one guided by any scriptural authority. Large groups offer more diverse studies in motives, styles of reasoning, and definitions of what works. The presence of authoritative scripture means that there will be many ways in which scripture can be interpreted. It would be a very dull reasoner who could not discover, somewhere in the Bible, a means of recovery from prophetic failure. Denial may take place, and reinterpretation of evidence almost always takes place, but additional resources—however unpredictable—can almost always be found. The great tool and appeal of millennialism is not tradition, the unifier, but reason, which is always productive of difference, especially when it is at work in the ample field of scripture, where plausible responses to prophetic failure multiply beyond the scope of any single theory. The diverse histories of the big apocalyptic movements make this clear.

Adventism appeared to have died, but it revived, with new explanations and new doctrinal associations, such as soul sleep and the seventh-day Sabbath. At least once a generation, Jehovah's Witnesses suffered massive prophetic failure, but they always found ways of interpreting scripture that could preserve their institutional life. The leadership's decisions about which methods to use were generally made in the harried, ad hoc manner typical of authoritarian organizations,[20] but some of them worked, in a way: people dissatisfied on one account were eventually replaced by people satisfied on another. The teachings and methods of one era were radically different from those of the last, but even this could be useful, because it enabled the Witnesses to affirm a tradition of revolution. They cite a Bible verse, a favorite among adventists of all kinds, about the light "that shineth more and more unto the perfect day."[21]

Groups of this kind often interpret a failure of prophecy in the way in which scientists interpret a failed experiment, as a learning experience. The president of the Watch Tower Society once testified in court about the organization's radical revision of a large set of interpretations. "Well," he was asked, "it was erroneous, was it not?" He answered: "Well, not all of it was erroneous. . . . As things become clearer it is much easier to understand the Scriptures. It is difficult to understand Scripture until things have transpired to fulfill those Scriptures."[22]

Persistence is the watchword. Endure to the end (Matthew 24:13), and probably it will come. Only one large millennial movement, the Worldwide Church of God, seems ever to have repudiated its ideas completely. From its beginning as the Radio Church of God in the mid-1930s, this group was a flamboyant expression of American entrepreneurship.[23] Its creator, Herbert W. Armstrong (1892–1986), was raised among Quakers but found no vital connection with God. He then "studied," as all millenarians do. He quarried many kinds of nineteenth-century isms, including adventism, seventh-day sabbatarianism, antitrinitarianism, British Israelitism (the idea that Britons are descended from the "lost tribes" of Israel), and the idea that God is actually a family of Gods. He gave these ideas his own, curious forms, and he built them into a modern church. His was basically an adventist successor group, with such obvious analogues to the Jehovah's Witnesses that he was at pains to deny the relationship. From the beginning he preached that the Second Coming was near. He joined the Witnesses in prophesying apocalyptic events for 1975 (and other times).[24]

Eventually Armstrong discovered a new way of advertising his group. He began traveling the world, conferring with officials of foreign governments, giving them expensive gifts, and generally making his 100,000-member denomination, its one college, and his syndicated television show look like features of a world-historical movement. But when he died, leadership passed to younger people, who began examining the Bible on their own. They concluded that he had been wrong about virtually everything; they admitted it; and they changed their teachings accordingly, until the church became a normal evangelical denomination. Despite heavy opposition, a hemorrhage of money (caused partly by principled abandonment of the church's policy on tithing), and the downsizing of headquarters from 1,000 to 40 employees,[25] they completed their work.

This revolution from the top—unpredictable and almost as curious as Armstrong's teachings—was patently sincere, although it lost the church half its members. There were several dramatic schisms of old believers, and even people who stayed with the church began to wonder why it should continue. The answer was, basically, that having returned to the traditional Christianity it had originally rejected, it had shown itself especially qualified to help people move forward.[26] Indeed, this church exemplifies the combination of forward and backward motion that has been pervasive in American Christianity.

The experience of the Worldwide Church of God was peculiar and perhaps unique, but when one looks closely at millenarian movements, that is what one finds: an array of vitally peculiar experiences, remarkably resistant to general theories. The most recent, and one of the most colorful, large-scale end time experiments was the May 21, 2011, prophecy. Eagerly if fecklessly covered by the national media, when they finally discovered it, the prophecy became the rare religious event that figured in the jokes of late-night TV hosts. The forecast emanated from a most unlikely source: Family

Radio, a network of several dozen Christian radio stations, and its president, Harold Egbert Camping (1921–).[27]

Family Radio was founded in 1958, when FM stations were relatively cheap to buy. It has always been run on a shoestring. But while other Christian organizations were feverishly modernizing, hoping to attract a general audience, Family Radio discovered a substantial niche market among people who wanted a strictly conservative, apolitical message, along with conservative religious music. Family Radio also benefited from the strange appeal of Harold Camping, who conducted an on-air Bible-answer program, *The Open Forum*, on Monday through Friday evenings.

Camping was not the ordinary motivational speaker. Slow, droning, excruciatingly digressive, arrogantly dismissive of even the slightest difference of opinion, Camping preached a dry, dogmatic Calvinism and a hyperrationalist method of Bible interpretation based on the idea that scripture, having been written by divine inspiration, must be interpreted solely by scripture, without regard to such things as the historical context or literary purpose of individual scriptures. Every word of the Bible was regarded as "spoken by God" in exactly the same way and as therefore immediately relevant to every other word—provided the reader was insistent enough about deducing its significance. Camping's method produced amazing results. Everything in the Bible now appeared to have a hidden meaning. Camping (a retired engineer, always friendly with numbers) discovered countless numerical patterns indicating that Christ would return in September 1994. He announced this in a book, which was ignored by the media but achieved a wide circulation. For a long time after the 1994 disappointment, Camping said nothing about his failure; then he pointed out that he had claimed his prophecy was only 99.9 percent likely to come true.

Then the Internet intervened, too late to permit easy access to his 1994 predictions but in time to ensure that his next deductions from scripture would be known worldwide. After 2000, they developed rapidly. Though no one could be more scornful of Jehovah's Witnesses than Harold Camping, his rationalism now led him to agree with certain findings of their own rationalism. He discovered that hell does not exist, that souls can die, and that the churches are ruled by Satan. And he set new apocalyptic dates: May 21 (the Rapture) and October 21, 2011 (the destruction of the physical universe). The interval was indicated by the fact that there are 153 days between May 21 and October 21, just as there are 153 fish mentioned in John 21:11. (Everything in the Bible must relate to everything else.) These dates were absolutely certain.

Camping's message struck a nerve with tens of thousands of people of all ages, ethnic groups, and social strata. Bands of his disciples descended on the streets of major cities, distributing end time pamphlets. Advertising caravans traversed the country. Believers bankrupted themselves to sponsor "Judgment Day—May 21, 2011" billboards, which appeared from Indiana to India. On the evening of May 19, Camping said good-bye to his radio audience, explaining that he wanted to spend the little time remaining at home with his family.

When May 21 failed to produce the Rapture, the great earthquake, and the worldwide devastation he had predicted, Camping explained that Judgment Day had begun, but invisibly. He also announced that, by the mercy of God, there would be no violent transition to the total destruction of October 21, which was, however, still certain to occur.

Many, perhaps most, of his followers stuck with him. In Bible lectures broadcast after May 21, Chris McCann, a Camping epigone, said of the events prophesied for that day: "In some small degree it didn't happen"; the fact that it didn't happen visibly was only "a minor point." This was all completely sincere. As McCann noted in comments broadcast on October 7, the Campingites were risking a lot on their prediction of a total end in only a few days. "We have our backs to the sea," he said. "This is it." If their prophecies were just "a ploy," "why would we make it five months from [May 21], not seven years or something, if we wanted to fool someone?" They made it October 21 because their reasoning led them there.

After October 21, however, there was a mass exodus of former believers. Camping himself admitted that he had been wrong about the timing (although he couldn't pinpoint his error—the reasoning still seemed perfect) and that the churches had been right in quoting Jesus's words about no one knowing the day or the hour of his return.[28] Nevertheless, Camping maintained, "the Church Age" was over. God had shown his unique approval of Family Radio by using its (failed) predictions to acquaint billions of people with the existence of the Bible.

Here were the outer limits of rationalism. Hardcore believers retreated to an earlier position; they continued to forecast the end, using Camping's mathematics to propose a series of new dates (e.g., Pentecost 2012). For being more Catholic than the pope, these believers were expelled from participation in Family Radio, which publicly regretted that it could not keep their websites from linking to its own. At this writing, the schismatics are struggling for adherents, and Family Radio has apparently held or reclaimed a sizable part of its audience, but it is struggling for funds. It has started selling stations. In the meantime, it retains its management, headed by Harold Camping, who continues to offer Bible interpretations on the air.

Whether his movement will continue, or in what form it may continue, cannot be guessed from social theory or even what we know of history. Evidently, it is easier to predict the end of the world than to predict the fate of an apocalyptic movement. One thing that history does appear to suggest is that witnessing the disconfirmation of other people's prophecies (or one's own) doesn't extinguish the desire to make and enjoy them, that as long as Americans are free to reason about the deep things of faith, they will continue to pursue the science of apocalypse and use it as their connection with God.

HIERARCHIES AND
REVOLUTIONS

At Christmas season 2011, the Roman Catholic Church mounted an expensive advertising campaign. Its goal was to reach people who had been reared in the church and reclaim them as communicants. Its leading feature was a beautifully constructed television spot emphasizing the continuity of the church, from its founding by Jesus and its "compiling" of the scriptures to the greeting of a modern American family (husband, wife, young children) by a friendly priest at a church door. The ad exploited a feeling held by both proponents and opponents of Christianity, the sense that the church you might visit today is basically the same church that existed in your youth, or a hundred years ago, or perhaps 2,000 years ago. To this church, the ad suggested, you should now "come home." A similar campaign followed a year later. Now a locker room was evoked—a sports allusion apparently having nothing to do with millennia past. But the message was the same: "We're saving your seat on the starting bench this Sunday. Welcome home."

No matter how the message is framed, however, the truth is that you can't "come home" again. The American Catholic Church of 2011 isn't remotely the same as the church of ancient Rome, or of the Council of Nicaea. It isn't remotely the same as the monarchical church of the Middle Ages, or the militantly antiliberal church of the 1870s, or even the American church of the 1950s. The Catholic Church in America is the product of many revolutions, and there is no reason to believe that revolutions have ceased.

In the early nineteenth century the (barely) Roman church was the heritage denomination of some old American families, such as the Carrolls of Maryland. It was a church that had been strongly influenced by Enlightenment ideas about the rational and practical aspects of religion. In that church, there was no emphasis on veneration of the saints or obligations to the pope. America's first Catholic bishop, John Carroll, whose cousin signed the Declaration of Independence and whose brother signed the Constitution, scoffed at the idea of the pope as a "universal administrator." Catholic clergy were so rare on these shores that historians refer to the time as the era of the priestless church.[1] Catholic committees often erected chapels, as they did in the early days of Jackson, for the use of any priest who came by—and they seem to have felt that this would do well enough for the time being.

The priestless (and liberal) church ended in the mid-nineteenth century with the strengthening of Catholics' hierarchical ties to Rome. The authoritarian papacy was recovering from its near-death experience with Napoleonic persecution, and there was a vast immigration to America from Ireland, hardly a hotbed of liberalism. For many years, the American priesthood was stocked from Irish seminaries. When priests "went home," it was frequently to Ireland. When other immigrant groups arrived, they relied on the church perhaps more than the church relied on them.[2] Special provision was made for people whose native language was not English and who might have special difficulty adapting to general American culture. In the mining town of Calumet, Michigan,

FIGURE 8.1. *First communion at St. Bernard's Roman Catholic Church, a German parish in Akron, Ohio, 1932. Plumes in the background identify members of the Knights of Columbus, the Catholic fraternal organization. Author's collection.*

there were six big Catholic churches: Irish, Slovenian, French Canadian, Polish, Croatian, and Italian. The "immigrant church," as it has been called, made much of its distinctiveness: it established its own schools, hospitals, and fraternal organizations and made large difficulties about intermarriage with Protestants. Busy parishes provided the rituals of life—baptism, confirmation, marriage, extreme unction—to masses of people whose Catholicism went without saying.

This was the foreign church that gradually became Americanized. In most communities, it was difficult for Catholics to live with their Protestant neighbors without developing strong habits of mutual recognition and respect. At the same time, there were many attacks by anti-"papist" forces. In the 1830s, "Maria Monk" whipped up a froth of anti-Catholic feeling with lurid myths about the secret life of Catholic convents. The 1920s witnessed the anti-Catholicism of the second Ku Klux Klan and an upswelling of bigotry against Al Smith, the Democratic nominee for president in 1928. Smith represented the conservative wing of the Democratic Party, but he lost many evangelical votes because of his Catholicism and his opposition to the evangelicals' not very conservative cause, prohibition. Despite all this, by the mid-twentieth century Catholicism had become as American as carpets in the nave. No one was more mainstream American than the most prestigious Catholic in the nation, Francis Cardinal Spellman of New York—the man who dealt with John O'Hara, the 1950s' symbol of the "indecent" novelist, by engaging him in an enthusiastic discussion of coin collecting.[3]

Yet while parents of baby-boom children were building new parishes in the suburbs, formal worship was still conducted as it had been in sixteenth-century Europe, with the Mass said in Latin while congregants watched, or made private prayers in their own tongues.[4] Few people "came home" to the sixteenth century; they simply went to their local church and listened (or didn't listen) to whatever the priest said there. Then, in 1962, Pope John XXIII convened the Second Vatican Council (Vatican II), which took action to modernize the church.

When a seriously hierarchical church takes action, radical things can happen almost overnight. This was a real revolution from above. Suddenly, altars were dragged from their traditional location at the front of the church and lodged, uneasily, someplace in the middle, where priests faced the congregation instead of God. Just as suddenly, the Mass was being said in English, not as an option, but as a requirement. Latin was firmly "discouraged." In some churches, priestly enthusiasts ordered votive candles to be extinguished, statuary to be junked, and marble pillars to be covered with black cardboard, so that the congregation would not be distracted by old-fashioned beauty and "superstition."

But as the international hierarchy enforced its vision of change, American Catholics were developing their own, often confused new viewpoints. Many regretted that the revolution hadn't gone far enough: priests were still commanded to be celibate; "unnatural" means of birth control were still forbidden; women were still kept from being priests. Many others, however, regretted that the revolution had happened at all. Some instituted covert masses, advertised by small signs in shop windows, at which anonymous priests dared to employ Latin, flouting their bishops. Others suffered in silence or stayed at home. Around everyone swirled a flood of radical teaching, most of it imported from the surrounding Protestant culture, but influential anyway: Catholic Pentecostalism (*what?!*); "folk" masses ("nuns with guitars"); and the devotion of several religious orders to anti-war, anti-imperialist, and feminist crusades—not to mention crusades against the Vatican.

Despite these developments, anti-Catholicism now appeared as strongly on the political left as it used to do on the political right. Popular songs, plays, and reviews satirized the church in ribald terms. Even Hollywood got into the act. Formerly the purveyor of all-American encomia to the goodness of priests, impersonated by Spencer Tracy and Bing Crosby, it now made movies such as *Mass Appeal* (1984), in which Jack Lemmon plays an alcoholic, time-serving priest whose soul is saved by a determinedly obnoxious young seminarian, inspired by revolutionary fervor—the Christ-figure in this movie.

Everything conspired to erode Americans' sense of Catholicism as a special religious and moral community. One of the heaviest blows to Catholic identity fell even before Vatican II: John Kennedy's election to the presidency. The fact that Kennedy could carry such evangelical states as West Virginia, North Carolina, and Missouri, which Al Smith had failed to win, suggested that his religion was just one of many on the American menu, no longer a unique source of values.

An event less welcomed by Roman Catholics was the Supreme Court's decision to legalize abortion. *Roe v. Wade* (1973) precipitated a protest movement that separated moral activists from ordinary church people and joined Catholic activists with the formerly antipodean evangelicals. Out of such national collaborations emerged the contemporary religious Right. As America's Catholic bishops moved to the left on virtually every public issue not directly related to sex or gender, many in the Catholic laity started feeling closer to their conservative evangelical friends than they did to their own church hierarchy. Catholics in general were paying less and less attention both to their church's voting advice and to its advice on sex. They now practiced birth control to the same extent as their Protestant neighbors, who, whether conservative or liberal, made no issue about it.[5]

Today American Catholics show a broad "convergence" with Protestants in every area from church attendance to divorce, intermarriage, and voting. Their proportion of American religious affiliation would have declined like that of the mainline Protestant churches had it not been for recent large-scale immigration from Mexico and Central America. This immigration is the church leadership's hope for the future—yet perhaps only a bare majority of Hispanic Americans consider themselves Catholic. There is no indication that today's immigrants will turn out to be any more observant than yesterday's. The church devotes an enormous amount of energy to fostering their culture and supporting their immediate political interests; nonetheless, the views of Latino Catholics tend to be more conservative, socially and theologically, than those of non-Latino Catholics and many Catholic clerics. This helps to explain why large numbers of Latinos have joined evangelical Protestant churches, often forming them where they did not exist before.[6]

Surveys indicate that for many years a majority of American Catholics have differed from the hierarchy on the question of married priests and women priests.[7] Catholics of every intellectual tendency have been alarmed and disgusted by what they have learned about sexual misconduct among priests and about the hierarchy's role in covering it up. The revelations themselves showed that a moral revolution had taken place: the church was no longer protected by the automatic deference once accorded it. The loss of morale—and the loss of money from the litigation that has bankrupted several dioceses—has been immense.

But another deeply damaging revolution had occurred years before in the responses of core believers to the church's top-down attempt to reform itself. Immediately after Vatican II, religious vocations dropped precipitously. In just three years, the number of women entering religious communities fell by almost two-thirds. The number of men enrolled in seminaries also headed sharply downward. In 1965 the ratio of seminarians to Catholics in general was fifteen times higher than it was at the start of the twenty-first century.[8] The situation remains very difficult. It has resulted in the closing of many parishes, the large-scale deployment of foreign priests, who are often not well understood by their congregations, and the effective secularization of many institutions formerly run by sisters.

The big drop in vocations is often explained as a result of the sexual revolution in the broader society. In fact, the religious revolution was already strong when the secular one had barely begun. One way of explaining it has to do with a decline in spiritual rewards. To become a priest or nun in the days before Vatican II meant sacrificing normal life for an institution that was distinctive and morally challenging. To make the same sacrifice in exchange for the normal, tedious duties of a church that was beginning to look like any other church—that was something different. If being a priest meant having to debate "situation ethics" instead of imposing penance, or having to "work with" fanatically "engaged" or superficially "committed" laypeople instead of running one's own school or parish, is it any wonder that vocations declined?[9]

The stories of J. F. Powers—the late twentieth century's most sensitive literary observer of the American Catholic Church—show what can happen when priests try to adjust to a Catholic world in which they, like many of their parishioners, no longer feel at home. One of Powers's literary creations is an apparently successful priest in a prosperous suburban parish. Father Joe had opposed the church's new ways of reaching out—"the various attempts to improve the church's image"—and, he believes, "he had been right." Though he hasn't suffered directly from the reforms, he sympathizes with those who resisted them—"a persecuted minority group if ever there was one." He sees the melancholy results of reform all around him: "Vocations, conversions, communions, confessions, contributions, general attendance, all down. And why not?" Catholicism has lost its self-definition: "We used to stand out in the crowd. We had quality control. We were the higher-priced spread. No more. . . . Tell the man in the next parish [a priest appropriately named Ed Smiley] that you fornicated a hundred and thirty-six times since your last confession, which was one month ago, and he says, 'Did you think ill of your fellow man?'" Yet when Father Joe hears that a former seminarian has lost his faith, he reflects that he himself isn't "exactly rolling in the stuff." He is always unhappy and frequently drunk.[10]

Powers's church leaders have lost their faith, usually without knowing it. Bishop Dullinger, the protagonist of two of Powers's best stories, is an example. A natural conservative, he is led to modernize his diocese without quite realizing what he is doing. Soon he discovers that there is no longer a place for him in the religious structure of which he was once the "keystone." He goes into a bewildered retirement. Only when he agrees to take over a local church (filling in for an absconding priest) does he find a new connection with God— the joy of Christian service. Unconsciously, undramatically, he is reconverted to Christianity. It's a mysterious event, and it isn't as easy as it sounds. Only providence could make it happen; the times, and the church, are all against it.[11]

Powers was hardly a typical conservative. He had gone to prison for refusing to participate in World War II, and he upheld the radical Catholic Worker movement as an alternative model of the religious life.[12] He shows Bishop Dullinger as inspiring his fellow Catholics by working beside, not above, them. But the defining moment of the bishop's return to Christ is his destruction of the New Age, post–Vatican II posters he finds in his temporary church: "Peace, Joy, Love, and so on." The posters are "amateurish," and he "dispose[s]" of them. Amid these callow, contemporary attempts at religious devotion, an old-fashioned professional like Bishop Dullinger may still have something distinctive to do.[13]

Religious professionalism remains important for American Catholics, despite their unhappiness about the hierarchy's defiance of their views on many things. Their affection both for the church and for its allegedly reactionary pontiffs remains. They felt genuine grief at the death of John Paul II, who is said to have pounded on the table to emphasize his refusal to hear anything more about women priests.[14] They have developed, among their other means of keeping in touch with God, an ability to separate issues from leaders and leaders from the discouraging qualities of their leadership. They have grown accustomed to agreeing to disagree, even about matters on which the church informs them they have no business disagreeing. There is no shortage of schismatic Catholic groups, both radical and hypertraditionalist. None of them has achieved any significant support. American Catholics, men and women, gay and straight, traditionalist and futurist, have generally stuck with the church. Disregard the slick ads about "coming home": the church still has the tools to locate broad veins of religious experience.

Commenting on this phenomenon, a reflective historian of American Catholicism has suggested that although the church has been "weakened," it has achieved both "a new volatility" and "a new vitality." Unexpectedly, Catholics have "found ways to challenge the positions of the church while still thinking of themselves as Catholics." Distinguishing the laity from the hierarchy, acknowledging both the autonomy of the former and the power of the latter, hasn't destroyed the church—although it has made its future even less predictable, if that be possible, than it was before.[15]

The difficulty with regarding the Roman Catholic Church as an image of America's general religious waywardness is the fact that it is not just American; it is also Roman. Who knows—who can divine—what American Catholicism might look like if its hierarchy didn't culminate in the Vatican, which in the 1960s (as at other times) acted as a disruptive force? But suppose there were a strongly hierarchical and traditional American church that had no dominant connection to anything except the faith of American adherents, a church that was never forced to contend with such troublesome dogmas as papal infallibility and clerical celibacy. Such a church would be worth studying to see whether tradition and hierarchy might be able to rescue American Christianity from its extreme volatility. This church would be particularly worth examining if it possessed some special, representative role in American life.

There is such a traditional, hierarchical institution. It is the Episcopal Church—a church that has always been available to provide images of Christianity in the public space, that has always been prepared, indeed, to act as the default church of America.

Thirteen or perhaps fourteen presidents of the United States have been associated with the Episcopal Church, more than with any other. Some were raised in it. Some accepted it as their own default version of Christianity. Some, such as Franklin Roosevelt, imported its style, if not always its substance, into their public lives. One, Franklin Pierce, became a humble convert after everything else had collapsed around him.[16] The "church of the presidents" is St. John's Episcopal Church in Washington; since 1816, when it was built, every president has worshiped there. Like Air Force One, a pew at St. John's is kept in constant readiness for the chief executive. Even off-brand presidents have resorted to the Episcopal Church. During the Civil War, Jefferson Davis, who considered himself a Christian of some kind but didn't even know whether he had been baptized, did what many other Americans have done: he suddenly decided that he had to join a church, right away. A special baptismal ceremony was arranged by an Episcopal priest for a Tuesday; Sunday was too distant.[17]

The Episcopal cathedral in Washington is called, by the Episcopal Church and everyone else, the National Cathedral. Its relics include the sepulchers of Woodrow Wilson (a Presbyterian), Helen Keller (a Swedenborgian), and Admiral Dewey (an actual Episcopalian). The funerals of Presidents Eisenhower, Ford, and Reagan were conducted in the cathedral, though only Ford was a (nominal) adherent of the church. What may be called the American Cathedral of 9/11 is St. Paul's (Episcopal) Chapel in lower Manhattan. The wounded and dying were taken to its grounds after the terrorist attack, and it was a center for recovery workers in the months that followed. Today, amid the mementoes of 9/11 that fill the building, one pew remains, that of George Washington, who had worshiped at St. Paul's two centuries before.

By the mid-twentieth century, the Episcopal Church had acquired a virtual monopoly of non-Catholic religious affairs in American movies. When Cary Grant, playing an angel (*The Bishop's Wife* [1947]), comes to earth in response to a clergyman's prayer, the prayer is made by a bishop of the Episcopal Church. When Henry Fonda, playing a heroic candidate for president (*The Best Man* [1964]), is asked whether he believes in God, he replies, "I was confirmed in the Episcopal Church." (He then confesses that he has come to believe only in "man," but by 1964 a humanistic Christianity was the best kind for Hollywood.) When Warner Brothers wanted to dramatize a funny, nostalgic story of the American family (*Life with Father* [1947]), it made the plot turn on the details of Episcopal practice, and it cast Edmund Gwenn (Kris Kringle in *Miracle on 34th Street*) as the gentle Episcopal priest. When the *Reader's Digest* wanted a big ending for a film about racial equality, it staged an Episcopal service in a quaint church in New England (*Lost Boundaries* [1949]). When MGM wanted to celebrate Americans' diversity and unity (*It's a Big Country* [1951]), its image of American religion was an Episcopal parish: "St. Thomas," in Washington, D.C., where even the president enjoys the service. And whenever a Hollywood film required a wedding and there was no reason for providing something specifically regional or ethnic, the rite was likely to be Episcopal.[18]

Seldom obtrusive but always at hand, the Episcopal Church offers itself to preside, as if by divine appointment, over any important American event, fictional or real, corporate or personal. Its offers have generally been accepted, despite—or possibly because of—the unlikelihood, the strangeness, the all-inclusive eccentricity of its adventures, beginning with the days when it was the least American of America's major churches.

In 1776 what is now the American Episcopal Church was the Church of England, American branch. In a number of the colonies, it was the church established by law and supported by taxes. Its head was the king of England. Its services were read out of the Book of Common Prayer, which was authorized by Parliament. Its ministers were ordained not by local people, as in Puritan New England, but by bishops who were appointed by the British government and who derived their religious authority from "apostolic succession," their consecration by bishops who were consecrated by other bishops, back to the first century. Buttressed in all these ways, the church was still the weakest in America.

Its rites may have been mandated by British law, but local people still had to support them financially, something they were very reluctant to do. The ordination requirement alone might have been enough to destroy the institution. Ordination required a bishop, but there were no English bishops in America. The government floated proposals to send one, but opposition was violent, even among American communicants of the church. No one wanted another high-priced agent of the crown. So applicants for ordination had to embark on a long trip to Europe, a trip that cost a fortune and that 20 percent of those who undertook it did not survive.[19] These hardships, besides the low pay and the likelihood of constant strife with one's parishioners to get even that, greatly discouraged American aspirants for the ministry. Parishes were equipped with clergy sent out by the bishop of London, men who were popularly suspected of being willing to emigrate because they were in trouble with drink or debts or because they enjoyed hunting and loose living.

Respect for the church was low in 1776, and it went lower. Wherever the church had been established, it eventually became disestablished. Most of its ministers were unsympathetic with the Revolution; others were sympathetic but respected their oath to the king. No matter: many were turned out of their jobs, exiled, or imprisoned. Leading revolutionaries, from Washington on down, were adherents of the church; nevertheless, it had to find some way to survive as an American institution.

In 1783 Samuel Seabury, a Church of England minister from Connecticut who had publicly opposed the Revolution and had been imprisoned in response, went to England seeking consecration as America's first bishop. The English bishops turned him down; the prayer book required acknowledgment of the king, which Seabury could no longer make. But the bishops of the Scottish Episcopal Church, reactionaries who didn't recognize the current king of England as their superior, agreed to consecrate Seabury as the first bishop of a revolutionary nation. Soon there were more bishops. In 1789 America's "churchmen" created their own constitution for their own "Episcopal" church, together with their own (kingless) Book of Common Prayer.

During its first generation, the new church seemed likely to fail. It consisted of a few strong personalities surrounded by demoralized believers and tepid attenders. Between 1805 and 1812, the diocesan convention in Virginia, formerly the church's hotbed (if there was one), didn't even meet. When it did, only a handful of clergy and laymen attended. One deacon rode away from one of these events saying to himself, "Lost, lost, lost."[20] Yet when forced to compete, the church found an audience.

An attractive feature of the church was its status as a heritage denomination. Some people remembered it as their spiritual home because their parents had done so, despite the fact that the church had changed. Being in opposition also helped. People in New England now had a respectable, historically associated, yet fully American church that they could attend if they fell out with their own heritage church, the Congregational. In America, success requires a separate and often an adverse identity. But the most important factor may have been one unusual person, Jackson Kemper.

Kemper (1789–1870) was "a high-bred gentleman" from the East Coast who was concerned about his denomination's near-total absence from the settlements west of the Alleghenies.[21] In 1835 he procured appointment as the first missionary bishop of the Episcopal Church. He spent the remainder

FIGURE 8.2. *Bishop Jackson Kemper, founder of churches: from a marsh called Purgatory to an apotheosis in stained glass (All Saints' Church, San Diego). Photo by John Gray III; used by permission.*

of his life planting Episcopal institutions on the other side of the mountain wall. An individualist and an enthusiast, Kemper convinced himself that the ancient forms of a hierarchical church were a perfect fit for frontier America. "How remarkably peculiar," he wrote, "how vastly important is the position of our Church! Possessing as we fully believe all those characteristics which distinguished the primitive fold:—A scriptural Liturgy—evangelical doctrines—and the apostolic succession—having the form of godliness *and* the power thereof—free from the false and worldly scruples and the time-serving policy of civil governments—independent— respected, and influential—in the midst of an intelligent, enterprising and commercial people."[22]

Kemper was hitting all the bases. He flawlessly identified what Americans are always seeking: a church that is progressive and enterprising, yet also scriptural and "primitive." As he slogged through the swamps and forests of what is now America's heartland, passing on one occasion "through a marsh called *Purgatory*, and crossing a river named *Embarrass*" (the Embarras River and a nearby swamp), Kemper was doing more than founding local parishes and dioceses; he was constructing a new church, generous and many-sided in ideas—broad enough to include a host of individualists like himself but therefore diverse enough to change incessantly.[23]

When today's Episcopalians "come home" to their local parish, the church that greets them will usually be one with an *altar* served by *priests* according to a demanding *ritual*, culminating in the *Holy Eucharist*. The priest may be male or female; the sermon may be an admonition for or against gay marriage, abortion rights, or the Democratic Party; but the ritual will assure the participants that this is an *Episcopal* parish and that when the service ends, they will *know*, as Episcopalians often say, *that they have been to church.*

Yet this distinctive experience was by no means distinctive of the Episcopal Church in the early nineteenth century.[24] Back then, an Episcopal clergyman (male, of course) was not a "priest"; he was merely Mr. Such-and-Such. At the front of his church stood a simple communion table that was normally used only once a month. The set texts of the prayer book were used, much to the disgust of Spirit-led Protestants, but Episcopalians resembled other Americans in their basic expectations of public worship. There would be songs, preaching, scripture reading, and windows you could look out through: no stained glass, no air of mystery. No one made the sign of the cross; no one used incense; and as late as the mid-twentieth century, a minister who tried to hang a crucifix behind the altar might very well be fired. During most of the nineteenth century, bishops were supported, if at all, by their own parishes. Some made their livings with a few acres and a cow.[25] No Episcopal cathedrals were built until the 1860s. The first was erected by extreme traditionalists, pioneers who lived on the western frontier: Minnesota.

Even in the penury of frontier life, a reaction (or revolution) had begun. Called in England the Anglo-Catholic movement and in America "ritualism," it demanded what most revolutionary movements within Christianity demand: a return to former faith and practice. In this case, the return was to practices that preceded the existence of an independent English church. Now there would be priests and altars and everything that went with them. The movement spread from a few intellectuals and a handful of ministers into the seminaries and then, top-down, to the congregations.

The church's national convention was urged by evangelicals and conservatives to repress this movement. In 1871 a committee of bishops proposed a canon that "prohibited by name all of the ritualistic practices that they could think of." The committee listed "incense, crucifixes, processional crosses, lights on or about the Holy Table, 'except when necessary,' elevation [of the bread and wine, by the priest during the Eucharist], the mixing of water with the wine, 'as part

of the service, or in the presence of the congregation,' bow-
ings or genuflections, except at the Holy Name, and many
other usages. They also proposed to forbid the introduction
of a choral service or vested choir by any minister without
the explicit consent of his vestry and the tacit consent of his
bishop." The committee failed; the church was already too
various to submit to a single rule. It had to "endure," as one
historian put it, "the tension which characterizes a comprehensive Church."[26] Now the most authoritarian and traditional church among Protestants was also one of the most
diverse and welcoming.

The ironies are delicious. The bishops were defending
the church of their past against the *advanced* thought of the
rising generation, which was struggling to return to a more
remote past, a past it had never experienced. Evangelical
defenders of the church's then-distinctive features were
arrayed against people who wanted to make the church
much more distinctive. The final irony is that the revolutionaries won, but in a way in which they didn't want to
win. They achieved a traditionalist church with a modernist
volatility, offering rich and tempting precedents for continued change. The national church made rules against ritualism but held back on actually enforcing them, so ritualism
gradually spread, even to congregations that had little or no
sympathy with the doctrines that justified it. As the twentieth century would show, almost anything could fit inside the
Episcopal box.

Unlike other mainstream Christian denominations, the
Episcopalians survived the Civil War without a permanent
rupture. Afterward, they survived successive waves of controversy—over Darwin, over socialism, over religious liberalism and modernism. There was a "high church" party and
a (gradually shrinking) "low church" party, the two divided
over how much ritual to use, but no one could predict the
ideology or social status of a given congregation by noticing

how often there were "yells, bells, and smells"—chanting, chimes, and incense. From the 1890s through the 1960s, most parishes probably considered themselves "broad church," a shifting target for definition, typified (or stereotyped) by a socially conscious, mildly left-wing rector, faithful to the church's central dogmas and the now-ordinary use of ritual but unsympathetic to "literalist" interpretations of the Bible.

In 1966 the church numbered 3.4 million reported members (the high-water mark, effected by the baby boom),[27] but its sole nationally known representative was Bishop James Pike, of San Francisco. Pike wrote, gave interviews, went on television, advertised political causes, and raised money to complete his cathedral, whose construction had been halted by the Great Depression. He also proclaimed that he no longer believed in his church's central doctrines, although he became a credulous believer in various New Age ideas and especially in spiritualism, conversing frequently with the other world.[28] Pike was threatened with a trial for heresy, but the matter was always side-channeled, and he eventually left the church. Soon afterward, he died in the Judean desert, having lost his way on an attempted visit to a "numinous" site. This sad, wayward figure had given, then denied, to his church a last, dramatic occasion to enforce its traditional beliefs.

In the 1970s, however, Episcopalians' live-and-let-live attitude was shattered by the revelation that the denomination's central leadership was no longer a purveyor of consensus but an inciter of controversy. The office of the presiding bishop, which had once existed mainly to arrange national conventions, had developed a large staff to manage the denomination's big-church social programs, some of which involved subsidies for radical political organizations. It was a long way from the time of Bishop Kemper, who had believed so much in the separation of church and state that he had refused to vote.[29] The national office, along with some local bishops, was not only moving with the tide of the 1960s but trying to lead it to shore. Supporting the national office required a lot of money, but demands for larger revenues were coming at a time of shrinking membership. Friends of the church are fond of saying that its numbers haven't really declined since the 1930s, and in a way they are right. By one reckoning, the church had two million members in 1940 and almost the same number in 2010. But that means its percentage of the population had fallen by 58 percent during the intervening period.[30]

Responses to the national office's pleas for funds were now so unfavorable that 100 "designated listeners" were dispatched to tour the country and, well, listen to what people had to say. The presiding bishop took early retirement. But progressives still held the initiative and the levers of national power. The prayer book and the hymnal were revised, not in particularly ideological ways, but in ways that were unsettling to people who thought they knew the old-time Episcopal experience. Dioceses were pressed to endorse abortion rights; some did, and so did the national convention, weakly in 1967 and very strongly in 1994. An even more divisive debate concerned the ordination of women. This was an especially hard matter for a church whose distinctive appeal was its embodiment of ecclesiastical tradition but whose membership was mainly moderate or liberal, politically. When women's ordination was approved by the national convention in 1976, dissidents started forming their own fellowships, associations, and "continuing Episcopal" churches, some of which maintain a vigorous existence today.

In the original church, attempts were made to do what Episcopalians had done during the ritualist conflict, when both sides learned that if nobody actually fired a shot, some way could be found to keep the church together. Now, however, the sides kept pulling farther apart. Liberal dioceses spent large amounts of money suing dropout parishes and attempting to seize their property. Sometimes they won and sometimes they lost, but they embittered more people all the time. In 2003 the leading party pressed its advantage by approving the ordination of a "practicing homosexual" as bishop of New Hampshire. In 2006 it followed up by electing a woman, and a pronounced theological liberal, as presiding bishop. Social conservatives were offended for predictable reasons; theological conservatives—who in the Episcopal Church have always included large numbers of gay people in flight to devotional and liturgical traditions from other churches' emphasis on domestic morality—were outraged by the two bishops' untraditional takes on doctrine. Emotions were additionally inflamed by the attempted interventions of conservative African bishops, who offered to take American conservatives under their wing. In 2012 a leading Episcopal journal observed that "New Hampshire Episcopalians seem accustomed to activism from the top"; several paragraphs later it mentioned that attendance in the New Hampshire diocese had dropped by 20 percent from 2000 through 2010.[31]

Both sides were stymied by their devotion to dogma, the conservatives by their reluctance to abandon an apostolic church and the progressives by their reluctance to suggest that Christian charity applies to everyone except conservatives. But these were official positions. The real news about the conflict within America's default church was conveyed by the many websites mounted by the disputing parties, sites displaying an extraordinary willingness to attack and abuse.

People who believe in overarching stories may find a way to explain the history of the Episcopal Church, although they will have to forget about the possibility of finding social and economic motivations for its religious disputes: Episcopal conservatives and Episcopal progressives live in the same kind of towns, have the same kind of incomes, represent the same kind of ethnicities, and sue one another in the same courts. The predictive question persists. Given the record of volatility established by America's most traditional Protestant denomination, who can predict the future of this church, or any other? Can you?

SERMONS IN STONE

Around the end of World War II, a publicity agent for the Congregational Church produced a book entitled *The Church Beautiful*. It should have been called *The Church Attractive*, because that is its emphasis: how to attract people to church and keep them there. One of its first commandments is that a church should look "like a church and not something else." A character in T. S. Stribling's novel *Unfinished Cathedral* (1934) puts the point even more forcefully: "A church, even a modern church, ought to resemble a church more and everything else less."[1]

This is still the most commonly expressed sentiment about church architecture. People don't like churches that "don't look like churches." The idea seems childishly obvious. It can be compared with another seemingly obvious idea, the most famous principle in American architectural history, Louis Sullivan's dictum: "Form ever follows function." "This is the law," Sullivan added—and it became the creed of modern architecture.[2]

Well, what is the function of a church? If you discover that function, you should be able to discover what the church should look like. But the history of American church architecture shows that form doesn't simply follow function; it also discovers function, and invents it.

A congregation usually bestows a larger amount of time and effort on its building than on anything else. The building shows what the congregation decides, after much consideration, a place of worship ought to be, out of all the multitude of things it could be. This particular collection of steel and stone is the congregation's way of defining and advertising a particular connection with God. That is why American churches look like so many things: Byzantine cathedrals, crusader chapels, theaters, schools, lecture halls, theme-park attractions, modern-art museums, television stage sets, rock-music venues, and all the other things that may or may not look like churches to you or me.

In the curious history of American church architecture, few documents are more interesting than an essay written by the Episcopal bishop Henry C. Potter advertising the new church he was constructing, the Cathedral of St. John the Divine. Potter declares that at the present time (1898), there aren't five church buildings in America that "are worthy of being mentioned." When Americans think of a church, he says, they picture "a huge auditorium, with a platform and a more or less dramatic performer, and a congregational parlor, and a parish kitchen." Unhappily, these are the religious forms you would expect Americans to create because they haven't identified the proper function of a church, which is "reverence": "We Americans are said to be the most irreverent people in the world, and of the substantial truth of that accusation there cannot be the smallest doubt."[3]

Evidently Potter had never met an Australian. But he had met an important idea: religious buildings are tools for defining and inducing specific kinds of religious feeling. The "reverence" he wanted to induce is "that upward reaching thought out of which comes penitence, and prayer, and faith, and," for good measure, "all the rest." What he meant was high-church devotionalism, as if "all the rest" could be derived from it alone. And he was right in saying that if you want to induce this kind of reverence, "a diet kitchen will not do that."[4]

In a sense, of course, all churches have the same function: they are places where Christians meet. America's early churches advertised that universal function; they were "meetinghouses." And they looked like houses: big, ugly, private homes. Sometimes the main door was in the middle of the long side of the church, because that made a more efficient entrance than a door that was dramatically, but inconveniently, situated at the far and narrow end. Over the years, churches grew more dignified, more distinctive, and more resolutely focused on the minister standing on his elevated platform. There was no thought of such distractions as organs or stained glass, either in New England or in the Church of England colonies. You were there to listen to the clergy pray and preach; the only structural distractions were the clear glass windows, useful for shedding light on the minister's manuscript but showing nothing to the audience except the monotony of the surrounding village.

Variations on the boxlike, congregation-plus-preacher church were characteristic of America until the beginning of the nineteenth century. Even Church of England buildings, loathed by Puritans for their "idolatrous" rites, had no idolatrous decorations besides the Ten Commandments or some other edifying text carved above the communion table. Yet the Church of England and its Episcopal successor were the custodians of architectural traditions that associated public worship with something more than meeting and preaching. In the late seventeenth century, the classical columns and sky-pointing spires of Christopher Wren's London churches had shown what Protestants could do with the old symbols of rational authority and medieval devotion. None of this was structurally or "functionally" necessary, yet it suggested there were ways to God other than assembling a congregation and listening to a preacher. It suggested that there was a cosmopolitan potential in Christianity, a potential notably lacking in the primitive meetinghouse.

In the eighteenth century, the British government forced toleration of its own church on the Congregationalist provinces, and Church of England edifices appeared even in Boston. The style of London was imitated in such structures as the Old North Church (1725), later famous for Paul Revere's ride. The imitation was crude, but it gave the king's church a competitive advantage, a way of inspiring thoughts and identifying associations that the Congregational meetinghouses didn't have. Gradually Puritan churches acquired some of the same features. After the Revolution, English neoclassicism imperceptibly merged with the neoclassicism of America's own "Greek revival," a style that could be adopted by anyone capable of paying for a wooden church with wooden columns. Now when choosing a church, one need not decide between the simple and the sophisticated; one could have them both, in any denomination—Episcopal, Baptist, Unitarian, Universalist. And a wooden steeple would give any church the crowning historical touch.

The colonial New England church, the greeting-card church that people "remember" when they come home for Christmas, is usually not colonial and often not New English; some of the best examples exist in such places as Ohio and date from the nineteenth century.[5] But if you want to come home in that way, just walk down the street: you are likely to find a "colonial" church someplace in your neighborhood. The supposedly period style has proven remarkably tenacious, despite its limited functionality; it is far from the obvious form for churches with offices, Sunday schools, and restrooms. But today, when few congregations would think of building a new church in the style of Victorian Gothic (fine for Christmas cards but not for re-creation), and none would try to rebuild the original and authentic New England meetinghouse, many still revolt against modernity and insist on "something colonial." The conjunction of (asserted) historical authority and (apparent) immediacy and sincerity of design remains potent across the denominations. The form has its own functions.

When Henry Ford attempted to re-create heartland America in his outdoor historical museum, Greenfield Village, he naturally provided a church for the village green—and naturally, this structure was an imitation of a "colonial" church, columned and steepled, with plain, white-painted pews inside. Other styles would have been more historically appropriate to the old buildings that Ford collected, most of them from the Victorian period, but no one in Ford's position would have chosen a Victorian style. It wouldn't have identified the ideal form of the heartland place of worship. The church at Greenfield Village has no doctrine, no pastor, and no congregation; mainly, it's used for weddings. Yet tourists hush their voices as they enter its doors and gaze upon its pews. The architecture makes the church. Here is the triumph of form over substance, medium over message; here is a harvest of reverence from soil that Bishop Potter pronounced barren.

Nevertheless, the most peculiar, and most dynamic, mixtures of the modern and the archaic in church architecture happened during the nineteenth century, when the colonial style was eclipsed almost completely by styles that were less functional but more alluring, at least for a while.

The early churches of the Second Great Awakening—Methodist, Baptist, Campbellite, and so on—were functional: quick, cheap, and bare. They weren't functional just in the sense of being cheap and easy to build. They were theologically functional; they were assertions and embodiments of Christian sincerity. The mystery of grace might suddenly appear, but if so, it would appear in full public view,

FIGURE 9.1. *The Martha-Mary Chapel, Greenfield Village, 1929: always "old" and always new. Photo by Joseph Ho; used by permission.*

with no colored glass or Ionic columns to obscure it and no tricks of ornament to divert the attention of those receiving it. But only one generation was required for the new revival churches and the old, formerly established churches to join in the next architectural revolution (or counterrevolution, as revolutions in America often are): the medieval movement. To the Victorians, Gothic and Romanesque were the modern style. How did this happen?

Medievalism in church architecture came to America with strong sponsorship from high-church Episcopalians, as a means of restoring pre-Reformation devotionalism. Thick walls; narrow, pointed windows filled with stained or painted glass; curiously separated and variegated internal volumes (nave, transept, chancel, choir); historic symbolism, not simplicity, throughout—everything in the modern medieval church was meant to encourage religious thoughts and feelings very different from those of the old-time meetinghouse.

FIGURE 9.2. *Michigan Romanesque: the First Congregational Church, Jackson, Michigan. If there had been churches in the Midwest during the twelfth century, and they had been constructed with modern materials, this may be how they would have looked. Courtesy of the Jackson District Library.*

There, one spent hours hearing one man's expositions of the Word; here, one might also do that, but one had many other things to think about as well. Medieval churches offered what one architect called "a home, a holy place, a response to the inner voice, an utterance of all that is good, and lovely, and reverent."[6]

Of course, no one literally went home to Gothic (although some people felt they had); its antiquity was new, and the religious sensations it inspired could be variously interpreted. But that just meant it provided many more methods by which people could find new connections with God. This is what Christians of every denomination, social class, and social setting now demanded.[7]

Some first-generation American gothicists labored under a self-imposed duty to make copies of specific medieval churches. That ideal quickly dissipated. Gothic and its elder cousin, Romanesque, were constantly reinvented parts of a general refiguring of American taste, an effort not "to replicate historic stage sets" but "to create dynamic sanctuaries."[8] Yet to almost everyone they quickly became what a church was supposed to look like. Episcopalians and Roman Catholics were the most enthusiastic about darkness, mystery, and intricate displays of symbolism, but even a Baptist church, with little more of Gothic than pointed windows, hammerbeam ceilings, and strangely shaped spires, could try to project the weight and assurance of ancient tradition—not to mention the respectability that comes from being up to date.

With the aid of modern building methods, "medieval" churches could assume virtually any shape or volume desired, and modern wealth could make them comfortable. A British visitor to America's medieval churches noted with pleasure that "the pews [were] all wide, the seats cushioned, the floor carpeted, and the whole church comfortably heated."[9] No one except the most intentionally primitive evangelicals now worried about defining a church by its simplicity. Organs grew big, and bigger, with choirs to match. Singers began to be surpliced, as in the abhorred temples of the "papists." Unwilling to be consigned to a loft at the back of the building, musicians claimed a place up front. Many congregations now appeared to be worshiping the singers and the organ pipes.

New means of religious experience were developing, and architecture was helping to identify them. The peculiar combination of the medieval and the modern provided new emotional associations for each. Strong objections might still be made to some medievalisms (crosses on steeples or crucifixes anyplace) and some modernisms (the overprominent organ, with its suggestion of a concert hall). Purists never ceased to deride America's weird combinations of down home and high church. But resistance was futile. The mixture of then and now, historical and modern, was a delightful discovery; it was exactly what the churches needed. No respect for historical styles ever kept an American church from installing sofas and plants in both its "narthex" and its "parlor." And why should it? One of the functions of churches was to be genteel and comfortable, like the best private residences in town.

To see how dramatically religious form and function might change in America, consider Baltimore's Lovely Lane Methodist Church. The building commemorates the centennial of American Methodism. But while memorializing the primitive past, it demonstrates—even celebrates—the enormous revolution that Methodism had undergone during the past several decades. This was no longer a church that advertised its simple, direct, and exuberant methods. It was a church discovering that stability, fortitude, institutional eminence, and connections with the historic Church (not necessarily the Methodist Church) might also point the way to God.

Designed in 1884 by Stanford White, the classiest of classy New York architects, Lovely Lane is more than just one church. On the inside, it looks like an exceptionally well-appointed concert hall. On the outside, it looks like the eleventh-century Italian church it is trying to imitate—but not too hard. Lovely Lane, unlike the church of the Abbey of Pomposa, is a monument to sectarian strength and dominance. Real granite and real height aren't enough for it; every

FIGURE 9.3. *A mighty fortress: Lovely Lane Methodist Church, Baltimore. Source:* The American Architect and Building News, *March 26, 1887.*

architectural device is used to create a sense of final triumph. The stone is somber, nothing like the pastel material of the Italian model; the existence of the pleasant auditorium would never be guessed from the exterior. The lower stories of the tower are more massively medieval than those of the real medieval church, making the imitation stronger and more assured, and the tower is further strengthened by the massing of the body of the church against it. At the Abbey of Pomposa, the tower windows broaden gradually and cheerfully toward the top; the tower of Lovely Lane is well fortified all the way up.

This tower, be it noted, is obviously and ostentatiously unnecessary. Its effect is purely spiritual. It has nothing to do with the practical functions of a modern church and everything to do with its ability to identify and define a religious experience—in this case, the experience of a divinely appointed order and solemnity. Unlike its primitive ancestors among Methodist churches, Lovely Lane doesn't look as if it could ever be involved with so turbulent an affair as a religious revival.

The medieval movement offered much, but it couldn't offer all things to all people. That function was assumed, or attempted, by the structures of the big-church movement, which started soon after Lovely Lane was built. Even small churches could seem like big ones if they had enough classrooms encircling their auditoriums and enough kitchens, meeting rooms, and social-service offices in the basement or the annex. Wealthier institutions could discover as many religious functions as their "expansion plans" permitted.

Stribling's *Unfinished Cathedral* is a work of fiction, but it isn't far from its target: American Protestants' large "church plants." The brainchild of a Methodist bishop, Stribling's cathedral is intended to provide "restaurants, kitchens, cold storage, game rooms, library, children's library, moving-picture room, basket-ball court, gymnasium, running track, laundry, billiard room, lecture rooms, and, of course, on the first floor, the main auditorium and chapels." To the objection that churches ought to concern themselves with *religion*, the bishop replies, "There is no use deceiving ourselves. Unless our churches are turned into communal centers, we will lose our congregations. There was a time when religion was the product of the churches; it is now a by-product." He blames a generational shift in public opinion.[10]

Stribling appears to agree: doctrinal Christianity is finished. The big-church people in his novel are all progressive churchmen and forward-looking businessmen. The bishop's assistant in the cathedral project is a young minister whose seminary education has taught him that "no man may say" whether the Christian story is true, but "if there be no God the Christian attitude is best," because only belief in an "inspiring ideal" can move "nations" to their "destinies." He communicates this modern gospel to a conference of supposedly conservative Southern Methodists who turn out not to be conservative after all. On the strength of his agnostic sermon, he is appointed minister of a metropolitan church that can afford to pay him the contemporary equivalent of $200,000 a year. That church is interested in social service: "recreation camps for the poor, a new wing to the Methodist hospital, an American citizens' training course for the foreign population . . . the milk fund, and on and on." All these activities require money and management, and the church thinks the progressive young preacher is perfect for the job.[11]

This is mild social satire and strong social realism. The buildings erected by prosperous churches of the late nineteenth and early twentieth centuries delineate "the Christian attitude" as interpreted by the big-church movement. There is a "sanctuary" of normal size, often betraying, as the medieval connotations of the word suggest, the relentless infiltration of high-church fixtures from the ritualist denominations: chancel, stained glass, altar-like communion table.

Extending outward from this shrine and across the "campus" is a complex of wings, annexes, and tangentially related structures, a place for every social activity. The church itself has a limited capacity, but its "programs" have no limits; they can go as far as there is money to hire masons and carpenters.

Even in these conditions, historical styles predominated: Romanesque, Gothic, Tudor, colonial. Many a Christian has played basketball in a medieval church gymnasium. This was no mere pretense, no victory of form over function. It was a way of endowing the structure with all the religious affinities that its "real" function could not provide. The effect went the other way, too. Mainline churches that were losing their doctrinal solidity (as Stribling suggests and as the poll cited in chapter 3 confirms) gained a new sense of confidence from their architectural alliance with other large, heavy institutions (public schools, city halls, Masonic temples) that the community often supported more enthusiastically than it did the church. The fact that big churches were often run like other big institutions meant that this wasn't just a pretense. And when the big downtown churches started running out of congregants, their architectural form identified other functions, appropriate to the new needs of their neighborhoods. Classrooms, gyms, and offices became daycare centers, rec centers, preschools, and places to help the homeless. But that's getting ahead of the story.

The Depression and the Second World War were not favorable to the building of churches, big or small. Two great periods of expansion followed—the baby-boom era and the era of the megachurch, which was initiated by the former babies of the former boom. In both periods, architecture showed new ways of defining what a church should be. It also showed some new effects of Americans' ideas about how churches should be supported.

For practical purposes, churches can be separated into two groups: those that have inherited a large endowment and those that have not. Very old, very eastern, or formerly very wealthy congregations are most likely to have endowments sufficient to preserve them no matter what they do. If the endowment holds up, the clergy can be paid, the choir can be paid, and the termites can be displaced, without any special effort to maintain the membership. Well-endowed churches can follow whatever traditions or institute whatever radical reforms their ministers think up. Other churches have to survive, somehow. Nothing is more common than for congregations to borrow money in the summer, when contributions are low, and repay it after Christmas.

During much of American history, churches were supported mainly by the rental or sale of pews. There might be an auction of pews when the church was built, or there might be a periodic leasing accompanied by reassessment of prices in response to the current desirability of an "inside" or "outside," a "front" or "rear" seat. When extraordinary (that is, fairly normal) needs for money arose, special contributions had to be solicited. That was a nightmare. It was all a nightmare. Suppose you rented a pew at St. Paul's Episcopal Church, San Diego, but you didn't show up when the service began on Sunday. At precisely what point could the ushers seat a "stranger" in your pew? Well, a harried church committee decided, "strangers" could be seated if you weren't there when the choir reached the chancel.[12]

"Strangers"! The more you looked at it, the more unchristian pew rentals appeared. No matter how cheap the pews might be (and they were very cheap in most churches), the practice discriminated against newcomers and less prosperous people, who would probably be ushered to the least desirable places, in the back or behind a pillar. Certainly the concept of pews as real estate made it difficult to cope discreetly with the new needs for money that seemed to come up every year. Therefore, in the early twentieth century, another system was developed: the free church combined with the weekly envelope. Anyone could come and sit anywhere, even in the seats of the mighty, if the mighty weren't already in place, but every autumn, people would be asked to make a "pledge" for next year. If they did, they would be supplied with fifty-two envelopes in which to insert contributions sufficient to fulfill their pledge. If they didn't, they would be missing out on a new but fundamental ritual of faith.

This is now the general method of church finance. It provides a way for unendowed churches to estimate their annual budgets and regularize their income. Of course, some people pledge more than others, but their contributions cannot be gauged by the locations of their pews. Everyone is now the target of "free-will" financial appeals, which means that everyone is encouraged to feel that his or her money (and opinion) matters. This can be very satisfying to those who pledge. When the "envelope system" came in, ministers liked the fresh new money it often produced, but few of them enjoyed the consequence, which was a more volatile membership. People might be inspired to pledge more than their ordinary pew was worth, or they might be inspired to pledge less, or to leave their pew (which wasn't "theirs" anymore), take their cash, and pledge it to another church. Envelopes are easier to transport than pews.

After World War II, this truism had a startling illustration: baby-boom parents moved to new suburbs, and they carried their envelopes with them to their new churches. The structures built to attract them conveyed emphatic messages about the nature of a church.

First, the church is a good place for children; in fact, nurturing children may be its primary function. The "school wing" of the baby-boom churches was often larger than the "sanctuary."

Second, cheerfulness is next to godliness, not just for children, but for adults as well. People looking for the Miltonic "dim religious light," even in a Catholic church, were implicitly but strongly advised by the architects to seek it elsewhere. Any but cheerful functions were hard to identify in worship spaces that were relentlessly pastel.

Third, the church, unlike other institutions, is perfectly honest about its own techniques, and one of its most important functions is to display this honesty, as well as the cost-cutting methods that produced it. Formerly, a steel post would automatically be hidden inside a stone or wooden "pillar." Now every girder and panel must be displayed as a sign that the church is fully and frankly part of the modern world. All ceremonies, even the most doctrinally mysterious, must be fully visible to, and if necessary spotlighted for, the congregation, which should ideally be gathered on all four sides of the altar or other sacred space.

Once again, the progressive turned out to be the primitive. By revealing and even delighting in the nakedness of their technology, churches advertised their connection with the simplicity of the early Church. A girder was no longer just a girder, whose practical function is to hold up a roof; it now had a symbolic aura. If signs of other historical continuities were required, they could be provided just as candidly: stained glass (bright, modern, and nonrepresentational, or assertively childlike or folkish); brick veneer on *one* façade; pointed windows that were not quite Gothic but might illustrate the connection; a big steel cross on the lawn out front, supposing that the zoning laws permitted it.

Twentieth-century architectural tendencies have been carried further by the megachurches. A true descendant of the big-church movement, the megachurch comprises a "campus" replete with little kids' rooms; big kids' rooms; young people's gathering places; older people's forums; offices for "worship teams," "outreach teams," and other teams; outdoor and indoor eating areas; Social Gospel clothing and food dispensaries; and of course the "parking facility," which sometimes has its own "parking ministry." Inside the church itself, one sees—no hiding—all the equipment needed to connect a modern, media-savvy audience with the traditional God. There are auditorium seats, not pews; a stage, not a chancel; a platform for a band, not an organist; and giant TV screens, not hymnals, to make sure that people can keep up with the songs. What the congregation views is a set on which live performances take place.

In these loud, spotlight-swept auditoriums, there is little encouragement for private emotion, for mystical awe and reverence, but cheerfulness and ease are freely administered by access-friendly ramps and passages, attractive electronic messages, and squads of happy greeters. No one intended it, but architecture and the associated means of crowd-control define the megachurch as a place where you don't have time or space to contemplate the mysteries of the universe, or even the means to participate in worship, except as an audience, as one person among the thousands duly seated for a one-hour flight to God. The presence of those thousands is especially important in megachurches that eschew the pledge system, imitating the early Church, which presumably had no such accounting devices. These pledgeless churches are uncomfortably dependent on what they take in, week by week, from the crowds that attend them.

The ability of high-tech auditoriums to transform worshipers into an audience has become a serious concern of megachurch pastors themselves. But however much they may wish to change the pattern, the architecture remains restrictive. When you want people to participate in a communion service, how do you do it? Do you have the congregation form a long, long line from the upper balcony to the guitar-encrusted stage? At some megachurches, people entering the auditorium are handed a plastic container of grape juice and a bit of plastic-wrapped bread; then, at a designated time in the service, they tear open the containers and consume the elements. Worship leaders wince when they hear the tide of ripping plastic spreading across the room, but the architectural form seems to require that the sacrament not be a solemn or even a frequent function of the church. Form discovers function, but it may also exclude function.

Of course, a major function of the megachurch is to attract people who are not in the older, more solemn churches, people who are, perhaps, put off by churchiness in general. The irony is that faithful attenders of megachurches appear to spend more of their time in church than faithful attenders of traditional institutions, often learning a more challenging theology than the one currently offered by the mainline churches, with their *forbidding* Gothic architecture. Yet the megachurches are determined not to pose any architectural barriers to anyone who might be shy about Bishop Potter's "reverence." One way of doing that is to reverse the old maxim and make the church look—and to some degree, function—like anything except a church.

Intentionally unchurchly churches have many historical precedents. Americans may be the world's most religious people, but they have often shown themselves the friends of revolution against identifiably churchly customs, including church architecture. The Puritans, the early Baptists, and some of the early Methodists scorned the recognized, and recognizable, ecclesiastical buildings of their day. In the 1960s and 1970s, new springs of antichurch Christianity shot up. Hal Lindsey, the end time writer, appealed to the current of antichurch feeling when he saw portents of apocalypse in the activities of the mainstream denominations and especially of the National Council of Churches. "Satan loves religion," he wrote. "Religion is a great blinder of the minds of men."[13] (These sentiments didn't hurt the sales of his book among members of mainstream churches.) Today, dismissal and denial of "the churches" is one of the most predictable features of American Christianity. A typical way of advertising a new church is a billboard showing photographs of gloomy young adults, obviously dissatisfied with something, and the slogan "Don't Like Church? We Don't Either."[14]

Two generations ago, it was said that people were reluctant to enter a church unless they could read the sign and see whether it was "First Methodist" or "First Presbyterian."[15] Now "Methodist" and "Presbyterian" often appear in microscopic lettering, while "All Are Welcome!!!" can be read a block away. But denominational churches have been finding friendlier terms for themselves than "First Methodist" for almost a hundred years—billing themselves, for instance, as "church homes."[16] The phrase suggests a place where you can drop in, have some coffee, and chat with your friends, as opposed to dressing up and participating in a formal religious exercise. Today, one of the most successful networks of contemporary churches, the Vineyard, has made it a ritual to stop the service after thirty minutes so that congregants can step outside for coffee and bagels and then return for the rest.

Easily accessible, unthreatening, reassuring in their external similarity to sports arenas, shopping malls, and other palaces of pleasure, the most contemporary "church homes" pose no architectural or ritual obstacles for people who lack the desire to go to a traditional church. But while people who attend these churches can be counted, there are no statistics about people who are not attracted to them, people for whom their very architecture rules out a connection with God. History, solemnity, symbolism, the dark night of the soul—all these may be ways to God, but they won't be found in places designed to omit them. "When your mother has just died," one middle-aged Christian said, "you need a *dark* place to go."

The slow crumbling of the big denominations created a niche for the nondenominational fellowships and megachurches. It's a big niche, but it is still a niche, still an attempt to strike oil with a certain kind of tool, in a certain part of the territory. Other niches are opening up, in other areas. The Internet finds or makes them. Any church that wants to put its picture on the Internet has a chance of attracting people who—though they may not have known it before—would like precisely that kind of church.

Surprisingly, many churches that look as if history had abandoned them are now proving attractive as "destination" churches. You can tell by the battered Gothic architecture that these (mainly inner-city) churches have survived with difficulty from more cheerful times. What you see on the Internet is a "historic sanctuary" (everything is "historic" in America if it goes beyond one generation) joined to a poignant series of schoolrooms, meeting rooms, gyms, and chapels, surrounded by crime-repellent walls and bars but retaining a door where poor people can go to receive food, medical care, and the kind of welcome you can't get elsewhere. This is the Social Gospel, in one of its most powerful yet least appreciated manifestations. But some people are attracted to it, and it doesn't take millions of them to keep it going.

Startling survivals are also seen among ideologically dissident churches, many of which are getting along quite well, thank you, because they have found new meaning in their historic buildings. The architecture isn't just a sample of history anymore; it's a modern beacon. Mariners' Church, an old inner-city Episcopal congregation in Detroit, discovered that it could gain enough support from traditionalists in the metropolitan area to resist the demands of the bishop, a modern liberal, for the church to recognize his authority. When he came to the church to conduct a service, the congregation responded by summoning the police, leaving him to walk away in the rain carrying his shepherd's crook.[17] And the congregation won, after a long court battle. Despite the huge political and social changes that Detroit has experienced during the past two generations, Mariners' remains the city's recognized, though nonofficial, shrine, with exhibits of Great Lakes shipping, windows dedicated to Detroit historical figures, and a blessing of the fleet at each year's start of navigation. It even found fame by an allusion in Gordon Lightfoot's top-forty ballad "The Wreck of the *Edmund Fitzgerald*," which calls it a "cathedral." It isn't a cathedral, and it doesn't even look like one, but if it hadn't been able to claim that it was historically and architecturally significant, it would certainly not exist today. The architecture found new functions for the church itself.

Church architecture is a tool and often an experiment. You can't tell how it will work. Our Lady of the Angels, the Catholic cathedral in downtown Los Angeles (2002), was built at tremendous expense for a generally impoverished Latino community. During its construction, it was roundly condemned, both for its cost and for its bulky, what-is-this? design, which combines the church proper with meeting rooms, offices, a cafeteria, a mausoleum, a spacious parking lot, and security emplacements to ward off downtown vagrants. This description suggests a Catholic megachurch, but the impression vanishes as soon as one enters what used to be called a nave. The interior is overwhelming in its size but also in the gravity of its ornaments, chief of them a series of immense wall hangings depicting the saints of the church, standing above the congregation. The combination of solemnity and ultramodernism administers the kind of shock that can provoke chance visitors into piety.

Such an inside-outside effect is conspicuous in many other churches that ostentatiously do not look like churches when you view them from the street. The Catholic cathedral in San Francisco, St. Mary of the Assumption (1971), is an enormous white concrete formation that from the outside looks like a church mainly because it doesn't look like anything else. Its upper reaches have no more practical function than a Romanesque steeple on a Congregational church. Yet the outside makes you want to see what's on the inside, and when you go in, you discover something more about what a church can be. The central space, high but wide, offers not

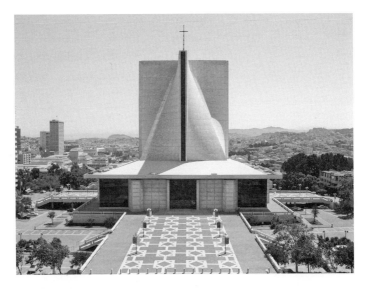

FIGURE 9.4. *Saint Mary's Cathedral: a concrete cloud hovering over San Francisco. Courtesy of the Cathedral of Saint Mary of the Assumption.*

FIGURE 9.5. *Saint Mary's Cathedral: beneath the cloud, the simplicity of open chapels (background, left and right) and the geometry of public worship (center), large yet close. Courtesy of the Cathedral of Saint Mary of the Assumption.*

only a close approach to the altar but access to broad views of the city beyond and entrance to eight small chapel-like areas, realms of private devotion. The church provides a real as well as a symbolic transition from one scale of experience to another.

Such effects, however, are not routinely produced by modernist or postmodernist church architecture. An unfortunate example is, or was, the Episcopal Cathedral of Christ the King (1968), in Kalamazoo, Michigan. Built near the junction of two freeways, it was intended to advertise Christianity to passing motorists, many of whom probably wondered why a warehouse should be built in such an ugly way. The cathedral was a brick box with tower-like protrusions at the roofline, leading even people friendly to the congregation's modernist theology to say that the building resembled a sick pig with all four feet in the air. Inside, it was a concrete box, centered on a concrete altar, with small, movable chairs instead of pews, arranged so as to compel the congregants to become a community, or at least to stare at one another. But congregants became fewer and fewer, despite all efforts to combine modern liberal preaching with exercises in quasi-medieval piety. (The church installed not one but three meditational labyrinths on its property.) In 2007 the tiny remaining congregation (twenty or so on a normal Sunday) sold the cathedral to a prosperous megachurch. The new owners immediately constructed an enormous addition, which has the virtue of transparency: it looks exactly like a megachurch—or a big-box electronics store.

The former cathedral is now a "historic facility . . . available for rental" by the megachurch. Its "beautiful mix of retro, modern and contemporary architecture" serves "as a striking venue for a variety of Christ-centered events including: weddings, funerals and other significant events."[18] Function follows form. Only experience can answer the question, How many followers will avail themselves of the functions?

10

THE MORTAL WORD

"The singing," said a tourist exploring America in the 1870s, "tends to become the most important part of the [church] service. One gentleman, a Unitarian in Boston, told me that he had to change his seat from near the door, to avoid the disturbance caused by people going out when the choral-singing was over, and before the sermon began. They tell a story about some minister, who announced that, as the singing had occupied longer than usual, the sermon would be postponed till some more convenient season."[1]

In today's churches, music continues to compete with sermons, or to put this in the language of "contemporary" churches, with the "messages," "reflections," "comments," and "perspectives" offered by the worship leaders. It isn't just the tunes and singers that provide the competition. The words that people sing are probably more important in propagating, reviving, and *making* American Christianity than any others, except those of the Bible itself. And the biblical phrases that people remember are often those they found in hymns. Songs are more than expressions of religious experience; they are primary means of constructing religious experience—and churches, too.

Good hymns are based on an irony: individual people write them from their own experience, yet thousands or even millions of other people can sing them with emotional authenticity. This has been true since Bible days. The biblical Psalms were written for communities of worshipers, and for thousands of years they have been repeated in public worship, yet many of them are as personal as a modern poem: "But as for me, my feet were almost gone; my steps had well nigh slipped. . . . When I thought to know this, it was too painful for me."[2]

It is a remarkable fact that successful hymn writers have often been very eccentric individuals. The life of hymns is a cycle of inspiration between the Christian congregation and some of its most unusual people and between those people and their own religious experience, experience that can come with the surprise and intensity of a presence entering from another world. That is how it seemed to Julia Ward Howe when she woke before dawn with the lines of a song beginning, as she said, "to twine themselves" in her mind, and she searched for a pen to record them before they disappeared.[3] This was the origin of "The Battle Hymn of the Republic," which despite its eccentric inspiration and its unique interpretation of the book of Revelation became one of America's unofficial national anthems.

A fuller exposition of the curious process of hymn writing was offered by Charles Price Jones (1865–1949), an African American preacher, a prolific songwriter, and the founder of a Christian denomination, the Church of Christ (Holiness). The American sense of "holiness" is hard to define. It isn't literal moral purity, which is impossible to attain; rather, it's an assurance of sanctification and an especially intimate experience of Christ, and of being part of the Body of Christ. Jones knew how to express the many implications. Like John Bunyan, his illustrious predecessor in the lifeways of radical Protestantism, Jones understood the limitless resources of "ordinary" language, and he was adept at using them to enchant and surprise his readers and listeners, never just to lure them in. One of the surprises was his direct testimony about himself, his individuality, his eccentricity. By surprising people with himself he created a community in which everyone could reveal surprising qualities, in which anyone could share the eccentricity of a friendship with God.

Jones readily admitted that he was "an extremist." He said, "This sounds foolish; but once in a while someone must be a fool for Christ's sake." But he showed how the "extremist" and the "fool" could establish a connection with God in which other people might participate. He said, "I had no idea at all of taking up holiness as a fad, or an ism, or a creed, or the slogan of a 'cult'. I just wanted to be personally holy. I just wished to make my own calling and election sure to my own heart by walking with God in the Spirit." But then he "became convinced by the Lord that what [he] needed, all His people needed." The question became, How could he get his congregation to "see it"?

Jones locked himself in the parlor of a friend's house in Jackson, Mississippi, and besieged the Lord in prayer. At last he slumped down, exhausted, confessing that he could "pray no more." And immediately, he said, "the Lord flooded me with blessing":

> Surely the heavens were opened. The Spirit spoke within from the holy of holies of my redeemed spirit, and said, "You shall write the hymns for your people." This He said six or seven times till it was fixed in my mind. I got up and went to the organ in the corner of the room, wrote a song titled "Praise the Lord," ruled off a tablet, set it to music, and sang it before I left the room.[4]

Jones continued writing hymns, hundreds of hymns, and these songs inspired his followers to continue in the face of

adversities that would make few other people burst out singing: violent rejection by the black Baptists with whom Jones
and his people had originated; attacks by hooligans and bul-
lies, who fired into their meetings; attacks by racist mobs,
who burned their church; the daily, undramatic labor of
maintaining a congregation made up largely of people beset
and poor; and the constant sense—sharp and chronic in
Jones himself, an inveterate conductor of self-inventories—
that one may not have the inner resources to go on. Jones's
songs enabled him and his faithful church people not just to
endure but to rejoice in a continual tension between spiritual
need and spiritual triumph. And it wasn't just his Holiness
friends who felt that way; his hymns made connections with
evangelical Christians everywhere, white and black. Some
are staples of evangelical experience today.

Explaining the origin of one of his songs, Jones said that
when he wrote it, he felt he was "coming short of [his] high-
est privileges of service in Christ." He "prayed in that song
for deeper grace, deeper wisdom, more perfect conformity
to and willingness to do God's will." Out of this confession of
personal need emerged the hymn that has gained the largest
response from other people:

> *Deeper, deeper in the love of Jesus*
> *Daily let me go;*
> *Higher, higher in the school of wisdom,*
> *More of grace to know.*
>
> *Oh deeper yet, I pray,*
> *And higher every day,*
> *And wiser, blessèd Lord,*
> *In Thy precious, holy Word....*
>
> *Deeper, higher, every day in Jesus,*
> *Till all conflict past,*

Finds me conqu'ror, and in His own image
Perfected at last.

Jones believed that "the simplicity and the happy lift of the melody," which he also composed, "had something to do with [the song's] popularity." But he was thinking more about the words when he said, "If ever there was an inspired song I feel that 'Deeper, Deeper' was inspired." Then he added, with his gift for critical self-consciousness, "Anyway, so I felt when it was written." There was something about the words that made an "inspired" connection with him, and could make that connection with others as well. "The Spirit gave me a song with which to express the need of my soul. And, Oh, how many need to sing it with me!" The many have sung it with him ever since.

The strangeness of words in song—their ability, sometimes, to speak to individuals as if from the Holy of Holies— appears in an eerie little anecdote from the years just after the Civil War. It was related by the tourist quoted at the beginning of this chapter. He encountered a young black man on a road in the South,

> a negro lad who sang . . . a weird hymn, in which the following verse occurred,

> *You'd better mind how you fool with Christ*
> *In a moment you'll be as cold as ice,*

> paused, and said, "I saw six converted on that verse."[5]

The anecdote isn't about theology, ethnicity, or socioeconomic circumstances. It's about the discovery of words that have power and can be shared.

At first, American Christians looked for those words in repetitions of the past. The first work published in English

America was the *Bay Psalm Book* (Cambridge, Massachusetts, 1640). It offered direct, and mostly bad, versifications of the biblical Psalms. The badness doesn't appear to have affected its sales, which were large; the book returned a better than 50 percent profit on investment.[6] Because the Puritan settlers of Massachusetts considered singing an important way to God, they expected the words they sang to be slavishly imitative of his Word.

Such expectations were ended by Isaac Watts (1674–1748), "the father of English hymnody." An evangelical Christian but also an intellectual and a poet, Watts escaped from bondage to the biblical text; he demonstrated that there are many more ways to God than one. The hymns he created were investigations of individual experience, seen in the dramatic light of the broader Christian story:

> *Am I a soldier of the Cross,*
> *A follower of the Lamb?*
> *And shall I fear to own his cause,*
> *Or blush to speak his name?*

> *Must I be carried to the skies*
> *On flowery beds of ease,*
> *While others fought to win the prize,*
> *And sailed through bloody seas?*[7]

Every Sunday, the hymns of Watts and his eighteenth-century followers are sung by multitudes of conservative Christians throughout America, while the words of these writers' brilliant contemporaries—Swift and Pope, Addison and Johnson—have almost vanished from popular knowledge. In Sinclair Lewis's encyclopedic satire of American Christianity, *Elmer Gantry*, even preachers know that their sermons are ordinarily forgotten as soon as heard, but everybody remembers the standard hymns.[8] The most strongly continuous expressions of Christianity in America are the reading of the King James Bible and the singing of the standard hymns.

Few hymns that Americans sang in the eighteenth century were written in America—certainly Isaac Watts's were not—but they became as perennially American as the apple tree. No church repertoire that is touched at all by the Protestant tradition omits Watts's "Joy to the World," John Newton's "Amazing Grace," Augustus Toplady's "Rock of Ages" (the song that the congregation usually sings in western movies), or Charles Wesley's "Hark! the Herald Angels Sing." Wherever there is a pew (not a movable chair or an auditorium seat) in an American church, these songs will be found in the book that sits in the little rack; the organ will play, and the congregation will rise and sing. Some churches that ordain only "contemporary songs" at the start and finish of a service never fail to use a "traditional song" during the offertory.

Yet the practice of even standard church music has changed greatly over time. A century and a half ago, hymnbooks generally provided the words only, sometimes with brief headings indicating each song's "measure" (the number of syllables per line), so it could be fitted to any of the scores of tunes available for that measure. This presentation might seem to favor trained musicians, with good memories for melodies, over the normal church attender, who has often been pictured as not knowing what to sing and leaving it all to the choir. That picture is more likely to be true of congregations today than it was of congregations in the distant past. Some big-city churches had choirs, and paid them, but many churches had no choirs at all; some still didn't believe in using them, or musical instruments, either. Nevertheless, almost every kind of church had its hymnbooks, popular though unofficial, and even nonmusical people enjoyed reading them at home as devotional poetry.

There was no shortage of hymns. The 1849 Methodist

hymnal contains 1,227, many more than today's hymnals, and people had no more difficulty memorizing much of this repertoire than they have in remembering popular songs today. In communities where books were few, a preacher or elder might need to "line out" a hymn, giving the words so the congregation could give them back—a dreary exercise, though one that shows the people's desire to share what they could not read. But even on the frontier, Methodist circuit riders reported that people "could, nearly every soul of them, sing our hymns and spiritual songs." At Cane Ridge, where "singing was the most enjoyable group activity," people gathered around those "slain by the Spirit" and sang hymns to revive them.[9] Towns were named after hymn tunes (China, Maine; Leoni, Michigan) and in honor of hymn writers (Olney, in several states, in recognition of William Cowper and John Newton, coauthors of the *Olney Hymns* [1779]).

But today's traditional hymns and traditional ways of treating hymns owe more to reformers than to appreciators. In seventeenth-century New England, choirless congregations sang out loudly, emitting notes as they remembered them and making a mess of established tunes. The eighteenth century wrought a revolution: Watts's hymns, the training of voices, and the use of three- or four-part harmony. The last two innovations were a plot by senior ministers and much resisted by the laity.[10] The next great reform of American religious music came in the early nineteenth century. Its most important figure was Lowell Mason (1792–1872), director of music for Lyman Beecher's Hanover Street Church, in Boston. Beecher considered music an important means of supporting evangelical Christianity and combating Unitarian modernism.[11] Mason was disgusted by what he regarded as the indifferent quality of church singing and church songs, and he determined to do something about it.

He was too fastidious about the songs. The enduring eighteenth-century hymns generally merited their authority, however inartistically they might be sung. At present, there is a considerable revival even of backwoods American hymns, some of great power. In any event, Mason looked to Europe for models of harmony, style, and performance, and he became a leader in the singing-school movement that disseminated musical training to tens of thousands of lay-people across America. Singing schools and "institutes" expanded the repertoire of church music, and like most religious innovations, they offered large ancillary benefits. They gave participants a welcome means of meeting new friends, while improving their taste and expanding their role in the local church.

Two of Mason's followers, George Root and William Bradbury, instructed thousands and created songbooks for millions. Bradbury (1816–1868) put the philosophy into a single phrase: "*new music,* and GOOD music."[12] Like Charles Finney, he associated Christianity with conversion and revival, and revival with a constant stream of new impressions—hence a constant stream of hymnbooks: *The Golden Chain, The Golden Censer, Golden Trio, Fresh Laurels* . . . He composed such now-standard but once *new* melodies as the tunes inseparably connected with "Jesus Loves Me" and "He Leadeth Me."

The career of George Root (1820–1895) exemplifies a new, non-European influence: commercial sheet music, made readily available by cheap methods of printing. To Americans of an earlier time, his career might have seemed fantastically unlikely. Reared on a farm in a remote part of New England where people still regarded instrumental music as a dubious enterprise, Root went to Boston, became a church organist and instructor, traveled to Europe for further training, and in the 1850s established himself as a writer of memorable popular music characterized by the *New York Times* as representing "that sentimental and not too lofty type which pleases the general public." He ran a music publishing company, and he composed Civil War songs, such as "The Battle Cry of Freedom" and "Tramp, Tramp, Tramp," songs that sold hundreds of thousands of copies and were actually sung by tramping soldiers.[13] He also wrote hymns and gospel songs. His are the tunes, at once rousing and touching, for "Jerusalem, Thou City Bright" (1855) and "When He Cometh" (the "Jewels Song" [1866]):

> *When He cometh, when He cometh*
> *To make up His jewels,*
> *All His jewels, precious jewels,*
> *His loved and His own:*
>
> *Like the stars of the morning,*
> *His bright crown adorning,*
> *They shall shine in their beauty,*
> *Bright gems for His crown.*

Root's direct command of human emotions—fresh in its time—managed to please both the general public and the University of Chicago, which awarded an honorary doctorate to the former farm boy.

The religious music of Bradbury, Root, and their many colleagues, competitors, and immediate successors—Fanny Crosby, Elisha Hoffman, P. P. Bliss, and a hundred others—is extraordinarily hard to characterize. It has been attacked with astonishing violence by academic writers, who have been willing to use such adjectives as "crude," "manipulative," "false and psychologically destructive," "escapist," "threatening, sadistic, bullying, regressive, [and] self-centred," as well as permitting themselves to discuss "pathetic false modesty," "pervasive sado-masochism," "regressive and infantile posturing," "thumb-sucking egotism," and even "the childish claiming of Jesus as a friend."[14] True, this music lacks the complexities of high-church devotionalism, and it isn't exactly "a little body of experimental and practical divinity," which is what John Wesley thought Christian music should be.[15] There are no sectarian disquisitions, as in "Rock of Ages" (1776), which gives listeners and singers a complete checkout on the Calvinist theory of salvation. Yet these songs often show a comprehensive knowledge of scripture, full ownership of the King James Version's horde of words, and an ability to give biblical expressions a new and enduring emotional resonance.

There is a farewell hymn published in 1882 that became standard among adventists and evangelicals:

> *God be with you till we meet again—*
> *Keep love's banner floating o'er you,*
> *Smite death's threatening wave before you.*
> *God be with you till we meet again!*

The scriptural allusions in this song—to 2 Kings 2:8 and Song of Solomon 2:4 in the stanza just quoted—are too obscure to register on most modern Christians. The author, indeed, was a college president: Jeremiah Rankin, of Howard University. But three generations ago the song wasn't too obscure to be used with dramatic effect. In small congregations, at the end of the service, people sometimes performed an impromptu dance to its earnest, pensive music, each person reaching to shake hands in turn with all the others until everyone had been bidden a last farewell, "till we meet at Jesus' feet."

Such songs define the elusive character of this ostensibly simple, commercial music. Like much music that works well on the stage—the songs of Stephen Foster, for example—it has an edge to it; it has a bittersweet quality that comes from an intensification of opposing emotions. It treats death, isolation, even lack of faith, not only with hope but with a sense of triumph. In Dwight Moody's 1874 crusade in Britain, the most popular song was Fanny Crosby's "Pass Me Not" (1868).

The solemn words, with the briskly confident tune by Howard Doane, are still very popular in conservative churches in
America:

> *Pass me not, O gentle Savior,*
> *Hear my humble cry;*
> *While on others thou art calling,*
> *Do not pass me by...*
>
> *Let me at thy throne of mercy*
> *Find a sweet relief,*
> *Kneeling there in deep contrition,*
> *Help mine unbelief.*[16]

Evangelical music broadened the spectrum of emotions
that a church, or a piano-equipped parlor, could make available to Christians, potential Christians, and even determined
anti-Christians—including H. L. Mencken, America's foremost opponent of Christianity, who enjoyed not only Bach but
also ordinary gospel songs, which he sang, enthusiastically, all
his life.[17] The emotional specificity, the delicately but firmly
delineated variations of this music are indicated by the fact
that few of the lyrics are ever sung without the melodies traditionally associated with them; they belong with those tunes.

The biggest revolution in American church music took
place in 1855, with the production of an innovative hymnal,
the *Plymouth Collection,* the work of Henry Ward Beecher
and his music director, John Zundel. The book carried the
prestige and broad appeal of the famous church and famous
pastor—evangelical but essentially nondenominational. Yet
the achievement of the *Plymouth Collection* was more basic.
It was the first widely circulated hymnal, designed for general congregational singing, that printed the music along
with the words.[18] Today it may seem remarkable that this

should ever have been seen as anything remarkable. But it was. It was something new.

Like many other revolutions in American Christianity, however, the *Plymouth Collection* was in a way—its own way—nostalgic, even preservationist. Among its 1,400 offerings were many eighteenth-century songs, most notably works by Isaac Watts (218 selections) and Charles Wesley (81). In his introduction Beecher claims that he tried to restore hymns that had been "mutilated" by earlier editors. Yet these good intentions didn't stop him from revising some songs and shortening many others, either to make them fit on a page or to make church services shorter and peppier.[19] Occasionally he added things. "Amazing Grace" appears with a "coda" that has nothing to do with the song. Thus Beecher both resisted and continued the fashion of revising the past, a fashion that rules without hindrance in today's hymnals.

One reason for the *Collection*'s success was its incorporation of the "revival melodies" that, Beecher says, had been vetoed by stuffy hymnbook editors but had still not been "driven out from among the people." He was happy to put himself at the head of a people's insurgency. Among the "homebred and popular" tunes that he included are the exquisite "Pleading Savior" and the indomitably rural-American "Hindustani Air" (the music for "Happy Land"). Putting his complaint as strongly as possible, Beecher charged that city churches often left hymns to the music director and the choir, who in return provided "worthless, heartless trash," so "devoid of character" that the songs "may be sung a hundred times, and not a person in the congregation will remember them." This stuff, he said, had no "merit" except professional "correctness." As a result of earlier reforms, the choir was now singing beautifully for the choir, without any appreciation of the myriad ways in which music can be "a means of religious feeling" and "imagination."[20]

That was Beecher's reason for finding and conserving the old church songs:

> The melody clings to them. On the way home snatches of it will be heard on this side and on that; and when, the next Sabbath, the same song is heard, one and another of the people fall in, and the volume grows with each verse, until at length the song, breaking forth as a many-rilled stream from the hills, grows deeper and flows on, broad as a mighty river! Such tunes are never forgotten. They cling to us through our whole life. We carry them with us upon our journey. We sing them in the forest. The workman follows the plow with sacred songs. Children catch them, and singing only for the joy it gives them now, are yet laying up for all their life food of the sweetest joy.[21]

Here is one of the most persuasive dreams of the old-time religion, a vision of experiences that, once discovered, can always be restored. That dream suggested the organization of Beecher's collection. The songs are arranged by subjects, and the subjects are not just doctrines or church occasions but emotions and their causes: "Trials and Temptations," "Praise, Joy, Conflict, Etc." Each of those subjects takes many more pages than "Institutions and Ordinances." The *Plymouth Collection* looks forward, too: there are 156 songs under "Missions and Reform."

Pressing his insight about music as a tool for discovering the varieties of Christian experience, Beecher took another step: he joined each song to one recommended tune, thus establishing a "best" emotional connection that in some cases became canonical. Today it is hard to imagine "All Hail the Power of Jesus' Name" without the stirring music of "Coronation." Scores of other tunes are possible, but that is the one that worked. Scripture is notable for its lack of stage directions. One can imagine God saying, "Behold, the man is become as one of us" (Genesis 3:22) in a number of ways—stern, regretful, alarmed, ironic—and the interpretation will vary accordingly. By joining words to music, the *Plymouth Collection* showed nonprofessional readers and singers a definite tone and interpretation, a strong interpretation that might not have occurred to them if they had selected the tune from a grab bag of metrical possibilities. The *Collection*—and the popular songbooks that followed its lead, and enhanced the standard repertoire—identified new and enduring ways of experiencing Christianity.

By 1912 those ways were so well established that the avant-garde writer Vachel Lindsay could begin a poem by saying that it was meant to be sung to "The Blood of the Lamb"—the tune of a revival song by Elisha Hoffman (1878)—and expect everyone in his audience to know exactly how it went. Sinclair Lewis displayed the same expectation about the songs he mentioned in *Elmer Gantry*. There were hundreds of songs like that, the salient results of all the musical revolutions that had happened since Isaac Watts. By 1930 more had been added by composers for mainline churches and by such latter-day revivalists as Homer Rodeheaver, a skilled musician who managed the music program and contributed hymnals for the Billy Sunday crusades. "What would Billy Sunday have been without Homer Rodeheaver?" someone—many people—asked, although it was a tribute to Sunday's artistry that he was able to remain the center of attention: Rodeheaver managed choirs of as many as 2,000 voices.[22]

Much of the standard collection endures, with important modifications, in the hymnbooks of the mainline Protestant and conservative evangelical churches. Here are songs meant to reach anyone, in any mood, on any occasion—almost. But no accumulated tradition, no set of religious measures, could ever be complete. The standard collection included few songs from African American authors or churches, partly because the collectors lacked the requisite knowledge and partly because the lyric and choral performance styles on which many African American songs depend were beyond the capabilities of other churches. This deficit began to be made up by memorable contributions of the 1960s and the following decades ("Sweet, Sweet Spirit," by Doris Akers, is a good example), but the barriers remained high. Other barriers restricted musical exchange with the most liturgical Christian traditions. The standard collection included an uneven representation of songs from the Episcopal and Catholic churches—churches that have had their own problems with mainstream Protestant hymnals. Episcopalians have always done their best to exclude commercial evangelical songs. Fanny Crosby has never darkened their portals. Anglicans and Anglo-Catholics contributed such standard offerings as "Good King Wenceslas," "The Navy Hymn," "Jerusalem the Golden," "For All the Saints," and "The Church's One Foundation," but songs about Mary, the Eucharist, the church year, and the mysteries of devotionalism were useless for America's predominantly evangelical churches.

The Catholics had a less fortunate history. For long a small minority culture in the English-speaking world, they made some important additions to the standard collection,[23] and they developed their own devotional songs, largely Eucharistic and Marian, often exploiting Protestant tunes. In 1903, however, Pope Pius X dealt a savage blow to musical creativity in a rescript banning almost everything except Gregorian chant and sixteenth-century ("classic") polyphony from the Mass. Music that suggested popular or "theatrical" forms was out, as were female voices in the choir. In America, the edict was met with apathy or disgust. Efforts to work around it were common, but without distinction.[24] The ban disappeared in the wake of Vatican II—an unfortunate moment, because at that time, even the majority, Protestant music was reverting to the lowest common denominator.

Hymnals are always being revised, but in the later twentieth century the revisions turned into a revolution against the standard hymnal itself. As the mainstream churches deserted their theological battlements, they also abandoned their more challenging biblical and conceptual outposts, the demanding ideas and allusions that were often the most interesting features of the standard offerings. Hymns were dropped or altered for reasons that would have baffled composers of the simplest gospel songs.

In 1965, when a Methodist cleric published a book assailing his church's supposed conservatism, he spent much of his time lampooning the standard hymnal. A special target was a stanza from "Sweet Hour of Prayer" (lyrics by William Walford [1845], with music by William Bradbury [1861]):

> *Sweet hour of prayer! sweet hour of prayer!*
> *May I thy consolation share,*
> *Till, from Mount Pisgah's lofty height,*
> *I view my home and take my flight:*
> *This robe of flesh I'll drop and rise*
> *To seize the everlasting prize,*
> *And shout, while passing through the air,*
> *"Farewell, farewell, sweet hour of prayer!"*

This, says the modern preacher, is "little short of gibberish. . . . If you didn't know this is part of a hymn which has comforted countless souls, you might take it for a message in a code which defies all efforts to break it."[25] Somehow, though, the "countless" nineteenth-century Americans who littered the countryside with Pisgah Churches had managed to break the code; they knew that Pisgah was the mountain ascended by the dying Moses, to view the Promised Land. People who didn't know what "Pisgah" meant were welcome to look it up. "Get you a dictionary," said Charles Price Jones in his advice for singers, "and learn. . . . Do not be too lazy to know."[26] One of the functions of churches and church music was to start an experience without necessarily completing it. And by the modern clergyman's own admission, when people knew what "Pisgah" meant, their souls were comforted.

But by the mid-twentieth century, the dominant culture of Christianity had little to do with intellectual struggle. In many churches, the bland were seeking the bland. The 1982 revision of the Episcopal hymnal, hailed at the time as a challenging new thing, marks most lyrics as "alt.," for "altered." Some of the alterations were dictated by political correctness, but many others were just meant to get rid of the *hard* words.

One of the last verbally complex yet generally accepted American hymns is "God of Grace and God of Glory" (1930). It was written by Harry Emerson Fosdick, a champion of modern liberal Christianity who still knew the value of a verbal challenge. His hymn asks God to "save us from weak resignation / To the evils we deplore," a mouth-filling yet intellectually satisfying pair of lines. Like Mount Pisgah, "deplore" has never been seen again in American hymnbooks. Now if a song has a difficult stanza, it is dropped, as are the lines just quoted from most renditions of Fosdick's hymn. Virtually all modern hymnals try to cut traditional offerings down to three or four stanzas, and the most intellectually and scripturally provocative lines are the first to go.

These revisions have happened simultaneously with changes in the Bible versions sponsored by churches and churchlike entities. After the King James Version (1611), the first new and widely used translation of scripture was the Revised Version (RV; British, 1881–1885). Its successor, the Revised Standard Version (RSV; American, 1946–1971), combined a high degree of accuracy with a strong sense of the dignity and historical associations of the text. The translators abandoned words in the King James Version that were no longer in common use, but in general they stayed close to the diction of that earlier text. The RV and RSV had a great influence on scholars, but little on congregations. In 1960 the ceremonial language of the American Protestant church was still almost universally that of the King James Bible. Conservative congregations still cling to it, as if it were inspired. But beginning with the New English Bible (1961–1970), the mainstream churches showed that they were looking for something different. Today they have joined the megachurches and Bible fellowships in a willingness to back almost any version that can be called "modern" or "contemporary" (i.e., easy to read).

The National Council of Churches strongly sponsors the New Revised Standard Version (1989). Catholic churches often feature the Jerusalem Bible (1966) or its offspring, the New Jerusalem Bible (1985; every translation now requires a "new" form). These versions are chiefly characterized by flatness and a pedantic scholarship that nevertheless prevents neither errors nor a general dumbing down.[27] Evangelicals have produced their own popular translations: the New International Version (1973–1978, 2011—scholarly and not entirely flat but biased by conservative theological formulations) and a plethora of allegedly fresh and relevant paraphrases, such as The Message (1993–2002).

The most popular recent translations are based on the principle of "dynamic equivalence," which means abandoning a literal, "word-for-word" rendering of a passage and substituting what is thought to be its modern-language parallel. Fortunately or unfortunately, this means that the modern-language reader tends to receive what the modern-language reader expects. If you open the Good News Bible (1966–1976) and turn to the first chapter of the Song of Solomon, you will see this:

> Take me with you, and we'll run away; be my king and take me to your room. We will be happy together, drink deep, and lose ourselves in love. No wonder all women love you!

One receives quite a different impression from the literalness of King James's translators:

> Draw me, we will run after thee: the king hath brought me into his chambers: we will be glad and rejoice in thee, we will remember thy love more than wine: the upright love thee.

The second passage offers an emotional challenge in every phrase and a mystery in many; the first passage would fit comfortably into a movie made for adolescents (no wine allowed). It mirrors a certain kind of modern world. The Good News Bible, which is endorsed by everyone from the Catholics to the Southern Baptists, has sold tens of millions of copies.

In some sense, that means its methods "work." But no figures are offered for the people it repels. Allan Massie, a British writer, made a memorable comment on Bible translations and their connections with readers: "I once argued the matter with a Bishop of the Episcopal Church of Scotland who defended the use of the new modern versions in church. 'I find,' he said with a degree of complacency, 'that it is usually people who no longer attend Church who object to the change.' 'Might this be why they no longer come to Church?' I asked, but my question was brushed aside."[28]

It is impossible to say whether modern language and modern music inspire more people than they irritate or bore. What is certain is that religious leaders think they do. Modern versions of the Word have therefore become the dominant tools of evangelical and megachurch worship, and nothing is more common than for mainstream churches to feature them in the afternoon "contemporary" service that "supplements" the "traditional" morning service, while insinuating a contemporary Bible and a contemporary songbook into the traditional service itself.

The (no doubt unfair) assumption is that the target audience possesses a limited vocabulary that it has no interest in expanding and that prospective Christians' only interest in religion lies in immediacy, sincerity, and spontaneity. Oddly, however, there is always the sense that self-consciously "contemporary" services are indeed self-conscious and need to be *performed.*

This could be said of virtually all religious services; they are tools and technology of some kind, and used for a purpose. Yet in traditional services, no matter how complicated, contrivance is, paradoxically, much less noticeable. The contrivers lived long ago. You don't see them parking their cars in the lot next door and entering the church with notes for yet another revision of the service. Worship teams, youth teams, outreach teams, mission statements, a new version of the Bible—these are things that have to be created right now, almost before your eyes, or they will not seem contemporary. The sense of contrivance and performance is especially acute in contemporary church music. A Methodist pastor puts it well: "Some contemporary music is very good, but it's more for the soloist than for the congregation."

Much of the contemporary repertoire has been influenced—at a considerable distance—by African American music. During the past fifty years, a great deal has been done to draw together the traditions of "white" gospel and "black" gospel and make them mutually accessible. Well-produced recordings and videos, such as those promoted by Bill and Gloria Gaither, have done much to ensure the national popularity of a kind of fusion gospel sound. But the dynamic balance of performance and participation, vitally important in African American churches, has seldom been maintained in other congregations. Even small black churches often have superb performance traditions; they produce singers and musicians who accomplish rigorously demanding musical tasks, while continuing African American traditions of exuberant audience involvement. But few contemporary evangelical churches—even megachurches with large musical programs—have been able to achieve this productive tension.

Many contemporary songs have choruses in which all can join, but those sections are almost always simpler and more repetitive than even the most rudimentary choruses in the older repertoire. The real emphasis is on the musicians' development of the verses and the bridge, in the kind of performance familiar to people who attend rock or pop concerts. A solo provided by the lead musician is usually expected to provide a time for meditation, but in any secular case it would simply be considered an instrumental interlude. The chord progressions are reassuringly familiar to the rock or pop audience, while the instruments themselves are the usual rock-concert apparatus: guitars always, and usually drums, keyboards, and electric bass. Loudspeakers, projectors, and electronic instruments are highly visible, as at a rock concert—on the stage, next to the preacher, often dominating the preacher.[29]

Most standard hymns and gospel songs can be accompanied either by a guitar or by a symphony orchestra; they can take almost any mood or coloration.[30] This can be said of very little contemporary Christian music. Slow it down, and it doesn't become more reflective; orchestrate it fully, and it just gets louder. Audience response is similarly unnuanced. It matches the response in concert venues, where music is appreciated for its energy, its volume, and its length. Many "contemporary" churches open their services with thirty to forty-five minutes of music and offer more music later on. Probably few people passing on the street would guess that the sound was part of a religious ritual. It doesn't sound like *church*. But the people standing and singing along inside often want much more of it. For them, the music isn't a "performance"; it's the Worship part of the service.

Obviously, this tool has struck a vein. People who aren't comforted or inspired by it have no more reason to argue that it isn't comforting and inspiring than the clergyman had to baffle himself with the mysterious appeal of "Sweet Hour of Prayer." What works in American Christianity is seldom what anyone would have expected to work, and it has never worked for everyone. Those for whom it doesn't work find it as mysterious as adventism or Pentecostalism or even Roman Catholicism—as those are construed by the people unreached by them. And no one can calculate its longevity. No one can say how long the new evangelicalism, in which not looking or sounding like a church is an essential function of a church, will continue to give millions of Americans a powerful connection with God.

In some circles, the reaction is already strong against it. Many pastors still preach from the King James Bible, and some now make it a battle cry. Younger evangelical pastors sometimes comment—though not in public forums—that they would love for their congregations to sing "Come, Thou Fount of Every Blessing" (1758) and hear "sermons about theology" delivered in "real theological language," but they fear their congregations wouldn't accept it. Church members often voice the same preferences, regretting that their pastors won't "move on to something more interesting." At some point, these people may get together.

In the meantime, there has been a technological revolution even more important than the invention of the electric guitar. The Internet has been the means by which millions of Christians, both contemporary mainstream and contemporary evangelical, have learned that American Christianity has more resources than those they encounter at ten o'clock on a typical Sunday morning. The Internet will show you that there were such people as Isaac Watts, Charles Price Jones, and Fanny Crosby; it will show you performances (competent as well as incompetent) of the songs they wrote; it will show you deep as well as cheap theology; and it will show you how to buy the songs, the sermons, and the Bible commentaries that are not "contemporary." By making religious history—the history of the Word as spoken, read, and sung— immediately accessible, the Internet multiplies opportunities for creative rediscovery of roads already taken—in short, for historical change. An old road is a new one, when you find it for yourself, and any road can start you on a journey to the ends of the earth.

But this thought introduces, for a final time, the problem of making predictions about America's religious life.

UNFINISHED
CATHEDRALS

During the past two centuries, nothing has been more fervently denounced by evangelical Christians than the Church of Jesus Christ of Latter-day Saints. One can hardly imagine an evangelical bookstore without a stock of anti-Mormon literature. Yet Mitt Romney, an active Mormon, carried all the evangelical states with ease during the 2012 presidential election. Even a few years ago, no one could have predicted this strange transformation, any more than people in 1820 could have predicted the rise of Mormonism, or anything like it, from the burned-over district of western New York.

In the same way, probably no one in 1960, when the first Catholic president was elected, would have predicted that within fifty years, despite the vast resurgence of evangelical Protestantism, there would not be one Protestant on the Supreme Court—and, more important, that almost no one would notice or care. Of course, no pundit predicted the resurgence either.

The brightest people sometimes make the worst predictions and generalizations. In 1927 Sigmund Freud published *The Future of an Illusion*. The illusion was religion; its future, according to Freud, was bleak. A century before, John Adams had complained that the great figures of the Enlightenment had thought the same thing. In 1835 Alexis de Tocqueville snickered solemnly about all the intellectuals (except himself) who had predicted the withering of Christianity under the fierce heat of modern democratic education. In 1899 Mark Twain predicted that within two generations, Christian Science would become the second-most important religion in the world and "the governing power in the [American] Republic." And speaking of the Mormons: in 1992 Harold Bloom, a well-known literary critic, argued that they would "soon" become "the Established Church of the American West" and by 2000 would help to "transform our nation" into an authoritarian religious regime.[1]

In the nineteenth century, America's most popular lecturer appears to have been Robert Ingersoll, who gave his mainly Christian audiences reason after reason for thinking that their beliefs were doomed. The audiences came, paid, listened, and went home, happy to have been entertained; they then returned to church on Sunday. Something similar seems to have resulted from the past fifteen years of best-selling books by scientific atheists.

The lesson is not that the atheists were wrong (or right) or that Mark Twain knew nothing about Christian Science—he was very well informed. It's only that the patterns we seek when we make predictions cannot be found, and fixed, within the intricate web of individual choices and priorities, deep values and immediate responses, that are constantly at work in American belief and practice. It is a fabric so rich and wide that its complexities can scarcely be imagined, yet it can tremble at the touch of a William Miller or a Mary Baker Eddy.

Or at the touch of some secular invention. The Internet has become a tool of religious change and, possibly, of revolution. I have mentioned several of its functions. It provides an accessible perspective on the past and thus a critical perspective on the present, and it shows how rich in religious options the present really is. It gives people a new ability to find a church that, whether it challenges or consoles, is the church for *them*. In the late nineteenth century, towns such as Jackson, Michigan, offered a menu of religious choices. By the late twentieth century, Ralph Ellison was able to liken all American cultural options to information stored in a (then-primitive) computer—accessible to any kind of person.[2] In the twenty-first century, the Internet allows everyone, everywhere, to select a church anywhere in the nation and enjoy its otherwise invisible fellowship. On most Sundays, most people associated with megachurches are probably "attending" online. They know, and the megachurches know, that this isn't really "going to church," but it's a connection with church, and it often leads people to unite more firmly to a religious community. The community, however, is first identified by its presence on the Net. Even tiny congregations now feel the need to define themselves online. The elderly leader of a little congregation in the Lake Superior country expressed a nearly universal feeling. She was asked whether her church had a good website. "I know, I know!" she said. "I know we have *got* to do something about that!" Indeed they do.

Some devout believers think they know better about all this. They think they have identified—without benefit of electronic methods—the true form of Christianity, together with all the good things that will happen if only people will embrace that form. Their ideas of truth vary greatly in substance, but the form is almost always that special American combination of the primitive church and the progressive church. True, original Christianity, which is simultaneously the only Christianity that can lead America into the future, has been sketched by persuasive representatives of both the religious Left and the religious Right.[3] Their sketches differ, although each assumes a coincidence of the biblically true and the socially useful that only a preexistent faith can recommend. There is no reason to think that any of these visions will prevail.

It is possible, however, to meet people who may be shaping some of Christianity's future, by what they are doing day by day.

Carol Phillips is the pastor of two churches whose address is Bridgeport, Illinois. One, First Presbyterian, stands at the head of Main Street; the other, Pisgah(!) Presbyterian, is out on the prairie, a few miles south of town. In 1910, during its big oil boom, Bridgeport was known as the most wide-open town on the B&O railroad. Now it is quiet, small, and getting smaller, with few businesses and many Social Security checks. Reverend Phillips is a cheerful, energetic woman who believes that "the Lord has a sense of humor." She works hard to maintain the modest membership of her churches. Her goal, she says, "is to keep a little corner of Christendom here in Bridgeport." One way of doing that is "missions." By "missions" she doesn't mean revival campaigns; she means the practical work her congregation does to help other people—hurricane victims in New Orleans, old people around Bridgeport who need ramps on their houses so they can keep living at home. This, she believes, is what gives the congregation "vision" and inspires it to defend its embattled province of the Kingdom. So far, it's succeeding.

The largest church in San Diego, California, is the Rock, a megachurch founded by an articulate and charismatic former football player, Miles McPherson. He is African American, and his congregation is a fair representation of San Diego's many ethnicities. The Rock experienced large growth a few years ago; now it has leveled off, and the leadership is reflecting seriously on the difference between an institution providing life-changing evangelism and an institution ministering to people who have already been converted. This appears to mean a shift from "outreach" to "inreach." The church has

FIGURE 11.1. *The Rock Church, San Diego, fully prepared for Sunday services: band instruments, a rotating platform, 3,500 seats, and a larger collection of permanent lighting (sixty-three Vari-Lite fixtures) than any other venue in Southern California. Photo by Stephen Cox; image used by permission of the Rock Church.*

outreach groups for every conceivable purpose, from running (its runners' ministry has 700 associates) to home building in Mexico, but it has fewer family groups, Bible study groups, and so forth than most other megachurches. The Rock has a core group of thousands of adherents, but even within the core, there is considerable "churning" as people are drawn in, evangelized, and then depart for who knows where. What would maturity and stability look like for such a church? That is what the people at the Rock want to find out.

On the surface, no two churches could be more different from each other than the Rock and Pisgah Presbyterian. The salient fact, however, is that in each case individuals matter, and matter very much, whether they are leaders or the people whom the churches need to find, inspire, and make into leaders if they can. Because individual decisions are so important, no generalization about American Christianity or prediction about its future has much hope of being right, even if it recognizes (as I, for one, think it must) both Pisgah and the Rock.

And that's not to mention something that includes all apparent opposites: the religious marketplace on display in most large cities of America. One of these markets of Christianity can be seen within a short drive from the Rock. It's a downtown neighborhood known for its restaurants, bars, hordes of young people, and devotion to countercultural activities. Here one might expect to find no churches at all. Instead, one finds a sizable Roman Catholic church, welcoming both Latino and "Anglo" communicants; a Pentecostal church of similar composition; a Pentecostal church with services in Spanish; a Southern Baptist church with congregants of all ethnicities; an evangelical church notable for its enthusiastic singing of nineteenth-century hymns and gospel songs, translated into Vietnamese; a Lutheran church; a non-Roman, gay-oriented Catholic congregation whose "cathedral" is a tiny chapel of the Disciples of Christ church; a Kingdom Hall of Jehovah's Witnesses; and the most traditional Episcopal church in southern California, with a congregation that includes strong representations of gays, African Americans, Latinos, Asian Americans, and Pacific Islanders. Even more churches might be listed. This marketplace of faith is open every day, offering goods ranging from the most "traditional" to the most "progressive" religious experience; and success or failure in the market shows up plainly, in a new roof or a cracked sidewalk, a sudden increase or decrease in the availability of parking spaces in the street outside.

This book has considered a variety of metaphors for Christianity in America—marketplaces, cornfields, islands, menus, rabbit catching, and my own favorite, prospecting for oil. None is universally applicable, although some of the best metaphors, such as the neighborhood marketplace that I just described, are also realities. The Rock Church is massively real and statistically successful, but it also appears to symbolize the unknown future of the new religious movements it represents. Reverend Phillips's two little churches, the offspring of farmers with teams of oxen and a faith in primitive Christianity, present a living picture of modern interests and mainstream survivalism. Then there's the overshadowing form with which this book began: the uncompleted Church of St. John the Divine. The fact that the great cathedral hasn't been finished, and probably never will be, can be taken as a comment both on American Christianity and on all attempts to analyze it. Every one of them, including this book, is an unfinished structure, missing an uncountable number of arches and buttresses.

Perhaps it's appropriate to conclude with the image of one of the smallest churches in America. It stands on U.S. Highway 41, an hour's drive northeast of Reverend Phillips's churches. Its address is Farmersburg, Indiana. Its name is the Taylor Prayer Chapel.

The chapel was erected by Russell Taylor (1899–1995), a Methodist minister, in 1956.[4] It is built of concrete blocks, painted white—materials that make it appear recent and utilitarian as well as quaintly old-fashioned. Like the Cathedral Church of St. John the Divine, it imitates the cruciform plan of a medieval cathedral. It has a nave, twenty-six feet long; a chancel, three feet deep; and two transepts, seventeen feet wide (together). It is the wrong shape for a country church, and the wrong size for a cathedral. But (contrast it with the Church of St. John the Divine) its transepts are completed; its spire is completed; the whole structure is completed. Reverend Taylor knew what he wanted and what he could afford, and he built and finished what he could: a place where Christian experience can happen, and continue to happen, in

FIGURE 11.2. *The Taylor Prayer Chapel, Farmersburg, Indiana: a mightier fortress than you would guess. Photo by Stephen Cox.*

whatever ways it may shape itself for the people who choose to visit there.

The chapel sits next to a ten-foot highway embankment, from which a quick exit is needed; the semis go pretty fast on 41. When you walk inside, you see light wooden pews for about twenty-five people, an altar with an open Bible and a picture of Jesus, and a boombox on which, if you want, you can play religious music (CDs stacked nearby). It's an entrance to a variety of religious experience that would have interested William James.

Sometimes people use the chapel for weddings, and they can contribute for that or not, as they please. Some do and some don't. There is a box by the door where you can leave your own contribution, if you want, and a book where you can enter any comments, prayers, or thanksgivings you care to write. Many people visit the chapel and don't write anything; many others record their thoughts. You can read back through their comments, year by year.

Some people pray for healing for themselves. Many more pray for friends or relatives who are sick, or out of work, or "on drugs." But most people just express their appreciation for the chapel itself. They say it is beautiful and they are glad that it is there, and that they are there too. They never think it necessary to mention their denomination or their local church, if any. They just reveal that something important happened to them, and that the chapel made it possible.

The most interesting feature of this little cathedral may be the door. It has no lock. For almost sixty years the door has been open, twenty-four hours a day, 365 days a year. Occasionally there's a theft. Years ago, somebody stole the Bible—but thirteen years later, it was returned. People are unpredictable. Vandals, who are almost as prevalent in the hinterland as they are in New York City, have not been much of a problem. Strangely, the chapel is a sacred space, even for people who recognize no other sanctities.

The visible sign on the chapel's tiny steeple asks, "Have You Prayed about It?" "It" can mean a multitude of things, and the question itself can be answered in a multitude of ways. So can the invisible sign that says, "What do you make of this? How can you explain this place?"

Here are questions more imposing than the massive form of St. John the Divine, or the massive accumulation of statistics about the sociology of American religion. But if the questions in that invisible sign are ever adequately answered, we will know that Christianity in America has run its course, that nothing more can be expected, that the revolution of American Christianity is at last at an end.

NOTES

CHAPTER 1: RUINS OR FOUNDATIONS?

1. Qtd. in Douglass Shand-Tucci, *Ralph Adams Cram: An Architect's Four Quests* (Amherst: University of Massachusetts Press, 2005), 191. For information about the construction process, see also "The Cathedral of St. John the Divine," *Pacific Monthly* (1906): 437–440; and Ralph Adams Cram, *My Life in Architecture* (Boston: Little, Brown, 1936), 167–184. For the dimensions of this church, compared with those of its competitors, see Shand-Tucci, *Ralph Adams Cram*, 270, 543. According to its plans, the Church of St. John the Divine is the largest cathedral in *volume*, 16,822,000 cubic feet.

2. Frederick William Faber, "Faith of Our Fathers" (1849), a hymn sung at the funeral of Franklin Roosevelt in 1945.

CHAPTER 2: FINDING OIL

1. Edward J. Larson, *Summer for the Gods: The Scopes Trial and America's Continuing Debate over Science and Religion* (Cambridge, MA: Harvard University Press, 1997), presents the full account.

2. Stephen Cox, *The New Testament and Literature: A Guide to Literary Patterns* (Chicago: Open Court, 2006).

3. Robert D. Putnam and David E. Campbell, *American Grace: How Religion Divides and Unites Us* (New York: Simon and Schuster, 2010), 122.

4. Ibid., 111–112, 122–123.

5. Paul E. Johnson, *A Shopkeeper's Millennium: Society and Revivals in Rochester, New York, 1815–1837* (New York: Hill and Wang, 1978), 120. Johnson, who produced a highly influential explanation of American revivalism, exemplifies the both-at-once approach; see, for instance, 136–141, 201–203. He proposes to "take religion seriously," to study revivalism as "a religious solution, addressed to religious problems," yet he also proposes to find "the secular origins of religion" in the quest for "social control." Another influential book broadens its explanation beyond the middle class but attributes the mighty Christian temperance movement simultaneously to social "confidence" and social "anxiety"; see W. J. Rorabaugh, *The Alcoholic Republic* (New York: Oxford University Press, 1979), 176, 189, 202, 210–213.

6. Rodney Stark and Roger Finke, *Acts of Faith: Explaining the Human Side of Religion* (Berkeley: University of California Press, 2000), 57–79.

7. Laurie Goodstein, "Percentage of Protestant Americans Is in Steep Decline, Study Finds," *New York Times*, October 9, 2012, http://www.nytimes.com/2012/10/10/us/study-finds-that-percentage-of-protestant-americans-is-declining.html?emc=eta1 ("Seismic"); the Pew Forum on Religion and Public Life, "'Nones' on the Rise" (2012), http://www.pewforum.org/uploadedFiles/Topics/Religious_Affiliation/Unaffiliated/NonesOnTheRise-full.pdf. Caution must be used when reading statistical reports on American religion. Goodstein, for example, headlines the idea that "for the first time since researchers began tracking the religious identity of Americans, fewer than half said they were Protestants." When I ask young members of today's large and growing evangelical fellowships whether they are "Protestants," they ordinarily look puzzled and say they are not; they are simply "Christians" or "nondenominational," although their beliefs and practices are more Protestant than those of the mainline Protestant churches. The real import of recent studies is that people in their late teens and early twenties (ages 18–22) have only a 66 percent rate of religious "affiliation," something looser and less demanding than "adherence" to a church. But polling samples cannot hope to represent the diversity of American religious opinion. The reports of the Pew Forum, as well as those of Putnam and Campbell, are based on phone interviews with 0.001 percent of the American population. When these respondents are subdivided by age, class, race, gender, geography, occupation, and denomination, the samples dwindle almost out of sight, and so does their credibility. Furthermore, people discussing religion often tell interviewers what they think the latter want to hear. Thus, Putnam and Campbell (546–547) find that only small minorities of Catholics, evangelicals, and Mormons (how many Mormons could possibly have been asked?) believe there is only one true religion. In view of the histories and teachings of these people's churches, this report is literally incredible. The results of Finke and Stark's study, by contrast, are distinguished by the richness and diversity of historical data supporting them.

8. Roger Finke and Rodney Stark, *The Churching of America, 1776–2005: Winners and Losers in Our Religious Economy*, 2nd ed. (New Brunswick, NJ: Rutgers University Press, 2005), 23, 246. Finke and Stark's figures for church adherence include their estimates for the numbers of minor children of adult church members, a subject on which religious denominations have various standards of reporting.

9. Ibid., especially 235–283.

10. *Yearbook of American and Canadian Churches*, ed. Eileen W. Lindner (Nashville, TN: Abingdon, 2012), 369.

11. Stark and Finke (*Acts of Faith*, 208–213) divide churches into five categories in respect to their "tension" with their environment and their demands on their members, from undemanding "liberal" churches to "moderate," "conservative," "strict," and "ultrastrict" ones. Thus they group Episcopalians with Methodists ("liberal") and Pentecostals with Mormons ("strict"), despite the fact that few members of these churches would recognize the affinity, and many would vigorously reject it.

12. Calculated from the denomination's statistics for America in its annually published yearbook. See *Year Book of the International Bible Students Association* (Brooklyn: Watch Tower, 1941), 71; *Yearbook of Jehovah's Witnesses* (Brooklyn: Watch Tower, 1942), 41; ibid. (2000), 38–39; ibid. (2001), 38–39.

13. See the church's website, http://herchurch.org.

14. Bob Jones Sr. qtd. in Douglas Carl Abrams, *Selling the Old-Time Religion: American Fundamentalists and Mass Culture, 1920–1940* (Athens: University of Georgia Press, 2001), 28; Anne Bradstreet, "To My Dear Children," in *The Works of Anne Bradstreet*, ed. Jeannine Hensley (Cambridge, MA: Belknap/Harvard University Press, 1967), 241, 243–244.

15. Anson Rogers Graves, *The Farmer Boy Who Became a Bishop* (Akron, OH: New Werner, 1911), 168.

16. Finke and Stark, *Churching*, 166; *Yearbook of American and Canadian Churches*, ed. Constant H. Jacquet Jr. (Nashville, TN: Abingdon, 1970), 211–212; (1971), 203–207.

17. Paul Harvey, *Through the Storm, Through the Night: A History of African American Christianity* (Lanham, MD: Rowman and Little-field, 2011), 72.

18. Charles Edwin Jones, *Black Holiness* (Metuchen, NJ: American Theological Library Association/Scarecrow, 1987). Harvey gives a good picture of the African American creation of churches (*Through the Storm*, esp. 8–19).

19. William James, *The Varieties of Religious Experience: A Study in Human Nature* (1902; repr., New York: Modern Library, 1936), 7–8.

20. Ibid., 4, xvii.

21. Ibid., 120, 511.

22. Johnson, *Shopkeeper's Millennium*, 140–141; George R. Knight, *William Miller and the Rise of Adventism* (Nampa, ID: Pacific Press Publishing Association, 2010), 15–20; Gary Land, "The Historians and the Millerites: An Historiographical Essay," *Andrews University Seminary Studies* 32 (Autumn 1994): 227–246.

23. Minnie Kennedy on Aimee Semple McPherson, in Lately Thomas, *Storming Heaven: The Lives and Turmoils of Minnie Kennedy and Aimee Semple McPherson* (New York: William Morrow, 1970), 100.

24. Stark and Finke, *Acts of Faith*, 86. As the authors themselves observe (122), people who join the churches frequented by their family and friends often *later* identify the purely religious needs they were seeking to satisfy—genuine needs, but previously unidentified.

25. Charles Grandison Finney, *Lectures on Revivals of Religion*, ed. William G. McLoughlin (1835; Cambridge, MA: Belknap/Harvard University Press, 1960), 9, 13, 275.

26. Dr. Frank Madison Reid III, of Bethel African Methodist Episcopal Church in Baltimore, qtd. in Putnam and Campbell, *American Grace*, 210–211.

27. Bernard Ruffin, *Fanny Crosby* (N.p.: United Church, 1976), 158, 172.

28. Fanny J. Crosby, *Memories of Eighty Years* (Grand Rapids, MI: Baker Book House, 1986), 111–112; Ruffin, *Fanny Crosby*, 68. The lyrics are by Isaac Watts (1707).

29. Ruffin, *Fanny Crosby*, 123, 125.

30. Fanny Crosby, "Blessed Assurance" (1873).

31. Julia Duin, "Serpent-Handling Pastor," *Washington Post*, May 29, 2012.

CHAPTER 3: THE MAINSTREAM AND THE CATARACTS

1. Historical information about Jackson and its churches is derived chiefly from King D. Beach, "I Wouldn't Change Lives with Anyone" (manuscript), 178–191; Charles V. DeLand, *DeLand's History of Jackson County, Michigan* ([Jackson, MI]: B. F. Bowen, 1903), 202–218; Charlotte Lockwood and Juanita M. Riedel, *Church on Main Street: A History of the First United Methodist Church, Jackson, Michigan* (Jackson, MI: First Methodist Church, 1984); Gilbert S. Loomis, *One Hundred Years in St. Paul's* (Jackson, MI: St. Paul's Episcopal Church, 1938); Richard Arthur Santer, "A Historical Geography of Jackson, Michigan" (PhD diss., Michigan State University, 1970); "First Presbyterian Church, Jackson, Michigan: 1883–2008," http://jacksonfirstpres.com/FPC-History-125years.pdf; *History of Jackson County, Michigan* (Chicago: Inter-State, 1881), 224, 512–523; *Jackson Michigan: Its Early Days* (1878; repr., L'Anse, MI: Mike Joki, n.d.); "Jackson Michigan: Sights and Scenes along the Michigan Central Line," entire issue of *Headlight* 2 (Aug. 1895); and Jackson city directories, 1867–2010.

2. Benjamin Franklin, *Autobiography, Poor Richard, and Later Writings*, ed. J. A. Leo Lemay (Washington, DC: Library of America, 1997), 667.

3. Roger Finke and Rodney Stark, *The Churching of America, 1776–2005: Winners and Losers in Our Religious Economy*, 2nd ed. (New Brunswick, NJ: Rutgers University Press, 2005), 156.

4. Edwin Scott Gaustad, *Liberty of Conscience: Roger Williams in America* (Grand Rapids, MI: Eerdmans, 1991), 90–96.

5. Finke and Stark, *Churching*, 157.

6. DeLand, *DeLand's History*, 213.

7. Finke and Stark, *Churching*, 202–203.

8. Peter Cartwright, *Autobiography of Peter Cartwright* (1856; repr., New York: Abingdon, 1956), 99.

9. Cf. the grudging concessions of Paul E. Johnson, in *A Shopkeeper's Millennium: Society and Revivals in Rochester, New York, 1815–1837* (New York: Hill and Wang, 1978), e.g., 118–121, 152–161, who is otherwise insistent (193n14) on capitalist "control" of churches through capitalist board members. Johnson is apparently under the illusion that churches are actually run by their trustees.

10. Loomis, *One Hundred Years*, 16.

11. Lockwood and Riedel, *Church*, 27; Loomis, *One Hundred Years*, 29.

12. On Protestants' symbolic differentiation from and competition with Catholics, see Ryan K. Smith, *Gothic Arches, Latin Crosses: Anti-Catholicism and American Church Designs in the Nineteenth Century* (Chapel Hill: University of North Carolina Press, 2006).

13. Arlan K. Gilbert, *Historic Hillsdale College: Pioneer in Higher Education, 1844–1900* (Hillsdale, MI: Hillsdale College Press, 1991), 29–30; DeLand, *DeLand's History*, 206, 208.

14. Edwin Scott Gaustad, *The Great Awakening in New England* (Gloucester, MA: Peter Smith, 1965), 38, 40–41, 74–75, 109.

15. William Ellery Channing, in William Henry Channing, *Memoir of William Ellery Channing* (London: John Chapman, 1848), 1.411.

16. Ibid., 1.350.

17. The last explanation is featured in John B. Buescher, *The Other Side of Salvation: Spiritualism and the Nineteenth-Century Religious Experience* (Boston: Skinner House Books, 2004), 119.

18. Gilbert, *Historic Hillsdale*, 20.

19. Acts 17:24.

20. *History of Jackson County*, 520–522.

21. 1 Samuel 28:7–24. Buescher, *Other Side*, offers a good history of spiritualism.

22. Advertisement, ca. 1930. In the 1850s and 1860s, the abolitionist-spiritualist utopian settlement Harmonia was built in the county just west of Jackson (Margaret Washington, *Sojourner Truth's America* [Urbana: University of Illinois Press, 2009], 277–280).

23. Mary Baker Eddy, *Science and Health With Key to the Scriptures* (Boston: Trustees under the Will of Mary Baker G. Eddy, n.d.), 16.

24. Mark Twain, *Christian Science* (New York: Harper, 1907), 84–86.

25. Andrew Carnegie, *Autobiography* (London: Constable, 1920), 338–340; Andrew Carnegie, *The Gospel of Wealth and Other Timely Essays* (New York: Century, 1900), 42 (cf. Matthew 20:1), 37 (cf. Deuteronomy 8:3), 30, 19 (altering Luke 2:14), 15.

26. "Tenth Anniversary of the Pastorate of Frederick Spence, D.D." (Jackson, MI: First Methodist Church, 1928), 12; Lockwood and Riedel, *Church*, 38, 42.

27. "Tenth Anniversary," 14.

28. Beach, "I Wouldn't Change," 178–181.

29. "Tenth Anniversary," 6.

30. Ibid., 14.

31. From 1940 to 1950, weekly church attendance reportedly increased only 2 percent, from 37 percent to 39 percent of the adult population. In the mid-1950s it rose to 49 percent, a likely effect of parents accompanying children to church. By 1975 it was back down to 40 percent. See *Yearbook of American and Canadian Churches*, ed. Constant H. Jacquet Jr. (Nashville, TN: Abingdon, 1991), 303–304.

32. Gaustad, *Great Awakening*, 20–21.

33. Loomis, *One Hundred Years*, 51, 64.

34. Sydney E. Ahlstrom, *A Religious History of the American People* (New Haven, CT: Yale University Press, 1972), 920; Joel A. Carpenter, "Fundamentalist Institutions and the Rise of Evangelical Protestantism, 1929–1942," *Church History* 49 (Mar. 1980): 62–75; Finke and Stark, *Churching*, 23.

35. Only 10 percent of the ministers were "Evangelicals," and only 10 percent were Baptists; the rest were mainly Lutherans (very overrepresented at 21 percent), Methodists (22 percent), Presbyterians (13 percent), Congregationalists (10 percent), and Episcopalians (6 percent). These statistics come from George Herbert Betts, *The Beliefs of 700 Ministers and Their Meaning for Religious Education* (New York: Abingdon, 1929), 24–60.

36. Ibid., 50.

37. Ibid.

38. 1 Corinthians 15:12–22.

39. Paul A. Carter, *The Decline and Revival of the Social Gospel: Social and Political Liberalism in American Protestant Churches, 1920–1940* (Ithaca, NY: Cornell University Press, 1954), 54.

40. J. Gresham Machen, *The Origin of Paul's Religion* (New York: Macmillan, 1921), 3. H. L. Mencken, a notorious foe of Christianity and particularly of fundamentalism, wrote that the fundamentalist Machen was to the fundamentalist Bryan "as the Matterhorn is to a wart" ("Dr. Fundamentalis," *Baltimore Evening Sun*, Jan. 18, 1937).

41. Finke and Stark, *Churching*, 246.

42. "Is God Dead?," *Time*, April 8, 1966; Jon Meacham, "The End of Christian America," *Newsweek*, April 3, 2009.

43. See, for instance, Galatians 1:6–9, 3:1, 4:9–11.

CHAPTER 4: THE MAKING OF REVIVAL

1. Revelation 21:2.

2. As described here, the last twenty-five seconds of the film are those that appear in the 1936 version, not the less interesting images incorporated in the 1948 rerelease.

3. George M. Marsden, *Jonathan Edwards: A Life* (New Haven, CT: Yale University Press, 2003), 31–32.

4. Ibid., 11; Iain H. Murray, *Jonathan Edwards: A New Biography* (Edinburgh: Banner of Truth Trust, 1987), 78–79.

5. Murray, *Jonathan Edwards*, 118.

6. Jonathan Edwards, *A Faithful Narrative of the Surprizing Work of God* (1737), in *The Works of Jonathan Edwards*, vol. 4, *The Great Awakening*, ed. C. C. Goen (New Haven, CT: Yale University Press, 1970), 152–155, 166–191.

7. Benjamin Franklin, *Autobiography, Poor Richard, and Later Writings*, ed. J. A. Leo Lemay (Washington, DC: Library of America, 1997), 669–670.

8. Edwin Scott Gaustad, *The Great Awakening in New England* (Gloucester, MA: Peter Smith, 1965), 36–41; Murray, *Jonathan Edwards*, 223–226.

9. Paul K. Conkin, *Cane Ridge: America's Pentecost* (Madison: University of Wisconsin Press, 1990), 89.

10. Peter Cartwright, *Autobiography of Peter Cartwright* (1856; repr., New York: Abingdon, 1956), 43–44.

11. Ibid., 43.

12. George R. Knight, *William Miller and the Rise of Adventism* (Nampa, ID: Pacific Press Publishing Association, 2010), 86–88.

13. Ibid., 180, 188–189.

14. Cartwright, *Autobiography*, 70–72. On the gates of hell, see Matthew 16:18.

15. On social factors, see Conkin, *Cane Ridge*, 103–104, 164. Conkin emphasizes the measures I mention here, as do Roger Finke and Rodney Stark in *The Churching of America, 1776–2005: Winners and Losers in Our Religious Economy*, 2nd ed. (New Brunswick, NJ: Rutgers University Press, 2005), 88–99, although their stress on planning and order may exceed the evidence; compare Conkin, *Cane Ridge*, 85–86.

16. Gregory Smith, "Palin V.P. Nomination Puts Spotlight on Pentecostalism" (Pew Research Center, 2008), http://pewresearch.org/pubs/949/palin-nomination-pentecostalism.

17. Charles Grandison Finney, *Lectures on Revivals of Religion,* ed. William G. McLoughlin (1835; Cambridge, MA: Belknap/Harvard University Press, 1960), 33, 54.

18. Alexander Pope, *An Essay on Criticism*, pt. 1, l.153.

19. Harold Frederic, *The Damnation of Theron Ware* (1896; repr., New York: Holt, Rinehart and Winston, 1958), 180.

20. Ibid., 173; Mark 9:24 (emphasis added).

21. Whitney R. Cross, *The Burned-over District: The Social and Intellectual History of Enthusiastic Religion in Western New York, 1800–1850* (New York: Harper and Row, 1950), 152.

22. Romans 7:14–25; Stephen Cox, *The New Testament and Literature: A Guide to Literary Patterns* (Chicago: Open Court, 2006), 127–134.

23. Cross, *Burned-over District*, 182–183.

24. Charles D. Pigeon, "Thoughts on the New-Haven Theology," *Literary and Theological Review* 5 (Mar. 1838): 158.

25. Finney, *Lectures*, 9.

26. Ibid., 9–10, 200–205.

27. Ibid., 14, 15, 52–71, 238–239, 284, 244.

28. Albert Dod qtd. in ibid., xxxviii.

29. Qtd. in ibid., l.

30. Charles Grandison Finney, *The Memoirs of Charles G. Finney: The Complete Restored Text*, ed. Garth M. Rosell and Richard A. G. Dupuis (Grand Rapids, MI: Zondervan, 1989), 78.

31. Edith L. Blumhofer, *Her Heart Can See: The Life and Hymns of Fanny J. Crosby* (Grand Rapids, MI: Eerdmans, 2005), 161, 151.

CHAPTER 5: STARS THAT RISE AND SET

1. See, for example, Sinclair Lewis's foreword to Paxton Hibben, *Henry Ward Beecher: An American Portrait* (New York: Readers Club, 1942), vii–ix.

2. Debby Applegate, *The Most Famous Man in America: The Biography of Henry Ward Beecher* (New York: Doubleday, 2006), 282.

3. 1 Corinthians 13:13.

4. Applegate, *Most Famous Man*, 300, 470.

5. Qtd. in ibid., 291.

6. Ibid., 440–442, 451, 455.

7. Bruce J. Evensen, *God's Man for the Gilded Age: D. L. Moody and the Rise of Modern Mass Evangelism* (New York: Oxford University Press, 2003), 10–11, 3.

8. Ibid., 14–47.

9. Kenneth W. Osbeck, *101 Hymn Stories* (Grand Rapids, MI: Kregel, 1982), 251–252. Elizabeth Clephane, the poem's author, based the work on Matthew 18:12–14 and Luke 15:4–7.

10. Martyn McGeown, "The Life and Theology of D. L. Moody," Covenant Protestant Reformed Church, Ballymena, Northern Ireland, n.d., http://www.cprf.co.uk/articles/moody.htm.

11. William T. Ellis, *"Billy" Sunday: The Man and His Message* (N.p.: L. T. Myers, 1914), 15.

12. Ibid., 18. Ellis's book provides one of the most detailed accounts of evangelistic techniques ever published, rivaling those of Cartwright and Finney.

13. "He himself," reported the *Louisville Herald*, "says he is an 'old-fashioned preacher of the old-fashioned gospel,' which is half true" (qtd. in Homer Rodeheaver, *Twenty Years with Billy Sunday* [Nashville, TN: Cokesbury, 1936], 101).

14. Qtd. in Ellis, *"Billy" Sunday*, 77.

15. Qtd. in ibid., 152–153; scripture allusions, Matthew 9:9 and Isaiah 55:7.

16. Ellis, *"Billy" Sunday*, 61.

17. Ibid., 299–300.

18. Ibid., 264.

19. In the 1960 film *Elmer Gantry*, Burt Lancaster attempts an imitation of Sunday's antics, including his base sliding, although Lancaster's unctuous manner is not at all like Sunday's.

20. Rodeheaver, *Twenty Years*, 142.

21. The late Paul Saltman, personal communication; Lately Thomas, *Storming Heaven: The Lives and Turmoils of Minnie Kennedy and Aimee Semple McPherson* (New York: William Morrow, 1970), 261.

22. Aimee Semple McPherson, qtd. by Roberta Semple Salter, and Aimee Semple McPherson, qtd. in Matthew Avery Sutton, *Aimee Semple McPherson and the Resurrection of Christian America* (Cambridge, MA: Harvard University Press, 2007), 77.

23. Ibid., 21.

24. Ibid., 51–52, 291n19.

25. For the colorful details see Thomas, *Storming*; and Lately Thomas, *The Vanishing Evangelist: The Aimee Semple McPherson Kidnaping [sic] Affair* (New York: Viking, 1959).

26. See the information provided by Sutton (*Aimee Semple*

McPherson, 34–36), who rightly observes that McPherson's "church welcomed all types of people."

27. Ibid., 280.

28. http://www.foursquare.org/missions, http://www.foursquare .org/news/article/foursquare_by_the_numbers_report_april_2013.

29. Marshall Frady, *Billy Graham: A Parable of American Righteousness* (Boston: Little, Brown, 1979), 313.

30. Paul K. Conkin, *Cane Ridge: America's Pentecost* (Madison: University of Wisconsin Press, 1990), 168.

31. Gilbert Tennent (on terror) and Stephen Williams (on Jonathan Edwards) qtd. in Iain H. Murray, *Jonathan Edwards: A New Biography* (Edinburgh: Banner of Truth Trust, 1987), 133, 169.

32. The late David Noel Freedman, personal communication.

33. Peter Cartwright, *Autobiography of Peter Cartwright* (1856; repr., New York: Abingdon, 1956), 232–233. Of the ninety sermons delivered by Billy Sunday in a typical crusade, only two appear to emphasize families (Rodeheaver, *Twenty Years*, 27–30).

34. Jacob Abbott, *Rollo at Play*, rev. ed. (New York: Sheldon, 1865), 79–86.

35. John Bunyan, *The Pilgrim's Progress* (London: Nath. Ponder, 1679), 2–5; Matthew 10:36–37.

36. The Rock, in San Diego, is one of these; see chapter 11.

CHAPTER 6: THE LOW WALL OF SEPARATION

1. James Madison, *The Federalist, No. 10*, in *The Debate on the Constitution, Part One* (Washington, DC: Library of America, 1993), 411.

2. Thomas Jefferson to Danbury Baptist Association, January 1, 1802, in *The Papers of Thomas Jefferson*, vol. 36 (Princeton, NJ: Princeton University Press, 2009), 258; Thomas Jefferson, Second Inaugural Address, in *The Writings of Thomas Jefferson*, ed. Albert Ellery Bergh (Washington, DC: Thomas Jefferson Memorial Association, 1907), 3.383.

3. George Washington, *The Diaries of George Washington*, ed. George C. Fitzpatrick (Boston: Houghton Mifflin, 1925), 4.50.

4. John C. Calhoun, Senate speech, March 4, 1850, *The Papers of John C. Calhoun*, ed. Clyde N. Wilson and Shirley Bright Cook (Columbia: University of South Carolina Press, 2003), 27.199–200.

5. Julia Ward Howe, "The Battle Hymn of the Republic" (1861); compare Genesis 3:14–15.

6. Peter Cartwright, *Autobiography of Peter Cartwright* (1856; repr., New York: Abingdon, 1956), 165.

7. The sickening facts are presented by W. J. Rorabaugh, *The Alcoholic Republic* (New York: Oxford University Press, 1979), 95–98, 113–119, 233.

8. Cartwright, *Autobiography*, 99, 128–129, 145–147, 180–181; Charles Grandison Finney, *Lectures on Revivals of Religion*, ed. William G. McLoughlin (1835; Cambridge, MA: Belknap/Harvard University Press, 1960), 416; Rorabaugh, *Alcoholic Republic*, 28, 81.

9. John Allen Krout, *The Origins of Prohibition* (New York: Russell and Russell, 1925), 164–168; Psalm 104:15; John 2:9–10.

10. Krout, *Origins of Prohibition*, 84–85, 119–123, 153–181. For later examples of church resistance to the prohibition movement, see Paul Harvey, *Freedom's Coming: Religious Culture and the Shaping of the South from the Civil War through the Civil Rights Era* (Chapel Hill: University of North Carolina Press, 2005), 55.

11. Rorabaugh, *Alcoholic Republic*, 232–233.

12. See, for example, Jack S. Blocker Jr., *Retreat from Reform: The Prohibition Movement in the United States, 1890–1913* (Westport, CT: Greenwood, 1976), 13–14, 32, 241. Paul E. Johnson offers a theory of social control by an agitated upper middle class; see Johnson, *A Shopkeeper's Millennium: Society and Revivals in Rochester, New York, 1815–1837* (New York: Hill and Wang, 1978), 128–141. Similar ideas have been used to analyze the problem that temperance tried to solve. An otherwise excellent book labors to *explain* people's desire to drink cheap liquor, as if that required an explanation (Rorabaugh, *Alcoholic Republic*, 149–183). The proffered explanation has to do with massive anxieties allegedly produced by the economic and ideological stresses of life in a capitalist republic, as opposed, presumably, to the restful lives of precapitalist sodbusters.

13. See Frances Willard, *Glimpses of Fifty Years: The Autobiography of an American Woman* (Chicago: H. J. Smith, 1889), 127 (a characteristically tepid discussion of religion); Blocker, *Retreat from Reform*, 31. The novelist and politician Upton Sinclair is an example of a socialist who waged a lifelong war against liquor. See his *Cup of Fury* (Great Neck, NY: Channel, 1956), which endured at least nine printings.

14. Blocker, *Retreat from Reform*, 19.

15. Ibid., 12. The figures pertain to 1890–1913.

16. Sidney E. Ahlstrom, *A Religious History of the American People* (New Haven, CT: Yale University Press, 1972), 653–669.

17. Cartwright, *Autobiography*, 270–287, 239, 114–115.

18. Walter Rauschenbusch, *A Theology for the Social Gospel* (New York: Macmillan, 1917), 111–112. *Christianizing the Social Order* (New York: Macmillan, 1912) is the title of another book by Rauschenbusch.

19. *Almanac of Theodore Roosevelt*, http://www.theodore-roosevelt .com/images/research/speeches/trreactionairies.pdf.

20. Rauschenbusch, "The Kingdom of God" (1913), in *The Social Gospel in America: 1870–1920*, ed. Robert T. Handy (New York: Oxford University Press, 1966), 264–267; Rauschenbusch, *Theology*, 17, 52, 55, 126.

21. Ahlstrom, *Religious History*, 802–804.

22. Qtd. in Herbert Wallace Schneider, *Religion in 20th Century America* (1952; repr., Cambridge, MA: Harvard University Press, 1967), 97–98.

23. Qtd. in ibid., 77.

24. Luke Eugene Ebersole, *Church Lobbying in the Nation's Capital* (New York: Macmillan, 1951), 121–122, 132–133, 138, 141.

25. Ibid., 125, 128, 134, 146–147.

26. Ibid., 33–35.

27. Ibid., 38–39.

28. Ibid., 48–56.

29. The remarkable story is documented by Roger Finke and Rodney Stark, *The Churching of America, 1776–2005: Winners and Losers in Our Religious Economy*, 2nd ed. (New Brunswick, NJ: Rutgers University Press, 2005), 218–224.

30. Schneider, *Religion in 20th Century America*, 84–85.

31. Jack Jenkins, "'Protest Chaplains' Shepherd Movement's Spiritual Side," *Washington Post*, October 10, 2011; Charles W. Dunn, ed., *The Future of Religion in American Politics* (Lexington: University Press of Kentucky, 2009), 28; Barack Obama, interview, WHO-TV, Des Moines, Mar. 12, 2012, http://whotv.com/2012/03/13 /backman-interview-channel-13s-john-backman-interviews -president-obama/.

32. Finke and Stark emphasize the role of liberal officials and seminaries in secularizing the mainline churches, thereby lowering the tension between them and their surroundings (see, e.g., *Churching*, 275, 302–303n12).

33. Martin Luther King Jr., *Strength to Love* (New York: Harper and Row, 1963), 13, on Romans 12:2.

CHAPTER 7: MILLIONS NOW LIVING WILL NEVER DIE

1. Charles Grandison Finney, *Lectures on Revivals of Religion*, ed. William G. McLoughlin (1835; Cambridge, MA: Belknap/Harvard University Press, 1960), 306. James H. Timberlake (*Prohibition and the Progressive Movement, 1900–1920* [Cambridge, MA: Harvard University Press, 1963], 34–36, 191–192n106) develops, though perhaps overdraws, the nineteenth-century preparationist picture.

2. Joshua V. Himes, "Memoir of William Miller," *The Midnight Cry* 1, no. 1 (Nov. 17, 1842): 1–2.

3. William Miller, *Evidence from Scripture and History of the Second Coming of Christ, about the Year 1843* (Troy, NY: Elias Gates, 1838), 36–55, 70; Daniel 8:13–14, 9:24–27; Ezra 6:1–14.

4. George R. Knight, *William Miller and the Rise of Adventism* (Nampa, ID: Pacific Press Publishing Association, 2010), 35–37.

5. Basic though not exclusive sources for Witness history are James M. Penton, *Apocalypse Delayed: The Story of Jehovah's Witnesses* (Toronto: University of Toronto Press, 1985); and Raymond Franz, *Crisis of Conscience* (Atlanta, GA: Commentary, 1983).

6. Charles Taze Russell, *The Divine Plan of the Ages and the Corroborative Testimony of the Great Pyramid* (Brooklyn: International Bible Students Association, 1913), 64; Charles Taze Russell, *Scenario of the Photo-Drama of Creation* (Brooklyn: International Bible Students Association, 1914), 89–96.

7. Penton, *Apocalypse Delayed*, 61.

8. *Special Colporteur Bulletin, Winter 1928* (Brooklyn: Watch Tower, 1928), 7.

9. Penton, *Apocalypse Delayed*, 96.

10. Ibid., 100–101; *Yearbook of Jehovah's Witnesses* (Brooklyn: Watch Tower, 1979), 30; Stephen Cox, "The Truth vs. the Truth," *Liberty* 17 (Sept.–Oct. 2003): 49–56, 76.

11. Internet Movie Database.

12. Hal Lindsey, with Carole C. Carlson, *The Late Great Planet Earth*, "movie edition" (Grand Rapids, MI: Zondervan, 1977), vii. Punctuation as in the original.

13. Ibid., v, xiii, 126.

14. Ibid., 81–86, 155.

15. Ibid., 43.

16. *The Hal Lindsey Report*, December 30, 2011, http://www.hallindsey.com/the-hal-lindsey-report-12302011/.

17. Miller, *Evidence from Scripture*, 35. The picture's pilgrim band owes a good deal to John Bunyan.

18. Joseph Franklin Rutherford, *Light* (Brooklyn: Watch Tower, 1930), 1.105–225, 2.19–67, on Revelation 8–10, 16.

19. Leon Festinger, Henry W. Riecken, and Stanley Schachter, *When Prophecy Fails* (Minneapolis: University of Minnesota Press, 1956).

20. Franz, *Crisis of Conscience*, 95–96.

21. Proverbs 4:18.

22. Nathan H. Knorr, in *Olin R. Moyle v. Fred W. Franz, et alia*, New York Supreme Court Appellate Division, 1943, transcript of testimony, King's County Index no. 15845-Year 1940, 1473.

23. For basic information, see Joseph Tkach, *Transformed by Truth* (Sisters, OR: Multnomah Books, 1997).

24. Ibid., 102–103, 155–160.

25. *A Short History of Grace Communion International*, http://www.gci.org/aboutus/history.

26. Tkach, *Transformed by Truth*, 196–197. In 2009 the church was renamed Grace Communion International.

27. Information in this section comes from a monitoring of Family Radio, its website (http://www.familyradio.com), and a variety of websites favorable or unfavorable to the movement, including http://departout.com, http://www.ebiblefellowship.com, http://groups.yahoo.com/group/Latter_Rain, and http://groups.yahoo.com/group/TimeandJudgment_May212011.

28. Matthew 24:36.

CHAPTER 8: HIERARCHIES AND REVOLUTIONS

1. James M. O'Toole, *The Faithful: A History of Catholics in America* (Cambridge, MA: Belknap/Harvard University Press, 2008), 46. O'Toole's account of "the priestless church" is revealing.

2. The church was capable of favoring one immigrant group over another—for instance, Irish over Poles—and even of calling for the federal government to curtail "alien non-resident labor"; see Melvin G. Holli, *Reform in Detroit: Hazen S. Pingree and Urban Politics* (New York: Oxford University Press, 1969), 12, 65, 67–68.

3. Bennett Cerf, *At Random* (New York: Random House, 1977), 272–273.

4. O'Toole, *The Faithful*, 118–120.

5. Ibid., 239–242, 251.

6. Robert D. Putnam and David E. Campbell, *American Grace: How Religion Divides and Unites Us* (New York: Simon and Schuster, 2010), 299–305; Roger Finke and Rodney Stark, *The Churching of America, 1776–2005: Winners and Losers in Our Religious Economy*, 2nd ed. (New Brunswick, NJ: Rutgers University Press, 2005), 257–261, 267–268. Statistics in this area are suspect; definitions of "Latino" and "Hispanic" vary greatly, and the immigrant population is constantly in flux and difficult to survey.

7. O'Toole, *The Faithful*, 249–250; Putnam and Campbell, *American Grace*, 238, 243.

8. Finke and Stark, *Churching*, 255–256.

9. The explanatory theory comes from Finke and Stark, *Churching*, 261–266.

10. J. F. Powers, *Wheat That Springeth Green* (New York: Knopf, 1988), 200, 198, 196. Advertisements for margarine used to call butter "the high-priced spread."

11. J. F. Powers, "Keystone" and "Farewell," in *Look How the Fish Live* (New York: Knopf, 1975), 44–76, 146–167.

12. Powers, *Wheat*, 332–333.

13. Powers, *Look*, 163.

14. O'Toole, *The Faithful*, 249.

15. Ibid., 265.

16. Roy Franklin Nichols, *Franklin Pierce: Young Hickory of the Granite Hills*, 2nd ed., rev. (Philadelphia: University of Pennsylvania Press, 1958), 527–528.

17. Herman Hattaway and Richard E. Beringer, *Jefferson Davis, Confederate President* (Lawrence: University Press of Kansas, 2002), 151–152.

18. For some examples of identifiably Episcopal weddings, see *Employees' Entrance* (1933), *It Happened One Night* (1934), *The Philadelphia Story* (1940), *The Palm Beach Story* (1942), *Father of the Bride* (1950), and *Arthur* (1981).

19. James Thayer Addison, *The Episcopal Church in the United States: 1789–1931* (New York: Scribner's, 1951), 50.

20. E. Clowes Chorley, *Men and Movements in the American Episcopal Church* (New York: Scribner's, 1946), 28, 39.

21. Addison, *Episcopal Church*, 141.

22. Jackson Kemper, *The Duty of the Church with Respect to Missions* (New York: Board of Missions, 1841). The scripture reference is to 2 Timothy 3:5.

23. Charles F. Rehkopf, "The Beginnings of the Episcopal Church in Missouri, 1819–1844," *Bulletin of the Missouri Historical Society* 9 (Apr. 1955): 270–273. The swamp and the river were in Lawrence County, Illinois.

24. For an apt summary, see William Wilson Manross, *A History of the American Episcopal Church* (New York: Morehouse, 1935), 266.

25. Chorley, *Men and Movements*, 41, 115.

26. Manross, *History of the American Episcopal Church*, 297; Addison, *Episcopal Church*, 213.

27. *Yearbook of American and Canadian Churches*, ed. Constant H. Jacquet Jr. (Nashville, TN: Abingdon, 1981), 239.

28. David M. Robertson, *A Passionate Pilgrim: A Biography of Bishop James A. Pike* (New York: Knopf, 2004), provides the standard, trying-to-be-sympathetic biography.

29. Greenough White, *An Apostle of the Western Church: Memoir of the Right Reverend Jackson Kemper* (New York: Thomas Whittaker, 1900), chapter 1 (unpaginated), http://anglicanhistory.org/usa /jkemper/white/01.html.

30. *Yearbook of American and Canadian Churches* (1981), 238; ibid., ed. Eileen W. Lindler (Nashville, TN: Abingdon, 2012), 371.

31. G. Jeffrey MacDonald, "A Softer Spotlight on New Hampshire," *The Living Church*, September 23, 2012, 4.

CHAPTER 9: SERMONS IN STONE

1. John R. Scotford, *The Church Beautiful: A Practical Discussion of Church Architecture* (Boston: Pilgrim, 1946), 8; T. S. Stribling, *Unfinished Cathedral* (1934; repr., University: University of Alabama Press, 1986), 329.

2. Louis Sullivan, "The Tall Office Building Artistically Considered," *Lippincott's*, March 1896.

3. Henry C. Potter, "An American Cathedral," *Munsey's Magazine*, May 1898, 249, 246, 247.

4. Ibid., 246–247.

5. Peter W. Williams, *Houses of God: Region, Religion, and*

Architecture in the United States (Urbana: University of Illinois Press, 1997), 1, 10, 161.

6. Robert Cary Long Jr. qtd. in Phoebe B. Stanton, *The Gothic Revival and American Church Architecture* (Baltimore, MD: Johns Hopkins University Press, 1968), 244. Stanton tells the whole high-church story.

7. Ryan K. Smith, *Gothic Arches, Latin Crosses: Anti-Catholicism and American Church Designs in the Nineteenth Century* (Chapel Hill: University of North Carolina Press, 2006), 65.

8. Ibid., 154.

9. David Macrae, *The Americans at Home: Pen-and-Ink Sketches of American Men, Manners, and Institutions*, rev. ed. (Glasgow: John S. Marr and Sons, 1875), 466.

10. Stribling, *Unfinished Cathedral*, 200, 84, 287.

11. Ibid., 46, 372–373, 375, 378.

12. Vestry records, St. Paul's, San Diego, January 26, 1899.

13. Hal Lindsey, with Carole C. Carlson, *The Late Great Planet Earth*, "movie edition" (Grand Rapids, MI: Zondervan, 1977), 119–120.

14. Evangelistic campaign, North Park, California, 2008.

15. Scotford, *Church Beautiful*, 10.

16. The expression already appears in Sinclair Lewis's *Babbitt* (New York: Harcourt, Brace and World, 1922), and in an especially clingy form: "your own church-home" (223).

17. *Created for the Ages: A History of Mariners' Church of Detroit* (Detroit: Mariners' Church, 2001), 182–186.

18. Kalamazoo Valley Family Church, "The Cathedral & Weddings," http://valleyfamilychurch.org/the-cathedral-and-weddings.

CHAPTER 10: THE MORTAL WORD

1. David Macrae, *The Americans at Home: Pen-and-Ink Sketches of American Men, Manners, and Institutions*, rev. ed. (Glasgow: John S. Marr and Sons, 1875), 465–466.

2. Psalm 73:2, 16.

3. Julia Ward Howe, *Reminiscences* (Boston: Houghton Mifflin, 1900), 274–275.

4. Quotations from Charles Price Jones in this section are derived from his "Autobiographical Sketch" and "The History of My Songs," in *History of Church of Christ (Holiness) U.S.A.: 1895–1965*, ed. Otho B. Cobbins (New York: Vantage, 1966), 21–32, 400–419.

5. Macrae, *Americans at Home*, 283–284.

6. Wilberforce Eames, introduction to *The Bay Psalm Book* (1640), facsimile ed. (New York: Dodd, Mead, 1903), viii.

7. Isaac Watts, "Am I a Soldier of the Cross?" (1724).

8. Sinclair Lewis, *Elmer Gantry*, in *Arrowsmith, Elmer Gantry, Dodsworth* (New York: Library of America, 2002), e.g., 547, 676–677, 754 .

9. Peter Cartwright, *Autobiography of Peter Cartwright* (1856; repr., New York: Abingdon, 1956), 61; Paul K. Conkin, *Cane Ridge: America's Pentecost* (Madison: University of Wisconsin Press, 1990), 93–94.

10. George R. Marsden, *Jonathan Edwards: A Life* (New Haven, CT: Yale University Press, 2003), 143–145.

11. Edith L. Blumhofer, *Her Heart Can See: The Life and Hymns of Fanny J. Crosby* (Grand Rapids, MI: Eerdmans, 2005), 130.

12. Ibid., 189, and 181 (on the favorable public response to newness).

13. "Dr. George F. Root Dead," *New York Times*, August 8, 1895.

14. J. R. Watson, *The English Hymn: A Critical and Historical Study* (Oxford: Clarendon, 1999), 490–497.

15. John Wesley, *The Works of John Wesley*, vol. 7, *A Collection of Hymns for the Use of the People Called Methodists* (Oxford: Clarendon, 1983), 74.

16. The reference is to Mark 9:23–24.

17. H. L. Mencken, *Happy Days: 1880–1892* (New York: Knopf, 1940), 178–186.

18. William J. Reynolds, "Henry Ward Beecher's Significant Hymnal," *The Hymn* 52 (Apr. 2001): 17–24.

19. An example is "Glorious Things of Thee Are Spoken," John Newton's "other" hymn (among his works, second in popularity to "Amazing Grace"), which Beecher cut from five to three stanzas, with the third stanza badly mutilated. Beecher's introduction classifies Newton, a favorite with many old-fashioned people of his day, as "useful" though not "poetical" (Henry Ward Beecher et al., eds., *Plymouth Collection of Hymns and Tunes* [New York: A. S. Barnes, 1856], iv).

20. Ibid., vi–vii.

21. Ibid.

22. Charles Merrill Smith, *How to Become a Bishop without Being Religious* (Garden City, NY: Doubleday, 1965), 77, repeating a common question; Homer Rodeheaver, *Twenty Years with Billy Sunday* (Nashville, TN: Cokesbury, 1936), 75.

23. Two instances are Frederick William Faber's "Faith of Our Fathers" (1849) and "There's a Wideness in God's Mercy" (1862).

24. An excellent source for this subject is Walter William Whitehouse, "The Musical Prelude to Vatican II: Plainchant, Participation, and Pius X" (PhD diss., University of Notre Dame, 2008), http://etd.nd.edu/ETD-db/theses/available/etd-04172008 -124519/unrestricted/WhitehouseW042008D_Vol1.pdf, and http:// etd.nd.edu/ETD-db/theses/available/etd-04172008-124519 /unrestricted/WhitehouseW042008D_Vol2.pdf.

25. Smith, *How to Become*, 84.

26. Deuteronomy 34:1–5; Charles Price Jones, "Inductive Lessons in Vocal Music," qtd. in Jon Michael Spencer, *Black Hymnody: A Hymnological History of the African-American Church* (Knoxville: University of Tennessee Press, 1992), 109.

27. To cite one instance, the NRSV replaces "firmament" in Genesis 1 with "dome," thus importing a concept far too late for the text.

28. Allan Massie, "Modern Translations of the Bible Clarify the Meaning but Destroy the Music," *The Telegraph*, November 14, 2011, http://blogs.telegraph.co.uk/culture/allanmassie/100057933 /100057933/.

29. For advice on this subject, I am grateful to Joseph Ho, a musician of wide experience.

30. George Root's war song "Tramp, Tramp, Tramp" is now the tune for an enduringly popular children's song, Clare Herbert Woolston's "Jesus Loves the Little Children" (ca. 1913).

CHAPTER 11: UNFINISHED CATHEDRALS

1. John Adams to Thomas Jefferson, March 2, 1816, in John Adams, Abigail Adams, and Thomas Jefferson, *The Adams-Jefferson Letters*, ed. Lester J. Cappon (Chapel Hill: University of North Carolina Press, 1959), 464–466; Alexis de Tocqueville, *Democracy in America*, ed. J. P. Mayer, trans. George Lawrence (Garden City, NY: Doubleday, 1969), 295; Mark Twain, *Christian Science* (New York: Harper, 1907), 72–73; Harold Bloom, *The American Religion: The Emergence of the Post-Christian Nation* (New York: Simon and Schuster, 1992), 263, 270.

2. Ralph Ellison, *Going to the Territory* (New York: Random House, 1986), 10.

3. For instances, see Peter J. Gomes, *The Good Book: Reading the Bible with Mind and Heart* (New York: William Morrow, 1996), acclaimed on the left; and Ross Douthat, *Bad Religion: How We Became a Nation of Heretics* (New York: Free Press, 2012), acclaimed on the right.

4. Information about the history of the chapel was kindly provided by Rosemary Taylor, the wife of Reverend Taylor's grandson.

INDEX